Liberalisation and Urban Social Services

Liberalisation and Urban Social Services
Health and Education

C.N. Ray

School of Planning, CEPT, Ahmedabad

RAWAT PUBLICATIONS
Jaipur and New Delhi

ISBN 81-7033-762-3

Published by
Prem Rawat for *Rawat Publications*
Satyam Apts., Sector 3, Jain Temple Road, Jawahar Nagar, Jaipur - 4 (India)
Phone: 0141 265 1748 / 7006 Fax: 0141 265 1748
E-mail : info@rawatbooks.com
www.rawatbooks.com

Delhi Office
G-4, 4832/24, Ansari Road, Daryaganj, New Delhi 110 002
Phone: 011-23263290

Typeset by Rawat Computers, Jaipur
Printed at Chaman Enterprises, New Delhi

Contents

Preface

The School of Planning at the Centre for Environmental Planning and Technology (CEPT) in Ahmedabad and the Department of Human Geography at the University of Oslo have collaborated since 1996 on various urban research projects. The joint programme was financed by the Norwegian Council of Universities' Programme for Development Research and Education (NUFU). We appreciate this financial support which, among other things, has enabled researchers at the School of Planning to conduct extensive fieldwork in Ahmedabad and other cities of Gujarat as well as to travel to Norway to get exposure to research groups in the Oslo area. This is one of several books presenting research under the joint NUFU programme.

Liberalisation and globalisation are two of the most quoted and researched topics of the day. So, when the Norwegian Council of Higher Education and the Department of Human Geography, University of Oslo proposed a project for studying the effects of liberalisation a decade after it was begun, it was felt necessary to focus on a lesser-investigated part of liberalisation. In this effect, a study on the impacts of the changes in the provision of social services by the urban local bodies was chosen.

Education and health are the two most important components of social services in India. Education that is expected to be equal for all, continues until the individual is capable of emerging as an independent member of the society.

Every person has the right to the full development of their abilities and it is expected that society will gain more from the educated than from the ignorant and uneducated members. Health is a basic right for attaining physical, mental and social well-being. Health and education are critical for economic and social development and without these, development can neither be broad-based nor sustained. For fast, shared and balanced economic development, education and health play a very important role. The ultimate aim of development is to create a better quality of human life, which is generally achievable by the attainment of social justice, modernisation and economic growth. In attaining these three important aspects, education can provide immense catalytic effects in the process. Good education, health, nutrition, and low fertility also help to increase income opportunities and reduce poverty.

During the early years of the last decade of the 20th century, the Government of India decided to liberalise the country's economy by various policy reforms leading to structural adjustment. An adjustment in the structure of the politico-economic system was identified as a necessary requirement for economic development in the country. Structural adjustment is defined as a process of market-oriented reforms in policies and institutions, with the goals of restoring a sustainable balance of payments, reducing inflation, and creating conditions for sustainable growth in per capita income. Structural adjustment is also expected to bring massive changes in the politico-economic system. Economic policies were re-examined critically and efforts were made to adjust them with the method of greater reliance in market mechanism.

Economic policies in India have undergone much change over the last few years, and more changes are in the process of being implemented. The central approach underlying these reforms, initiated in 1991, involves a greater reliance on the market mechanism, and this translates into a class of public policies including deregulation and reduction of government controls, greater autonomy of private investment, less use of the public sector, more opening of the economy to international trade, less restrictions on the convertibility of the rupee, and so on. While many critics had wanted faster reforms (and a quicker change basically in the same direction), there can be little doubt about the gathering force and the growing reach of the reforms, or about the break that has been initiated in the established conventions of Indian planning and policy making. Nothing quite like this has happened earlier in the Indian economy, since independence.

India is a country with more than 70 percent of the population living in rural areas. Urbanisation constitutes a mere 29 percent of the total population but it is in the metropolitan cities or the class I cities where most of the urban population lives. The high density of these cities makes the provision of urban basic services a monumental task, especially with a high rate of in-migration and mushrooming of slums. With the ushering in of the liberalisation era, the economy has become more open and market-oriented where the role of the government agencies is becoming less that of a benefactor and more of a manager. In this light, it is the huge section of the low-income households who will be most affected, being the most dependent on the services that the urban local bodies provide.

Ahmedabad is considered to be one of the most fortunate and better-managed cities in India. The seventh largest city in India, it has managed to avoid most of the pitfalls of larger cities by modernising its management strategies which began in the mid-nineties. Although the short-term results show positive developments, the long-term effects of such measures are yet to be ascertained. This book focuses on two basic services – health and education – that are the most neglected simply because their results are long-term and indirect.

The provision of physical and social services today is geared towards a public-private partnership or privatisation. With inadequate and crumbling infrastructure, most people are willing to pay for their provision only to have an assured supply and good maintenance. The city authorities, on the other hand, in a bid to attract investment, are trying to make cities as investment-friendly as possible. In this respect, most of the funds are moving towards physical infrastructure, roads and city beautification. Soft services, like health and education which were inadequate to begin with, are facing a further crisis.

This book tries to investigate this situation in the context of Ahmedabad. The basic contents of liberalisation have been dealt with at the beginning. The situation of health and education in India follows next. To bring out the comparative context, the situation has been covered both in terms of before liberalisation and after liberalisation. To understand the situation in Ahmedabad, a brief profile of the state of Gujarat as well as the city of Ahmedabad has been given initially. From there the study progresses to the situation of health and education services in Ahmedabad.

However, the focus of the book is not only on the provision of services by the municipal body but also on the utilisation pattern of the people and how this utilisation is changing with the change in the provision of these services. As such, the utilisation patterns of the people from six localities of slums and non-slums have also been investigated. The responses of the people show a change in the pattern of utilisation that is prevalent in both the slum and the non-slum areas.

I am extremely thankful to the Department of Human Geography, University of Oslo for the financial support. I owe my sincere gratitude to Prof. Jan Hesselberg, Department of Human Geography, University of Oslo for his constant encouragement and support for the last four years. I am also thankful to Mr. Amitav Kakoty and Ms. Preeti Gulati who were associated at different stages of this study and helped me in data collection and data analysis. Finally, I express my gratitude to Dr. R.N. Vakil, Hon. Dean, CEPT for his encouragement and the institutional support.

C.N. Ray

List of Tables

List of Figures

1

Introduction and Research Methodology

Social services have been identified as the most essential public services so far as human needs are concerned. Therefore, their importance is gradually felt by the concerned authorities as well as by the common people in almost all spatial set-ups: local, regional and national. But, the provision for social services and their accessibility are complex questions in development planning. Their efficiency is related to the conditions of institutions (both administrative and planning), the social preferences, economic situations, lifestyles of common people, their collective efforts, etc. Progress in the social sector is both a vital yardstick of and a key element in improving the quality of life. Health and education are critical for economic and social development, and without these development can neither be broad-based nor sustained.

In a country such as India, the government's policies and decisions affect the level of utilisation and preference for such services in the entire spatial strata -- national, regional and local -- in varying intensities. India claims herself as a democratic socialist country, where human welfare is seen as one of the most important objectives by the state, and this is mainly tried to be achieved by the provision of social services as public utilities. However, achievements in the post-independence era, in terms of these services, are not very satisfactory and because of this the Human Development Index (HDI) of the country is one of the poorest in the world (UNDP, 1998). Gains from the social services, their effectiveness and accessibility are directly related to some of the components of the index such as life expectancy at birth and literacy rate.

Urbanisation

According to many national leaders, although India is considered to be rural, we are living less in villages. By the turn of this millennium, 305 million Indians were living in nearly 3,700 towns and cities spread across the length and breadth of the country. This comprises 30 percent of its population, in sharp contrast to only 60 million (15%) who lived in urban areas in 1947 when the country became independent. During the last fifty years, the population of India has grown two and a half times, but urban India has grown by nearly five times. In numerical terms, India's urban population is the second largest in the world after China, and is higher than the total urban population of all countries put together barring China, USA and Russia. About one-third of urban India (71 million) lives in metropolitan cities (million plus) and the number of such cities in India has increased from 1 in 1901 to 5 in 1951 to 23 in 1991. It is estimated that the number will go up to 40 by 2001. Out of the total increase in the country's urban population of 58 million, between 1981 and 1991, 44 million persons were added to class I cities alone and 28 million to metropolitan cities.

Urban areas are marked as the engines of productivity and growth in the country. This is manifest in the increasing contribution of the urban sector to the national income. Growth of employment (main workers) in urban India during 1981-91 was recorded at 38 percent against 16 percent in rural areas and 26.1 percent in the country as a whole. However, the positive role of urbanisation has often been overshadowed by the deterioration in the physical environment and quality of life in the urban areas caused by the widening gap between demand and supply of essential services and infrastructure. Imperfections in the land and housing markets and exorbitant increases in land prices have virtually left the urban poor with no alternative except to seek informal solutions to their housing problems, leading to mushrooming of slums. It is estimated that about one-third of the urban dwellers live below the poverty line. About 15 percent of the urbanites do not have access to safe drinking water and about 50 percent are not covered by sanitary facilities. Traffic congestion has assumed critical dimensions in many metropolitan cities due to massive increase in the number of personalised vehicles, inadequate road space and lack of public transport.

Traditionally society was divided into the rural-urban form as urban centres had a distinct lifestyle in comparison to the rural way of life. The non-farm economic activities were also responsible for creating a different way of life, which was supposed to be more modern. This difference is now fast disappearing all over the country as it is happening in many developing societies. Recent historical experiences link growing towns and cities with industrialisation. However, dense living, with non-farm economic activities as the most common occupations, has occurred in many places around the world for a very long time in human history. Market and administrative towns never constituted a large proportion of a nation's or empire's total population. City life, as the common form of living, is a more recent phenomenon (Hesselberg, 2002).

In India, there was a strong Brahmanical anti-urban sentiment during the last century. Moreover, Gandhian opposition to urbanisation lived on as an ideology among politicians after independence. According to Ramachandran (1989), "there is strong reluctance on the part of politicians to discard the theory, incongruous though it may be today. An unhappy consequence of this duality [anti-urban sentiment and pro-urban bias in investments] is the widening gap between what is stated as policy and what is actually practised" (p. 325). The basic reason for the concentration of industrial and service activities, as the foundation of the rapid growth of cities particularly after the Second World War, is easy to find. Most industries are linked by one factory's output being an input to another. By locating both in the same area, cost and time are saved. Another reason is the common need for physical infrastructure and energy sources. The principle of economy of scale explains the relatively low cost per unit of production of these necessary factors of production. Furthermore, a concentration of people allows economies of scale in the costs of transport and consumption. The main determinant of rapid urbanisation today is not whether a society has positive or negative economic growth but whether the country has a low or high level of urbanisation. Thus, urbanisation continues with its own momentum in countries at the low end of level of urbanisation. The term 'overurbanisation' has been used to describe the high urban development, which is not in accordance with the level expected due to improvement of industrial production and national income. In China, for several decades, people were forced to live in rural areas, effectively hindering millions from migrating to towns, despite the country having experienced rapid industrial growth.

With the recent trend in the rate of urbanisation, and the present processes of liberalisation and globalisation, which strengthen the rate, it is likely that the figure will increase considerably in the next two decades. Presently, at least three-fourths of the world's population growth occurs in urban areas in the South. The doubling time of the urban population is less than thirty years. In South Asia, the World Bank (2000) estimates that in the coming years 95 percent of the population growth will be in urban areas. Moreover, in the period up to

2015, there will be a dramatic demographic change with many cities passing the one million mark, thus becoming metropolises. In Asia alone, there will be 15 mega-cities (defined as having more than 10 million inhabitants) (UNCHS, 2001). The shift to an urban world everywhere will soon be an established fact -- cities are "our common future".

According to official sources, the level of urbanisation in India was 17 percent in 1950 and 28 percent in the year 2000, and it will be 46 percent in 2030 (UNCHS 1996, 2001). At present, the population in India is growing at 1.5 percent annually, whereas cities grow at nearly double that rate, 2.8 percent (UNFPA, 2001). The rate of annual urban population growth is expected to be 2.5 percent during the period from 2015 to 2030 compared to an annual decline in the rural population of 0.2 percent. The national natural growth of population will probably be below 1.3 percent in the same period. If national economic growth prevails in India, it must be expected that the rate of urbanisation will continue to be considerably higher than the natural growth rate. Furthermore, the shift of population from smaller towns to larger will prevail. Moreover, the centralisation of political, administrative and economic power in the state capitals must be expected to 'metropolise' India even further. Migration to these leading places of opportunities is inevitable if market forces are "left to decide". India is thus no longer a typically rural country and planning ought to be based on this fact of ever-growing cities. The country is undoubtedly going through the urban transition, which ends in an almost completely urbanised society with the large majority of the population living in big cities. The level of urbanisation in Gujarat is above the national average with the official census figure (provisional) for 2001 of 38 percent (the figure was 34% in 1991). This is to be expected since Gujarat is one of the more industrialised states in India.

It is argued that structural reform and the associated development strategy launched formally in 1991 would accelerate rural-urban migration and give a boost to the pace of urbanisation. The proponents of the strategy believe that linking of India with global economy will increase the inflow of foreign capital as also facilitate indigenous investment, resulting in rapid development of infrastructure and industries. This is likely to give impetus to the process of urbanisation since much of the industrial growth and consequent increase in employment would be within or around the existing urban centres. Even when the industrial units get located in rural settlements in a few years, the latter would acquire urban status. Critics of the new development strategy, however, point out that employment generation through industrialisation may not be high. The reduction in infrastructure and industrial investment in public sector, necessitated by the need to keep budgetary deficits low, would slow down even the growth in agriculture and its demand for labour. This, coupled with open trade policy, is likely to destabilise the agrarian economy, causing high unemployment and exodus from rural areas. This would lead to rapid growth in urban population. Thus, the protagonists as also the critics of economic reforms seem to converge on the proposition that urban growth in the post-liberalisation phase would be high. Interestingly, the policy documents of the Government of India reflects this 'optimism' with regard to urban growth (Kundu and Mahadevia, 2001).

Globalisation and Urban Dynamics in Gujarat

Gujarat presents a unique case of globalisation among the Indian states. It has historically been linked with the international market through the migrant businessmen and their family-based interactions with the local entrepreneurial class. The exposure of the state's economy to American and European markets can, therefore, be traced back to the pre-independence era. The rapid growth of the manufacturing sector in the state, its export-oriented growth, etc., can be attributed, in no small measure, to exogenous factors and the capital brought in by the non-resident business community. Measures of structural adjustment and liberalisation launched in the early 1990s hold forth a big promise for the state in terms of industrial and economic development. It is often argued that the negative impact of the policies of structural adjustment on the urban economy of the state, if any, would be transitory in nature. Efficiency and accountability in the functioning of urban institutions, that were somewhat better in Gujarat compared to their counterparts in other states, are supposed to become the driving force in the new system of governance. These, in turn, are likely to have a positive impact on the employment and poverty scenario.

In the background of this perspective, many of the public sector organisations created during 1950s and 1960s for the provision of infrastructure and basic services are being criticised for blocking scarce capital resources without yielding adequate returns. Many of the infrastructural services, falling within the purview of the state governments, are gradually being thrown open to be managed on commercial lines or being transferred to private agencies. The state government of Gujarat, for example, has set up Gujarat Infrastructure Development Board (GIDB), which is expected to lay down urban policies and a perspective and encourage private investment within the framework. GIDB has projected a vision, which details out the blueprints for privatisation of infrastructural development (GIDB, 1999), to be operationalised through Gujarat Urban Development Authority.

The 74th Constitution Amendment Act has been hailed in Gujarat as a major step in dismantling the state level bureaucracy, taking power to the people and initiating a process of democratic administration and planning at the grass roots level. Importantly, the state has witnessed a high growth rate in the manufacturing sector in the post-liberalisation phase. But empirical investigations suggest that this falls in line with the long-term trend in the state economy. The growth in income from the manufacturing sector has been high, decades before the launching of the reform measures. During the 1970s, the annual growth rate of the manufacturing sector was 5.6 percent, which increased to 8.11 percent in the 1980s. It nonetheless went up to 12 percent in the 1990s, which could be attributed to reform measures (Hirway and Mahadevia, 1999). Because of this sector, the state's overall economic growth has remained high despite near stagnancy in the growth rate of the agriculture sector in the 1980s and the 1990s.

The share of the secondary sector in the state income has doubled in the last twenty-five years. During this period, the share of the primary sector has been reduced to less than half that of the early 1970s. Correspondingly, the figure for the tertiary sector has gone up to one and a half times. The growth of the state's economy, thus, seems to have been led by the manufacturing sector, which has registered the highest growth rate during the period (Hirway and Mahadevia, 1999). Importantly, the state has experienced a rapid growth of population, much above that of the country since the beginning of the present century. This could be attributed to, besides a lower death rate particularly of children, to a high rate of inmigration. There was a substantial decline in population growth rate during the 1980s, bringing it down to below national level for the first time. In the decade of the 1990s, once again, the state's annual population growth rate has gone above that of the country. As per the provisional population estimates of 2001, the two figures are 2.05 percent and 1.95 percent respectively. The pace of urbanisation in the state, on the other hand, has apparently been less than that in the country, except in a couple of decades. The urban population in the state during 1981-91, for example, has grown at 2.90 percent per annum, which is less than that of the previous decade, viz., 3.47 percent per annum Importantly, the corresponding rates for the country are higher, 3.09 percent per annum and 3.83 percent per annum respectively.

Looking at the present trend, one may infer that the rate of urbanisation in Gujarat is low and decelerating over time. It must, however, be pointed out that the population in the rural areas of the state has grown at a rate much below than that of the country, going down further in the recent decades. The annual exponential growth rate in the 1960s was 1.96 percent, which has come down to 1.80 percent in the subsequent decades. As a consequence, the rural-urban growth differential for Gujarat during 1981-91 works out as much larger than that of the country and, in fact, most of the other (large) states. The rural-urban growth differential was 1.46 in the state compared to 2.05 in the country during 1970s. The figure for the state has gone up to 1.51 in the 1980s, which is much above than that of the country, i.e., 1.29 percent. It would, therefore, be legitimate to argue that Gujarat has been one of the rapidly urbanising states in the country in recent years. It is the only state where the rate of net in-migration from outside has gone up significantly during the 1980s, both in rural as well as urban areas. The only other state, which shows an increase in the rate, is Haryana but here the increase is negligible. It is, thus, evident that arrival of workers from outside the state is an important factor that is responsible for the pace of urbanisation in the state.

The distribution of population in different size-classes of urban centres in the state is similar to that of the country. About two-thirds of the total urban population resides in class I cities having population of one lakh or more. Another quarter is in class II and III towns in the size-class between 20,000 and 1,00,000. A similar pattern is observed in the developed states of Karnataka and Tamil Nadu, as also at the national level. Some of the other developed states like Maharashtra and West Bengal have a much higher share of population in class I cities. The less developed states of Bihar, Himachal Pradesh, Madhya Pradesh, Orissa, Rajasthan and Uttar Pradesh, on the other hand, have a lower share of population in this size-class. One would, therefore, argue that the structure of urban population in the state of Gujarat is similar to that of the developed states in the country.

The population growth profile for different size-classes of urban centres, computed by considering only those towns that belong to a class in the base year, reveals an interesting pattern. The growth rates in class I cities work out to be higher than that in the lower order towns in the country. This was the case not only in the 1970s but also in the 1980s (Kundu, 1994). The only exception to this is the class VI towns that record growth rates higher than even the class I cities at the national level as also in several states. This is because many of these towns have been established through some public or private sector projects, administrative or military decisions and some other special considerations. Consequently, they do not fall in line with other towns in terms of socio-economic characteristics. Importantly, the class I cities in Gujarat exhibit a higher growth rate than the smaller order towns as noted at the national level. A similar pattern emerges in the case of a few other developed states like Karnataka, Maharashtra, Punjab and Tamil Nadu. In most of the less developed states, however, the class I cities are not having an edge over other categories in terms of population growth. Also, the class VI towns in the state have not grown at a faster rate than the class I cities, as is the case for several other states. This is because there are not many special purpose towns in class VI in Gujarat. The pace of urbanisation varies across the districts in Gujarat but the disparity is not as high as in some of the backward states in the country. The growth rates are fairly stable, ranging between 18 percent and 38 percent except for three districts (Kundu and Mahadevia, 2002).

Research Problem

Urban social services from the public system are not directly related to broad objectives of liberalisation but privatisation of such services has been going on for sometime in India. As a result of this new trend, the dependence on public system is reducing in urban as well as rural areas gradually. But, for the overall development, economic growth and provision of social services are not a one-way game. In general, economic growth leads to better provision of social services in a society, but it is also true that for economic growth, there should be a minimum level of social services and their efficiency. Economic growth and its sustainability will depend very much on minimum service levels. The level of social services (basic education, good health, etc.) will also determine the success of strategies for economic development such as adjustment of structure by liberalisation. Equal opportunity to access these services will determine the equitable nature of development, which will be participatory in nature.

While discussing about structural adjustment policies in the context of development, Amartya Sen (Dreze and Sen, 1996) comments that there must be an attempt to link the strategies of development to something more fundamental and, in particular, the ends of economic and social development. Why do we seek development? What can it achieve, if fruitful? How are the successes and failures of policies, including the 'reforms' of traditional policies, to be judged? It is only with an explicit recognition of the basic ends that debates on means and strategies can be adequately founded. What are the means that have to be employed to achieve these ends felicitously? While the debates on the current reforms concentrate on a particular class of means related to the use of and non-use of markets (such as incentives for private investment, reliance on international trade, and so on), there are many other means, especially dealing with the 'social' side of economic operations and successes, which typically tend not to figure in these debates. To the foundational lacuna of neglecting the scrutiny of the basic ends is, thus, added the more immediate gap of ignoring the examination of some powerful means that help us to achieve those ends. In fact, he argued that achievement of even the limited objectives of the current reforms would depend crucially on conscious and organised pursuit of the social means on which economic performance and results are frequently conditional.

Ideally, development policies should help every individual to improve their abilities in making use of economic opportunities in the present context. Education and health can be important enabling factors for individuals in the current situation in India and many developing countries. However, there was a remarkable neglect of elementary education in India, and this has now forced her to recognise the importance of basic education for the economic development of the country. According to Dreze and Sen (2002), education and health can be seen to be valuable to the freedom of a person in at least five distinct ways:

1. Both education and health are valuable achievements in themselves and the opportunity to have them can be of direct importance to a person's effective freedom.

2. They help individuals to have a choice to pursue different things. It can also facilitate a wide range of valuable activities in everyday life.

3. Greater literacy and basic education can facilitate public discussion of social needs and encourage informed collective demands; these, in turn, can help expand the facilities that the public enjoys, and contribute to the better utilisation of the available services.

4. Expansion of schooling can reduce the distressing phenomenon of child labour so prevalent in India. Schooling also brings young people in touch with others

and thereby broadens their horizons; this can be particularly important for young girls.

5. Greater literacy and educational achievements of disadvantaged groups can enhance their ability to resist their oppression, to organise politically, and to get a fairer deal.

The interpersonal influences of education and health are only one aspect of the social dimension of health and education. The latter pertains not only to the outcomes of health and education programmes, but also to the process of improving health and education levels. The case for social intervention in the provision of health and education is strong from several viewpoints. First, the interdependence of outcomes itself calls for social intervention (if only in the form of subsidies) since private decisions often overlook the positive externalities associated with improved health and education. This issue is particularly crucial in matters such as public health, especially the eradication of communicable diseases.

Second, social intervention is often required to overcome various 'market failures' that have been extensively analysed in public economics. For instance, the asymmetry of information between users and providers of health services often undermines the efficiency of the market mechanism in this field, and may even lead to the disappearance of market-based arrangements. The pervasive uncertainties involved in health matters, together with the inherent limitations of market-based insurance arrangements, have similar consequences.

Third, there is a strong case for public involvement in health and education matters from the viewpoint of equity and rights. This is not an issue of market failure, even in the broadest sense of the term, since ensuring equity or protecting rights is nowhere within the province of the market mechanism. The inequitable nature of private health and education arrangements in India is evident enough. So is their inability to guarantee basic entitlements such as "free and compulsory education for all children until they complete the age of fourteen years" (Indian Constitution, Directive Principles, Article 45). Entitlements of this type are important not only because they consolidate the bargaining power of those who are deprived of basic health and education services, but also because they shape broader notions of solidarity. There is, thus, a strong case for thinking about education and health in terms of fundamental rights, and this calls for social arrangements that go well beyond the market mechanism.

Last, but not the least, one crucial aspect of interpersonal influence of health and education relates to motivation. For instance, to send his or her child to school, one parent tends to be strongly influenced by the corresponding attitude of other parents in the neighbourhood, village, and caste or reference group. The motivation of children, too, is likely to vary depending on the behaviour of their peers. This feature also applies to personal attitudes towards family planning, dietary habits and work patterns, to cite a few other examples. The work culture in schools and hospitals is another important context where interpersonal effects have a paramount influence on individual motivation. The interdependence of personal decisions is, in fact, a pervasive feature of social life, which influences many aspects of everyday behaviour even outside the field of health and education, from relatively trivial ones such as the decision to wear a seat-belt to more momentous matters such as occupational and matrimonial choices.

The argument for social intervention in health and education matters has to be considered together with the equally real fact that the standards of public services in India are abysmally low. It is not to make a case for public provision of every aspect of health and education, or denying that private provision has a role. Rather, Dreze and Sen (2002) argued to see the promotion of health and education as irreducibly social concerns, even when particular services are effectively provided through private channels. In every modern economy, health and education are divided to a varying extent between public provision and private supply. However, this does not detract from the overarching importance of public discussion and social planning in these sectors.

The social dimension of health and education is evident even in the so-called market economies of Western Europe and North America. It is often forgotten that in these market economies, public expenditure generally accounts for 35 to 45 percent of GDP (rising to 50% or so in countries like the Netherlands, which are not bad achievers, to say the least). Further, the share of health, education and social security in the total government expenditure in these economies tends to range between one-half and three-fourths. These are, in other words, fundamental areas of state involvement, which also account for a major share of overall economic activity. Health, education and social security also have a high political visibility in western societies, as can be seen in the attention they receive in electoral campaigns, for instance. Even outside electoral campaigns, education and health issues (from abortion and AIDS to the school curriculum) are the objects of a great deal of public attention and media coverage. All these patterns, incidentally, persisted (and indeed, in many respects, intensified) through the Reagan and Thatcher years. These years, for instance, were a period of sustained increase in public expenditure on social services in many western countries, notwithstanding the free market rhetoric. The universalisation of basic entitlements to health care, elementary education and social security is perhaps the most significant social achievement of western market economies in the 20th century. The achievement is not confined to western economies. Cuba and pre-reform China, for instance, also made impressive progress in the direction of universal entitlements to basic education, health care and social security. China's post-reforms experience, for its part, illustrates the danger of social abdication in these fields. As the reforms ushered in through the floodgates in 1979-80, the market principles were suddenly extended to health and education, leading to a major decline in the accessibility and affordability of public services (Dreze and Sen, 2002).

The possibility of influencing social norms is well understood in the world of advertisement and propaganda. In drawing attention to this possibility, Dreze and Sen (2002) have not just suggested the extension of these techniques to health and education matters. That can indeed be done, as India's recent Total Literacy Campaign and Polio Vaccination Programme illustrate. More importantly, however, what is at issue here is the possibility of health and education becoming matters of broad-based public discussion and concern. Achieving this transformation of the politics of health and education is one part of the broader agenda of democratic practice in India.

Amartya Sen (Dreze and Sen, 1996) placed special emphasis on the need for basic social services/facilities. He referred to the famous speech of Jawaharlal Nehru (the first Prime Minister of India) on the eve of independence in August 1947. In this speech on India's tryst with destiny, Nehru reminded the country that disease and inequality of opportunity are the main barriers to future development. As Nehru pointed out, the elimination of ignorance, illiteracy, remediable poverty, preventable disease and needless inequalities in opportunities must be seen as objectives that are valued for their own sake. They expand our freedom to lead the lives we have reason to value, and these elementary capabilities are of importance on their own. Economic growth is, of course, important, but it is valuable precisely because it helps to eradicate deprivation and to improve the capabilities and the quality of life of ordinary people.

Education and health are the two most important components of social services in India. Education that is expected to be equal for all and continue until the individual is capable of emerging as an independent member of society. Every person has the right to the full development of abilities and it is expected that society gains more from educated than from ignorant and uneducated members. Health is a basic right for attaining the physical, mental and social well-being. Health and education are critical for economic and social development and without these two, development can neither be broad-based nor sustained. For fast, shared and balanced economic development, education and health play a very important role. A large number of social scientists believed that the ultimate aim of development is to create a better quality of human life, which is generally achievable by the attainment of social justice, modernisation and economic growth. In attaining these three important aspects, education can provide immense catalytic effects in the process. Good education, health, nutrition and low fertility also help to increase income opportunities and reduce poverty.

The lessons of economic and social progress across the world over the last few decades have forcefully drawn attention to the instrumental importance of education, health and other features of the quality of human life in generating fast and shared economic growth. This, in turn, can contribute to enhancing the quality of human life. They do have instrumental roles in making us more productive and helping us to generate more outputs and incomes. Improved standard of living leads to gain in health and education, freeing people from the trap of ignorance and exposure to disease.

Aim and Objectives

The aim of this study is to look into the details of urban social services (health and education) and the utilisation and preference for these services in Ahmedabad (Gujarat, India) in the context of economic liberalisation and structural adjustments at the national level. To this end, the major objectives of the study are to

- to study the liberalisation process and its relation to social services in India and Gujarat;
- to study the exiting social services provided by the urban local body and other public agencies in Ahmedabad;
- explain the utilisation and preference for health and education services; and
- identify the differences in utilisation and preferences in slums and nearby non-slum areas.

Scope

The geographical scope of this study is restricted to the area under the jurisdiction of Ahmedabad Municipal Corporation (AMC). However, the Ahmedabad urban area is now extended to a larger area. This area is under many small urban local authorities and adequate secondary data are not available which has forced us to restrict ourselves to the AMC boundary only. Conceptually, our study is focused on utilisation and preference for health and education services only as these two services play the most important role in present urban life of Ahmedabad. Other social services remain out of the scope of this study.

Sample Selection and Primary Survey

To capture the income group and settlement-wise differences, three low-income settlements were selected purposefully from three different locations: Lakhudi slum in the western, Omnagar slum in the northern, and Machhipir slum in the eastern part of the city to represent the major regions of Ahmedabad city. The non-slum areas are located adjoining these slums and people living in these areas are from middle and higher income groups. This method of settlement selection has helped to cover all the income categories, which were assumed as an important variable to study the utilisation and preference for social services in the context of post-liberalisation and structural reforms.

At the settlement level, households were selected on the basis of availability of the head of the family. A simple random sample was planned in the beginning, but in many cases, the head of the household was not available during the daytime, forcing a change in this sample selection process. However, during the field visits, it was observed that within settlements information variation is very limited to household details only. But, the entire fieldwork was affected as the AMC was demolishing some units in Lakhudi and Machhipir close to the main roads of these settlements. On the first day in Lakhudi slum, people were not ready to talk freely as they suspected the surveyors to be from the Municipal Corporation. However, after some informal discussions, they cooperated. Otherwise it would have been a very difficult proposition.

In adjoining non-slum settlements, the same sample selection procedure was followed. However, the people were very non-cooperative in sharing information related to their occupation, income and expenditure. They were suspicious about the purpose of conducting this study. In some cases, they expressed that the survey results may be used by government agencies, like the income tax department, and refused to answer. As a result, the total time taken for primary data collection was much longer than was thought necessary in the beginning. In some cases information given by the respondents was not clear and they did not allow enough time to crosscheck it for correction. Hence, some of the information remained a little confusing. This experience clearly shows that primary survey is still relatively easy in low-income areas as compared to middle- and high-income areas of Ahmedabad and it may be true for all other urban areas in India as well.

Limitations

The limitations of this study are as under:

- Analyses and inferences are drawn from a relatively small sample of 300 households selected from three areas only and they do not represent the entire city of Ahmedabad. Hence, it is difficult to generalise.

- The primary data were collected by using an interview schedule and in some cases many people were present when the head of the family was being interviewed. The presence of the other people might have influenced the respondent's answers. In some cases informal discussions were held with other people from these settlements to cross-check some of the data, but, even then, some discrepancies are expected.

- Disease-related information is noted as stated by the respondents without looking into medical reports or taking any clinical tests.

2

The Concept of Liberalisation

The economy of India took a self-sufficient course of development when the Second Five-Year Plan (1956-1961) was introduced in the mid-1950s. The subsequent quarter century was, however, marked by severe economic crises and a low rate of economic growth. Despite the attempt at within-system internal economic liberalisation in the mid-1980s under Prime Ministers Indira Gandhi and Rajiv Gandhi, India remained a comprehensively and stringently controlled economy, both internally and externally. Then, in 1991, India made a decisive shift to a more open and liberal economy, albeit gradually. The question at hand for examination is what and how much has changed in respect of India's external openness. Of course, it is true that the more prosperous economies today are open, but that does not settle the issue of causality. External openness does provide significant opportunities for growth, but it also carries huge risks. In any case, external openness by itself does not assure growth unless it is part of a larger strategy for economic growth focusing on investment in physical and human capital and on the provision of appropriate social and political institutions for macro-economic adjustment and conflict management.

The last quarter of the 20th century has seen a wave of economic policy reforms in the developing world, with one country after another taking the liberalisation cure, often imposed by the international financial institutions. This wave of reforms had been preceded by a quarter century of state-directed effort at economic development, during which time the goals of economic self-reliance and import substitution industrialisation were the hallmarks of development strategies in the less developed countries. The goal seemed particularly justified, given the long experience of these countries with colonialism and the agricultural nature of their economies. However, all this seemed to be overtaken by the subsequent surge of liberalisation.

During the early years of the last decade, the Government of India had decided to liberalise the country's economy by various policy reforms leading to structural adjustment. An adjustment in the structure of the politico-economic system was identified as a necessary requirement for economic development in the country. Structural adjustment is defined as a process of market-oriented reforms in policies and institutions, with the goals of restoring a sustainable balance of payments, reducing inflation, and creating conditions for sustainable growth in per capita income (Nagraj, 1997). Structural adjustment or 'liberalisation' policies, using trade, fiscal and monetary instruments, symbolise measures to stimulate structural change by reorganising production, focus on shifting emphasis from the state to the market and forging closer interaction between the national (domestic) and the global economy. Structural adjustment is also expected to bring massive changes in the politico-economic system. Economic policies were re-examined critically and efforts were made to adjust them with the method of greater reliance on market mechanism. The roots of the Structural Adjustment Programme (SAP) can be traced to the era of 'debt-led growth' of the 1970s and the focus of international and national policies on reduction of external debt, and subsequent incorporation of growth and to a limited extent the reduction of poverty.

In India, economic policies have undergone much change over the last few years, and more changes are in the process of being implemented. The central approach underlying these reforms, initiated in 1991, involves a greater reliance on the market mechanism, and this translates into a class of public policies including deregulation and reduction of government controls, greater autonomy of private investment, less use of the public sector, more opening of the economy to international trade, less restrictions on the convertibility of the rupee, and so on. While many critics had wanted faster reforms (and a quicker change basically in the same direction), there can be little doubt about the gathering force and the growing reach of the reforms, or about the break that has been initiated in the established conventions of Indian planning and policy making. Nothing quite like this has happened earlier in the Indian economy, since independence or after it (Sen, 1996).

The recent wave of economic policy reforms in the developing world has been seen as a necessary consequence of a changed world economic system. The key feature of the changed world economy is the element of heightened economic globalisation, which provides new external challenges as well as opportunities for development. As globalisation has accelerated, it has come to loom large in the perceptions of policy makers and adjustment to it, in the form of economic liberalisation. The phenomenon of economic globalisation provides the widest possible context for the examination of economic policy reforms. Economic globalisation here refers to the integration of economic processes across political borders so that the behaviour of economic agents is oriented to the global market rather than particular national markets; in short, it calls attention to laws of motion of the global market.

Economic liberalisation covers many aspects of policy, but the central issue at stake is the relative role of the state and market in the operation and management of the national economy. The contemporary movement in economic policy reforms has involved the retreat of the state and the shedding of many of its economic functions in favour of the market, which has been accorded a wider and increasingly important role. An interesting question pertains to what ought to be the appropriate relationship between the state and market for purposes of effective economic performance.

The end of the century also saw the beginning of globalisation as an important all-pervasive phenomenon. The two factors, which helped the process, were the revolution in informatics and information technology (IT), and the emergence of very powerful multinationals. The IT made it possible for the multinationals to easily supervise and control their operations anywhere in the world and take instantaneous decisions. All the countries are experiencing profound change in their economies under the impact of globalisation. To undertake a comprehensive review of the momentous socio-economic changes that took place during the last millennium is a daunting task. A century is a long period in the history of any country. The analysis starts by giving a bird's eye view of the state of the Indian economy on the eve of the British rule and the changes brought about in it by British colonisers up to the end of the 19th century. This is followed by a brief review of the growth of Indian economy during the British rule, and the growth of the economy in the post-independence period, i.e., from 1950-51 to 1998. The purpose is to specially focus on the evaluation of different policy regimes that existed during various periods and their efficacy and impact on the Indian economy. Finally, an attempt is made to conjecture on the challenges and opportunities provided by the process of globalisation in the 21st century.

The Indian Economy: A Historical Overview

Pre-Independent India

Early British Period

According to the contemporary Indian historians, the British rulers were responsible for bringing about profound changes in the Indian economy and polity during their two hundred years of rule (Bhalla, 2000). When the East India Company established trading relations with India, the economy was mainly agrarian. There existed the handicraft industry, which was developed far ahead of its European counterpart but this catered mainly to a specialised clientele. The socio-economic structure comprised of self-sufficient villages under the princely states. As the British gained political and economic power, they established a trade regime that was mainly extractive, i.e., exporting raw materials from India and importing finished products to India. Through a policy that pursued their own profits, they led to the collapse of the highly organised Indian industry and the agrarian village's self-sufficiency. The important changes brought about by the British in the agrarian structure included alteration in land settlements and right of sale and alienation of land. Except for some commercial crops needed for exports, very few systematic attempts were made to improve the technology of production in agriculture. But, a beginning was made in investment in irrigation during the late 19th century as a belated response to recurring famines. This helped to increase output of food and some commercial crops.

Changes in Industrial Policy

At the time of the ascent of the East India Company into political power in India, there was the start of the Industrial Revolution in Britain. While India provided enough raw materials, the British flooded the Indian market with inferior quality goods. To capture the market, where the existing Indian goods were of superior quality, the British made policy changes to gain monopoly over the market. Already, the handicrafts industry that had suffered after the collapse of the state courts that were their patrons was struggling. With the flooding of cheaper goods by the British, they were finally at their end. The British achieved this through several policy measures that included the forcing of British free trade on India, exporting raw material from India, imposing heavy duties on Indian manufactures in India, the transit and customs duties, building railways in India and granting special privileges to the British in India. The disappearance of the native Indian courts, change in tastes with the establishment of an alien rule, and the competition of a more highly developed form of industry were the main factors that led to a process of de-industrialisation. In addition, the absence of growth of indigenous modern industry forced the unemployed to move to the countryside thereby increasing unduly the pressure on land in India (Desai, 1986).

The Beginning of the 20th Century

The pursuit of such discriminatory policies by the British for the next century increased to encompass even the socio-cultural milieu with the result that by the beginning of the 20th century, India was an extremely poor country. Naoroji estimated the per capita income of India at Rs 30 in 1870 compared to that of England of Rs 450 in 1891 (Bhalla, 2000; after Heston, 1982). This was a trend that continued throughout the rule of the British with scholars claiming that both national income and per capita income not only remained stagnant but also declined in some cases.

Performance of Indian Economy since Independence from 1950-51 to 1990-91

India recorded a significant acceleration in the growth rates of Gross Domestic Product (GDP) and per capita income after independence. Between 1950 and 1999, the GDP of India recorded a growth rate of nearly 4.16 percent per annum at

1980-81 prices and the per capita income grew at a rate of 1.77 percent (Table 2.1) (Bhalla, 2000).

Table 2.1

Growth Rates of GDP and of Per Capita Income from 1950-51 to 1998-99 at 1980-81 prices

Years	GDP				
	Overall	Agriculture	Secondary	Tertiary	Per Capita Income
1950-51 to 1998-99	4.16	2.61	5.61	5.15	1.77
1950-51 to 1990-91	3.77	2.49	5.49	4.76	1.41
1967-68 to 1990-61	4.20	2.80	5.20	5.20	1.64
1950-51 to 1964-65	4.00	2.65	7.73	4.61	1.69
1967-68 to 1979-80	3.45	2.10	4.43	4.49	1.11
1980-81 to 1990-91	5.46	3.94	6.86	6.58	3.01
1990-91 to 1998-99	6.23	1.95	7.45	8.24	4.30

Source: Economic Survey, Various Issues, quoted from Bhalla, 2000.

The Plan Periods before 1991

After independence, India decided to use the strategy of Five-Year Plans to aid development. As such, the First Plan was launched in 1951, which was only a collection of existing schemes. From the Second Plan onwards, when Mahalanobis introduced the concept of industrial development through heavy industries under the public sector, India was on the road to modernisation. At that time, even the international development and donor agencies, concerned with the fate of the newly independent states, were propagating a westernised development model for rapid growth. This included the four points of urban industrialisation, open economies, modernisation and urbanisation. The result was an increased investment in infrastructure, roads, power, irrigation, communications, etc. Following this, there was rapid industrial development and growth of the Indian economy.

Along with growth of the primary and secondary sectors, there was also rapid demographic growth. With declining mortality rates and greater life expectancy, population growth escalated to the point of constraints in food availability. Although there was a peak output of food of 89.36 million tonnes in 1964-65, the following two consecutive droughts dealt a severe blow to food production. Imports and policy measures had limited success and by the end of the sixties, India was facing a balance of payment crisis (Bhalla, 2000). The added expenditure of financing two wars increased the pressure and India had to borrow from the International Monetary Fund (IMF) to solve the crisis.

The following years saw a slowdown in the growth rates of GDP as there was decreased public and private investment. There were two severe droughts again in the seventies, which led to major crises in the Indian economy. While the Green Revolution in the late sixties introduced new technology and scientific measures in agriculture, this was confined to the northern states.

> The technological breakthrough in agriculture during the mid-sixties resulted in significant increases in agricultural output and income. Rapid agricultural growth also led to a more rapid growth of manufacturing in agro-processing and consumer goods industries and in services and other tertiary sector through input, output and consumption linkages. More important, rapid agricultural growth succeeded in increasing the income levels of a large number of agricultural workers and thereby made a big dent in rural poverty in the green revolution areas (Bhalla, 2000).

With the problem of drought that led to food shortages, there were the problems of war expenditures, millions of refugees from Bangladesh who had to be fed, the reduction in foreign aid and the sharp rise in oil prices. The government took hard measures to combat the crises this time and managed to stop the situation from deteriorating by 1975. India became more open to exports and the migration of a large number of Indian workers to the Gulf countries helped in building up large reserves of foreign exchange so much so, that during the next oil crisis of 1978-79, it was not severely affected.

The eighties began with another severe drought that seriously affected foodgrain production. But with control measures in place, the Indian economy witnessed a turnaround and recorded very high growth during this period (Table 2.1). The growth rate of income increased to 5.46 percent compared to 3.45 percent during the seventies. Per capita income increased at 3.01 percent per annum compared with a paltry figure of 1.2 percent during the previous thirty years. While agricultural GDP grew at 3.94 percent per annum, income from the secondary and the tertiary sectors grew at 6.86 percent and 6.58 percent per annum, respectively. Again, while agricultural output grew at a rate of 3.47 percent per annum -- the industrial growth rate rose to 8 percent per annum, the highest in the country's history. Not only that, exports from India recorded a growth rate of 10 percent per annum in real terms. It seems rather paradoxical that the decade of eighties which saw unprecedented growth should be soon followed by the severest foreign exchange crisis by 1990.

Liberalisation

Until at least the 1970s, the Indian economy was seen as a classic case of post-war state-led economic development, within a mixed economy framework (Ghosh, 2001). This approach incorporated the major tendencies of Indian economic planning, including the emphasis on heavy industrial investment until the mid-1960s and the focus on state ownership/control of the 'commanding heights' of the economy (the basic and core infrastructure industries as well as other strategic and economically significant industries), as well as state regulation of many other aspects of economic activity even in the non-core areas. It also meant recognition of the role played in the subsequent decades of Indian development by the state in subsidising private investment activity in both industry and agriculture.

Over four decades, this broad mixed economy approach brought about some significant, if qualified economic successes, as well as glaring failures. The more striking successes were in terms of the substantial increase in aggregate growth rates over the pre-independence period, as well as the steady diversification of the economy and the building up of a substantial productive base in a range of modern industry. The most striking failures were in the persistence of absolute material poverty among a very large section of the population (such that even at present more than 30% of the population is officially described as below the poverty line) and in the inability to achieve basic human development goals such as education and adequate health provision for the entire population.

The basic elements of the changed economic regime since 1991 have included a system of more liberal imports and reduction/elimination of external trade controls generally; a progressive removal of administrative controls over capacity creation, production and prices, including a move to free markets in foodgrains and a cutting down of food subsidies; a strictly limited (and declining) role for public investment even in important infrastructure sectors, the privatisation of publicly-owned assets over a wide field; a focus on reducing implicit subsides by raising user charges over a wide range of public utilities and services; an invitation to MNCs to undertake investment (under substantially liberalised conditions relating to ownership, operation and profit repatriation); and financial liberalisation measures that have substantially reduced priority sector lending and subsidised credit and allowed greater capital market innovation.

Overview of Economic Reforms

A process of creeping liberalisation had been launched by consecutive Indian governments since the late 1970s, and especially after 1985. However, the current phase of economic reforms dates back to July 1991, when following a balance of payments crisis generated by the withdrawal of international credit and non-resident Indian (NRI) deposits, India's foreign exchange reserves collapsed. The government opted for conditional credit from the IMF to deal with the situation, necessitating policies of stabilisation, and an acceleration of 'structural reform' as well as its extension into the external and financial sectors.

Stabilisation

In theory, stabilisation required a sharp reduction in the fiscal deficit from its record high of 8.3 percent of GDP in 1990-91 to a targeted 3.4 percent of GDP over a short span of time. In practice, however, public expenditure reduction has involved a substantial reduction in the expenditure on capital formation, besides cuts in subsidies as well as certain other types of expenditures. The process of stabilisation also required a sharp reduction in the 'monetised deficit' of the government, or that part which was earlier financed through the issue of short-term, *ad hoc* treasury bills to the Reserve Bank of India (RBI), with the aim of giving the central bank a degree of autonomy and monetary policy a greater role in the economy.

Structural Adjustment

The principal aims of the structural adjustment policies adopted as a part of the reform process were:

(i) to do away with or substantially reduce controls on capacity creation, production and prices, and let market forces influence the investment and operational decisions of domestic and foreign economic agents within the domestic tariff area;

(ii) to allow international competition and therefore international relative prices to influence the decisions of these agents;

(iii) to reduce the presence of state agencies in production and trade, except in areas where market failures necessitates state entry; and

(iv) to liberalise the financial sector by reducing controls on the banking system, allowing for the proliferation of financial institutions and instruments and permitting foreign entry into the financial sector. Policies specific to the various sectors are considered below.

Industrial Policy

The post-reforms industrial policy has moved in three principal directions. The first was the removal of capacity controls by 'derestricting' and 'delicensing' industries, or abolishing the requirement to obtain a licence to create new capacity or substantially expand existing capacity. As a result of the dereservation of areas earlier reserved for the public sector and the successive delicensing of industries, there were only nine industries for which entry by private investors was regulated at the end of 1997-98.

The second area of industrial reforms related to the dilution of provisions of the Monopolies and Restrictive Trade Practices (MRTP) Act, so as to facilitate the expansion and diversification of large firms. The MRTP Amendment Bill removed the threshold limits with regards to assets for defining MRTP or dominant undertakings, thereby removing any special controls on large firms.

The third type of liberalisation in industry involved foreign investment regulation. The first step in this direction was the grant of automatic approval, or exemption from case-by-case approval, for equity investment of up to 51 percent and for foreign technology agreements in identified high-priority industries so long as royalty does not exceed 5 percent of domestic sales (8% of export sales). As a follow-up, the Foreign Exchange Regulation Act was modified so that companies with foreign equity exceeding 40 percent of the total were to be treated on par with Indian companies. Further, NRIs and overseas corporate bodies owned by them were permitted to invest up to 100 percent equity in high priority industries, with repatriability of capital and income. Foreign investors were allowed to use their trademarks in Indian markets.

Trade Liberalisation

A distinguishing feature of the economic reforms of the 1990s was the effort to eliminate import controls by rapidly reducing the number of tariff items subject to quantitative restrictions, licensing and other forms of discretionary controls on imports as well as by cutting the rates of tariff on a range of commodities. However, the process of tariff reforms has not been uniform across industrial sectors. Imports of capital goods have been substantially liberalised by placing them under the Open General Licence (OGL) category, by reducing tariffs and by offering concessional duties for 'project imports' and imports allowed at zero duty subject to promises of export to be realised. The same is true of imports of intermediates, access to which have been simplified and subjected to lower duties.

Reforms in Agriculture

The economic reforms did not include any specific reforms for agriculture. The presumption was that freeing agricultural markets and liberalising external trade in agricultural commodities would provide price incentives leading to enhanced investment and output in that sector. However, the pattern of structural adjustment and the government's macro-economic study since 1991 have actually been associated with a reduced rate of overall agricultural growth, declines in per capita foodgrain outputs and inadequate employment generation.

Exchange Rate Policy

In a series of steps the government has moved to a situation where there is a unified, market determined exchange rate of the rupee, which is fully convertible for current account transactions. In addition, various financial liberalisation measures have had direct and indirect implications for exchange rate management, since they affect the inflow and outflow of short-term capital into the country.

Until the East Asian crisis, the government appeared keen on moving to full convertibility of the rupee. The official Tarapore Committee, set up to draw up a road map for the process, had recommended that the implementation be spread over 1997-98 to 1999-2000 and suggested preconditions to be met sequentially for this. Besides fiscal consolidation, a mandated inflation target and the restructuring of bank capital, the road map prescribed a step-wise process of financial liberalisation.

Financial Liberalisation

An important area where major reforms have been continuously implemented is in the financial sector. The process started with the repeal of the Capital Issues (Control) Act, 1947 and the abolition of the Controller of Capital Issues. Companies could freely seek finance through the capital market, subject to the regulations of the newly created Securities and Exchange Board of India (SEBI). Indian companies were allowed to access international capital markets through Euro equity shares. A range of non-bank financial companies, including private mutual funds, were allowed to operate. Investment norms for NRIs were liberalised and foreign institutional investors (FIIs) were allowed to register and invest in India's stock markets, subject to an overall ceiling (30%) and a ceiling for each individual FII in a particular company's shareholding. In addition, the government did away with the higher rate of capital gains taxation that applied to foreign and NRI investment that chose to invest in the stock market. Besides these, a number of guidelines to ensure transparency in share issues were specified.

The other element in financial sector reforms was that the regulation of the banking sector in terms of controls on entry by private, domestic and foreign players, cash reserve ratios and statutory liquidity ratios, entry of financial institutions in the banking sector, priority sector credit provision and investments and activities, have been substantially eased. A range of new instruments has also been permitted.

Causes for the Genesis of Liberalisation

Planners, researchers and policy makers often discuss the causes, which lead to the initiation of structural adjustments/reforms. Many commentators have talked about the condition of Indian economy during 1990-91 as the immediate cause. The crisis that hit Indian economy during 1990-91 was the immediate cause for the series of reforms taken place later on. The Gulf War pushed up petroleum prices and India's annual petrol import bill rose. Due to stagnation in the industrialised nations, exports also did badly. India's international debt increased and during the late 1980s her debt was the fourth largest among developing nations (US$ 71,557 million). Debt service ratio increased up to 30 percent. India's international lenders began fearing that India would run into a debt crisis and decided that they should get away with their money while the going was still good (Basu, 1993).

Much of the discussion of the structural adjustment policy package applied in India since 1991 has tended to concentrate on its intellectual origins in the Fund-Bank 'Washington consensus' and its likely consequences in the specific Indian environment (Ghosh, 2001). It is now increasingly evident, however, that this may be an inadequate mode of considering the entire process. Some of the essential ingredients of the package have been retained in Indian practice, for example, in terms of greater emphasis on liberalised markets, a reduced role for direct public investment and a concerted drive to woo foreign investment through numerous concessions. But it is also certainly the case that the Indian combination of economic policies for adjustment has differed in some important ways from the 'textbook' Fund-Bank model, most particularly in the continuing internal imbalances of the government as well as in the possibility of continued external imbalances because of capital inflows, both of which point to the lack of 'adjustment' at least in the standard sense. Focusing on the ideal construct of the standard package is therefore not very illuminating any more. With some of the more recent data that are now available, it is now possible to attempt an assessment of the Indian structural adjustment package since 1991, based not on the supposed model, but on the policies that have actually been pursued.

There are at least two striking features of mainstream analyses of the economic reforms programme in India since 1991. The first, which is evident not only in official government publications (particularly of the Finance Ministry) but also in the English language financial press, is the generally unsupported statement that the 'reforms' instituted so far by and large have been successful both in achieving the medium-term goals of structural adjustment and in preparing the economy for 'take-off' in the new globalised environment. The second, which is not so much an assessment as a longing and wistful eastward gaze, refers to the bold examples of the successful East and South-East Asian economies, and suggests that emulation of their supposedly 'open' and 'market-oriented' policies would allow India also to benefit from the buoyancy evident in what is economically the most dynamic part of the world today. Not only are the countries in this region constantly cited as examples of the enormous benefits to be derived from 'globalisation', but their rapid growth is seen as a continuous reminder of the failures of our own past development strategy.

It is curious, however, that while both these sets of arguments are typically put forward by the same -- or similar -- groups of people, they are rarely put forward together in a way which would allow for a systematic comparison of the adjustment policies being followed in India and those which have been adopted in other East and South-East Asian countries. But such a comparison is necessary, because only in this way can we hope to come to a reasoned assessment of whether the package of economic reforms currently being implemented in India has any relation to the strategies that have allowed for the apparent economic success of these other countries in Asia. This section attempts such a comparison, albeit in a brief and relatively sketchy fashion.

Basu (1993) also mentioned the political instability and changes of government at the Centre in discussing the causes of adjustment. But he argued that it was not the immediate crisis but there was a structural need for the policy changes and most of the propagators of structural adjustment had lack of confidence on what was going on with the country's economy. Questions were more fundamental than immediate action on the perceived crisis. He also claims that 'socialist' India in the pre-reform period has failed to fulfil her basic objectives in elimination of poverty, equitable distribution of social justice, etc. According to him, the failure of the pre-reforms system provides the rationality to envision structural adjustment during those years.

Given the professed objectives and at times even claims of being 'socialist', India's performance in terms of poverty reduction and provision of basic needs is abysmally poor; and in fact India's growth record through the 1980s is not one to be dismissed. The national income growth averaged 5.2 percent per annum right through the decade. On the other hand, the percentage of households without access to safe drinking water in the country in 1981 was 61.81. The percentage without electricity was 73.81, and, most tellingly, the percentage without any literate member was 32.96 percent. By several measures India's literacy performance is beginning to trail behind that of Sub-Saharan Africa.

As far as poverty in general goes, it is difficult to make cross-country comparisons but with around 300 million poor, India is home to nearly one-fourth of the world's poor. On the infant mortality front India has made strides and with a figure of 92 in 1990 it stands ahead of Pakistan and Bangladesh but far away from China (29), Thailand (27) and Sri Lanka (19). Since so many of our policies over the last fifty years have been justified in the name of equity, this should make us realise that in economics what looks obvious may not be so. Policies that on the face of it look 'pro-poor' may be serving the interests of the wealthy. In many cases, benefits meant for the poor, like cheap credit and subsidised medicines, have been cornered by the relatively better off people, either by directly acquiring these provisions for their own use or by charging a higher price than the one fixed by the government, while selling these to the poor. One of the things that this demonstrates is that even when planning our basic needs programme, we must not be wished away. One of the India's gross failures in the past has been exactly this. The purpose of structural reforms is partly to make amends fcr this (Basu, 1993).

But many people talked more about the immediate crisis that leads to smothering the fact of the gross failure of the past system. Some critics also say that the perceived immediate crisis in 1990-91 was not a serious matter; it is only the lack of confidence that made the reforms to be happened. Supporting these points, few facts will provide valuable information. International debt and trade performance were the two perceived crisis-hit areas of Indian economy during those years. Basu (1993) argues, whereas many within India rose and alarm about these results (fourth position of India in terms of external debt), it is not clear that the absolute size of the debt is the right measure to look at. If we divide each country's debt by GNP, India, with a figure of 29.2, drops down to the 90th rank from fourth.

Basu also examined India's trade deficit as percent of GDP, and finds that it was also not an area of crisis as deficit was lower than in the early eighties (2.9 in 1990-91 while 3.4 in 1980-85). The claim that on the international front India has always lived precariously but there was no precipitous decline in the 1980s seems maintainable. This is what lends credence to the 'thesis' that the crisis of 1991 was a crisis of confidence.

The word 'reforms' was hardly seen in the literature on economic development or growth in the 1940s and 1950s. It did not make its presence felt even in policy making circles the world over till almost the 1980s. If the word is interpreted in a broad sense, the Indian economic history since India's independence could be classified into two reforms modes – the first spanning from 1955 and running through the years up to the middle of 1991, and the second is the one that is proceeding on since then. The first reforms mode itself is not that crystal pure in terms of the content of the policy strategies that were pursued. The second mode expectedly is evolving. Nonetheless, one could identify the essential building blocks of the two modes, as forming two different approaches to economic development.

It is obvious that the emergence of the reforms mode in the mid-1991 would not have happened, had the first mode been effective (Vasudevan, 2001). Indian economic and political thinkers were influenced by a number of streams of thought on economic development even before India attained political independence in 1947. The three famous plans of the 1940s – the Bombay Plan, the People's Plan and the Gandhian Plan – and the Indian economists' writings about the inflationary situation during the Second World War and in the post-war years, as also about the reconstruction and rehabilitation activities, were evidence of a cross-section of views on how India should fashion its development path after independence and the policies required to move ahead on the path.

It was, however, only in 1955 that a view, a majority one, on India's development strategy was formed and the political consent given to pursuing, what Mahalanobis called 'scientific planning'. This, however, did not mean that there were no dissenting voices on the chosen path at the time of the formulation of the development strategy.

The adopted development strategy (in 1955) was said to be in the tradition of the then fashionable balanced growth doctrine. As the economy then was not in a position to pull itself up by the 'boot straps' because of the resources crunch, priorities were assigned in order to develop 'steel first' with direct state intervention. The saving rate being low, the state had to resort to inflationary financing, and some, albeit limited, dependence on foreign sources. The consequential price increases were to be contained by price controls and allocative mechanisms.

By the end of the 1970s, however, it was evident that the rate of growth of the economy was unspectacular: it averaged about 3.5 percent a year, earning the sobriquet, the 'Hindu rate'. It was hardly enough to improve the living standards to double the levels that existed in the early 1950s, even by the end of the 20th century. The theoretical rationale behind inflationary financing, namely, that it will generate 'forced saving' did not materialise.

Shortages and bottlenecks reflected the presence of over-regulation, the absence of incentives, and the inadequate effective demand. Competitiveness abroad was hindered by protectionist policies and the lack of absorption of new technologies. Private initiatives were discouraged by barriers to entry and exit, restrictions on size and scope of activities, and absence of means of market financing. Public sector management was not allowed to be creative because of lack of incentives and excessive intervention 'from above'.

Although the 1980s was marked by some relaxation of the over-regulation, the difference made to the regime was not of kind but of degree. By the end of the 1980s the Indian economic experience was in some respects similar to the economic experiences of the erstwhile Soviet Union and some of the East European countries. These experiences showed that the 'jam tomorrow' as against 'jam today' argument, advanced in the name of state-directed planning, would work only for some initial years and not for long. This could be attributed to several reasons.

First, the state bureaucracy will increase, and render the synergetic interactions between the economic decision-making processes and the market forces, weak. In many cases, the bureaucracy will flourish and profit from a proliferation of regulations and controls. Secondly, the economic controls introduce distortions and vitiate allocative efficiency, thereby adversely affecting productivity. Thirdly, the initial successes of state-directed planning in the erstwhile USSR owed mainly to 'forced labour' and repression of civil liberties, especially in the 1930s and 1940s, but it was quickly realised that they could not be sustained for long, as information flows became sharp through new communication technologies, notably the radio and television. Finally, the idea that growth depends on technological strides and financial development, as captured in the writings of endogenous growth theorists and in the writings of McKinnon (1973), Shaw (1973) and Maxwell Fry (1978, 1988), was hardly in evidence in dirigiste regimes in general. In the case of India, however, the Green Revolution of 1968 proved to be an exception in that it was a major technology shock but it was limited to very few farm products. Financial deepening in India was constrained during the period of the first reform mode by financial regulations, and by concentration of decision-making powers at central levels.

Nonetheless, in some important respects, the Indian economic experience was different from the totalitarian/ planned economies (of the erstwhile USSR and East Europe). Fortunately, India did not opt for state ownership of all the means of production, and experimented with a 'mixed economy' pattern right from the mid-1950s. This has enabled the private entrepreneurship to flourish, albeit under constraints, in trade and industry. In fact, in agriculture and small-scale industries, the presence of public ownership was characterised by conspicuous near-absence. Even in the field of medium- and large-scale consumer good industries, private sector was allowed to be dominant. Moreover, a number of financial institutions specialising in certain areas (long-term project finance, housing finance, capital market) were set up with the initiative of the government and the central bank of the country right from the 1960s with a view to improving the domestic capital formation and widening the financial markets.

This development has provided some 'financial base' that could be utilised prospectively for financial deepening whenever liberalisation processes are initiated. Besides, the large geographical coverage of commercial banks in the 1970s and 1980s gave a good infrastructure for development of financial intermediation processes.

Finally, the availability of high skills formed partly owing to relatively cheap higher education at premier educational and technological institutions in the country provided a platform that could be utilised in the prospective shifts in technologies and management strategies.

It should, however, be recognised that these advantages merely suggested the opportunities for policy makers available to be put to good use in the prospective period. But, they were not the reasons for moving to the second reforms mode. The fact that movements in the major macro-economic indicators have shown a perceptible improvement over the 1980s should have in fact prompted a deferment in shift over to the second reforms mode. The severe balance of payments crisis triggered the initiative for discarding the prevalent policy frame and shifting to a reforms mode that would enable the country to accelerate growth on a sustained basis together with monetary and financial stability. Such a shift would also enable the economy to avoid the problems of debt – both external and internal. Therefore, high allocative efficiency in both real and financial spheres through incentives and dynamisation of market forces both at home and abroad has been made the main focal point of attention in this reforms mode.

Economic Reforms: An Assessment

Post-reforms Performance

The performance of the Indian economy in the post-reforms period has been extensively commented upon. Judged by the standard criteria of growth rates of national income and per capita income, external balance and inflation rate, the Indian economy has done well since liberalisation (Rangarajan, 2001). Between 1981-82 and 1990-91, the growth rate of the economy was 5.6 percent per annum. The year 1991-92 was an exceptionally bad year for reasons well known. Indeed, there is no justification to include that year as part of the post-reforms period, particularly while judging the effectiveness of the reform process.

It is interesting to note that between 1992-93 and 1999-2000 there was only one year in which the growth rate was less than 5 percent. The co-efficient of the variation of growth rate in the 1990s, is distinctly lower than in the 1980s. With a slowing down of the population growth rate, the per capita income growth rate in the 1990s has been 3.8 percent. Between 1992-93 and 2000-01, the industrial growth rate was 6.6 percent per annum whereas the growth rate in services was 7.9 percent. The gross domestic savings rate of the economy on an average during the period from 1992-93 to 1999-2000 has remained at

23.1 percent of GDP. Inflation rate as measured by the Wholesale Price Index, though high in the early 1990s, started declining from 1995-96 and the average inflation rate has been around 5 percent since then.

Concerns and Issues

The liberalisation process has come in for criticism from two opposite ends. First, there are those who feel that the process has been slow and not sufficiently comprehensive. These critics attribute the current slowdown in the growth rate to this factor. On the other hand, there are critics who view the reform process as misconceived, ignoring the basic realities of our country. There are four aspects of these criticisms, which deserve attention.

A major criticism of the liberalisation process is that the higher growth rate achieved has made no dent on poverty and unemployment. Based on the National Sample Survey (NSS) data on consumption expenditure, over years, certain methodologies have been evolved to estimate the number of people below poverty line. Estimates of the percentage of the people below poverty line based on various NSS rounds show that the combined rural and urban poverty ratio came down from 44.48 percent in 1983 to 38.86 percent in 1987-88 and further to 35.07 percent in 1993-94. However, based on the smaller annual samples, some analysts had come to the conclusion that there was a rise in the poverty ratio since 1993-94. This, if confirmed, would have been a disturbing trend.

However, recently, results of the large sample survey data on consumer expenditure for 1999-2000 have been released. These show a sharp decline in poverty ratio to 26.10 percent. Certain technical questions have been raised about the comparability of the latest survey data with the earlier surveys. The use of two reference periods in the latest survey, according to some, has vitiated comparability. However, some independent studies conducted using the data collected on consumption expenditure in the employment survey also show a decline in the poverty ratio after 1993-94, even though the decline is not as strong as indicated by the large sample survey on consumption expenditure. In the past, it has always been found that higher economic growth is accompanied by faster reduction in the poverty ratio. However, there has been a significant change in the sectoral pattern of growth in the 1990s. There has been a distinct slowing down in the growth rate in agriculture while the tertiary sector has grown strongly. The growth rate of agricultural production at 2.8 percent in the 1990s had been much lower than 4.1 percent in 1980s. While the trend of reduction in poverty ratio is reassuring, a further look at the pattern of growth has become essential, since agricultural and associated rural activities still constitute the major source of employment.

Employment figures indicate that between 1990-91 and 1997-98, overall employment grew only at an average rate of 1 percent with the employment in the organised and unorganised sectors growing at 0.6 percent and 1.1 percent respectively. Part of the explanation for this phenomenon lies in the imperfections in the labour market which induce preference for capital in relation to labour contrary to the pattern of factor endowments in the country. The abundant supply of labour must become the source of expanded output. Where there is a transition from one industry to another, appropriate social safety nets and retraining facilities must be put in place.

One of the major planks of the liberalisation policy has been to reduce the fiscal deficit. Of course, some people question the wisdom of focusing on fiscal deficit as an indicator of financial health. In seeking to defend higher fiscal deficits, the theory of Keynes is invoked. This is a case of applying a principle out of its context. Keynes was writing when a balanced budget was the order of the day, even at times of depression and he felt that, under those circumstances, a deficit was in order. But, what we are discussing now is not whether there should be a fiscal deficit or not but what order of deficit is desirable. In this respect, the original Keynesian framework is inadequate because the model did not take into account the implications of alternative modes of financing government expenditure. Borrowing from the market can have an impact on the interest rate, while financing through money creation has inflationary implications and at one step removed on nominal interest rate.

There has been some success in reducing fiscal deficit but not to the desired extent. Some are critical of the fact that whatever reduction had been brought about was almost by reducing capital expenditures. Total expenditures as a proportion of GDP came down by 3 percentage points between 1990-91 and 1997-98. This was achieved by a reduction in capital expenditures as a proportion of GDP by 2.1 percentage points and revenue expenditures by 0.9 percentage points. The revenue to GDP ratio has remained more or less at the pre-reforms level, despite significant tax reform measures introduced. No doubt, the best way of reducing fiscal deficit is by reducing revenue deficit. But, unfortunately, revenue expenditures have kept increasing. Wages, salaries and pensions have continued to rise. In many states, they account for almost the whole of state's own revenue receipts. Subsidies after an initial decline have remained at the same level as percentage of GDP. At state level, implicit subsidies have increased enormously. The fiscal deficit can be contained at a reasonable level only by widening the tax base and raising the ratio of revenue to taxes and by limiting revenue expenditures.

Yet another area of concern of the critics is that enough attention is not being paid to social infrastructure areas. Literacy levels have risen in India. Nevertheless, they remain well below what is desirable. Basic health facilities have not reached everyone. But, the fault for this situation cannot be laid at the doors of liberalisation. The distortions in priorities occurred much earlier. In fact, the very purpose of liberalisation is to reduce the role of the state as an entrepreneur and direct investor and expand its role in areas such as social infrastructure, where state alone can play a dominant role. The need for expanded state intervention in areas of education, health and sanitation cannot be underestimated. It is necessary to generate the surplus to fulfil the socio-economic obligations. It is also to be noted that better education and health are a function of not only levels of expenditures but also the efficiency with which such expenditures are incurred. For example, according to the Human Development Report, 1991, both Sri Lanka and India had a similar human expenditure ratio of 2.5 percent of GDP. Human expenditure per capita in 1988 was $ 10 for Sri Lanka while it was $ 9 for India. However, in the ranking of Human Development Index, Sri Lanka occupied 75th rank, whereas India was lower down at 123rd rank. Part of the reason for the difference in the ranking could be enhanced expenditure at a certain level over a longer period. The Human Development Report itself admits: "Even government expenditure cannot be considered in isolation. Its impact depends not just how much money is spent but on how and in what environment it was spent."

The fourth area of concern has been the growing disparities in income among states. Differences in growth rates among states have become more pronounced after liberalisation. During the 1980s the growth rate of State Domestic Product (SDP) ranged from a low of 3.6 percent per annum to a high of 6.6 percent. In the 1990s, the variation has been from a low of 2.7 percent per annum to a high of 9.6 percent. Some of the highly populous states have registered very low growth rates in the post-liberalisation period. Tax devolution formulas as well as Planning Commission allocations of grants and loans are heavily weighted in favour of population and the inverse of per capita income. Nevertheless, the populous states have grown weakly in the last seven-year period and this has contributed to the increase in the overall poverty ratio also. Many of these states have not been actively involved in the liberalisation process. If the regional disparities have grown, it is at least in part a reflection of the quality of governance. It is interesting to note that the ranking of the states according to income growth rate differs considerably between 1980s and 1990s. The rank correlation coefficient between the two periods is only 0.283. This implies that some states, which have grown slowly in the earlier period, have had higher growth rates in latter period.

As one surveys the period since 1991-92, it becomes clear that the economy has shown distinct improvement in several areas. The broad philosophy of promoting a competitive environment must be pursued. At the same time, if the growth momentum is to be maintained, some areas need focussed attention. Mention was made earlier of the problems arising from the slowdown in agriculture. A comprehensive agricultural policy encompassing a higher level of public investment, a shift from subsidies to investment in terms of public expenditure, consolidation of holdings, a proactive programme to foster exports, intensified agricultural research to raise yields and evolving a better cropping pattern needs to be thought of. Growth in agriculture has several implications for the economy. It leads to a reduction in poverty, a greater expansion in employment given the Indian situation and a more broad-based growth.

Second, as mentioned earlier, fiscal consolidation is a necessary prerequisite for sustained growth. The finances of the state governments are particularly under greater pressure. The appropriate level of fiscal deficit has a relationship to the level of household savings and more particularly to the savings in financial assets. Even as of now, very nearly, the whole of the household savings in financial assets is appropriated by the public sector. There is validity in the argument that government expenditures should shift in favour of capital expenditures. Unfortunately, the trend has been in the opposite direction. Containing the growth rate of revenue expenditures has become essential. In a developing economy like India, where a significant proportion of people remains poor, subsidies are an essential component of government expenditures. However, they need to be targeted appropriately, so that they accrue only to the deserving. We must make an effort to evolve a consensus on how to deal with subsidies, user charges and reducing revenue expenditures. This is indeed the task of the political managers of the economy. With different parties in power in different states, it should be possible to achieve a significant degree of consensus on this issue of fiscal prudence.

Public sector still continues to dominate the economy in several important sectors. Even as attempts are being made to disinvest wherever feasible, there is no doubt that we must pay adequate attention to improving the functioning of public sector enterprises where their presence is essential. In fact, in certain areas, disinvestments can only follow the strengthening of the enterprises. This is very much true in the case of electricity generation and distribution. Many committees and commissions have studied these problems. It is high time that a policy package is put together and implemented for bringing about a significant improvement in the efficiency of public sector enterprises. Clearly, the lesson of Indian development experience is that monopolies, whether of state or private sector, do not lead to efficiency.

The need to create, promote and sustain a competitive environment is absolutely essential. India is no longer a country producing goods and services for the domestic market alone. Indian firms are becoming and have to become global players. At the minimum they have to meet global competition. However, even as we do create conditions for more effective functioning of the enterprises, some of the issues discussed earlier, such as emphasis on agriculture, fiscal consolidation and public sector reforms need special attention. The recent slowdown in the growth rate of the economy points to the importance of the role of investment and effective governance. These two factors are interrelated. The strong growth exceeding 7 percent per annum, which was witnessed for three consecutive years beginning 1994-95 was fuelled by heavy investment. Investment is the major driving force of growth. An environment should be created which is conducive to investment.

All investment decisions are based on future prospects. Continuance of economic policy is basic to sustaining expectations in the right direction. Equally important is the confidence in the future course of the economy. It is in this context that governance becomes a key concern. Policies have to be right. But that is not enough. They must be pursued with vigour and conviction. They have to be implemented with single-minded devotion. This is one lesson that we have to learn from China. In any economic system, state can play many roles. One can at least identify three important roles: (1) as a producer of goods and services, (2) as a regulator of the system, and (3) as a supplier of 'public goods' or 'social goods' like primary education and health. The decreasing role of state as a producer of goods and services and the increasing role of market in such areas simultaneously enhance the role of state as a 'regulator' and 'facilitator'. The regulatory role comes into play in order to maintain competitive conditions in the market and to ensure that everyone follows the basic rules of the game. This is indeed an important aspect of 'governance' and may warrant appropriate legislative changes.

Liberalisation programme to be successful must ensure that the benefits accrue to all sections of society and that it commands the acceptance of a wide constituency. Efficiency and equity should not be posed as opposing considerations. They must be taken together to produce a coherent pattern of growth. There is no conflict between the process of liberalisation and the social obligations of the state. There is nothing inherent in the liberalisation process, which should hinder the special responsibilities of the state in relation to the poor and underprivileged. In fact, a more efficient economy, which should be the outcome of the process of liberalisation, would enable the state to meet better its responsibilities in the socio-economic arena.

Economic Reforms Strategy for the Next Decade

In the years immediately following the start of the SAP, or later, India did not suffer any drop in total GDP, high inflation or sizeable increase in unemployment unlike in many other developing countries which carried out SAP with or without stabilisation measures. The stabilisation programme had some negative effect because of the compression of imports and of government expenditure but, on the whole, the SAP had a positive impact. In the nineties the growth rate of GDP could reach the level of 7 percent per annum (Table 2.2). After three years of high growth, the economy entered a period of downswing and deceleration in growth with the onset of political instability and the East Asian crisis. Still, the rate of growth of GDP hovers around 5 percent. The average rate of growth in the 1990s up to 1996-97 (including the early years affected by the BOP crisis of 1990-91 and the stabilisation attempt) is not much higher than that of the 1980s. But, there is a significant difference. This rate has been achieved in the context of a slowdown in the world economy and has been sustained along with a remarkable build-up of our foreign exchange reserves. Indeed, in the external sector, there is a remarkable transformation. Three significant developments may be noted: (a) a tremendous increase in foreign investment; (b) a very large flow of remittances with a realistic exchange rate; and (c) remarkable growth in exports until the beginning of the world economic slowdown and no balance of payment problem after 1991-92.

Table 2.2
Growth of Gross Domestic Product
(at constant prices, 1990-91 to 1996-97)

Years	Rs in Crore	Percent
1990-91	2,12,253	5.36
1991-92	2,13,983	0.82
1992-93	2,25,240	5.26
1993-94	2,39,145	6.17
1994-95	2,57,700	7.76
1995-96	2,76,132	7.15
1996-97Q	2,96,845	7.5

Annual average rate of growth, 1980-81 to 1989-90 = 5.69. Annual average rate of growth, 1990-91 to 1996-97 = 5.75. Q = Quick Estimates.

The most significant gain from the reforms so far carried out is the capacity to grow at a fairly high rate without running into BOP problems, provided of course reasonably sound fiscal policies are followed. As Bimal Jalan, the RBI Governor, has pointed out, in 30 of the 36 years preceding 1990-91, we had some BOP problem or the other. Now, it can be said that we have achieved self-reliance in one important respect. Ironically, the extreme left is saying that we have come under the dominance of IMF and the World Bank, whereas the fact is, unlike in the past, we do not need to go to the IMF at all, and can carry on even without World Bank loans. During the next decade, to sustain a high rate of growth, we need, among other things, to maintain a high growth of exports and obtain large and growing remittances and sizeable foreign investment. For this purpose, we have to have a fairly open economy with a realistic exchange rate and the efficiency of our economy has to be further increased. Therefore, there is no doubt that the major reforms carried out from 1991-92 to 1996-97 were in the right direction. In the subsequent two years some more reforms have been carried out, but owing to political instability and quick changes of government, the reform initiatives have not been quite consistent and in some areas the action has not been carried out on a sustained or consistent basis.

State-Level Reforms

The major reforms and the policy changes to be effected at the state level during the coming decade are: (a) power sector reforms; (b) improvement in the roads and extension of road network; (c) removal of hindrances to a maximum possible extent to the free movement of goods; (d) closing down or sale of loss-making public enterprises; (e) reduction in subsidies in respect of consumption of power by the agricultural and domestic sectors along with other reforms in the power sector; (f) at least partial privatisation of the road transport (passenger) services; and (g) higher outlay on primary and secondary education, health and family planning and significant improvement in the standards of these services. The obstacles to reforms are to some extent lack of understanding, short-term political considerations and lack of financial resources. Understanding of issues is growing, but there seems to be no improvement in the financial conditions of the state governments.

While the reforms of state-level public enterprises would help to some extent, it is absolutely necessary to raise the ratio of revenues to SDP by at least 1 to 1.5 percentage points. Correspondingly, on the other side, administrative expenditure and the size of the administrative staff would have to be drastically reduced. All in all, the ratio of government's revenue expenditure to SDP should be brought down by about 1 percentage point. These changes would ensure that the revenue deficits of the state governments would be wiped out and that all their borrowings could be used for capital formation. Most of the capital formation can be for infrastructure development and human development, with public enterprises not requiring any investment because most of them would be gradually phased out.

The initiation of reforms started after devaluation of rupee twice on July 1 and July 3 in 1991, which resulted on an aggregate devaluation of 18 percent. New industrial policies were announced. Tariff rates were lowered down. Temporary reprieve had been earned in the form of borrowed foreign exchange of 4.8 billion dollars from IMF, immediately. Flow of money into the country from NRIs residing in different countries started in a massive way since May 1992. Gradually, many multinational companies started investing in India in various fields/sectors ranging from power (Enron) to passenger cars. A private initiative in infrastructure sector was also thought seriously and concepts of BOT, BOOT infiltrated and negotiation took place with many private agencies for investment in road sector. Ideas of public-private partnership were given importance even at the city level. People started talking about competition of cities in attracting investment and new constitutional amendments, empowering local governments (74th for urban and 73rd for rural) were conceived. Private investment in cities, particularly in the mega-cities, increased rapidly (e.g., investment in private housing provisions during the early years of the decade was so high that it created recession in building industry of the city).

Neogi and Ghosh (1998) have studied the impact of liberalisation on performance of Indian industries. This study shows that productivity growth and efficiency level have not improved as per expectation during the post-performance period and the distribution of efficiency is skewed. The capital intensities in terms of capital-labour ratio are growing at faster rate during the whole period of 1989 to 1994, particularly during the post-reforms period. N. Taneja, former member of the Indian Statistical Service, reported that industrial employment has been adversely affected in post-1991 primarily due to failure of the government to provide a level playing field to domestic industries. His analysis shows that industrial employment has been hit hard in units having investment of more than Rs 1,000 million. Likewise, Tendulkar and Jain (1995), by using NSS data found that there was a sharp increase in rural poverty whereas a moderate rise took place in urban poverty.

Liberalisation in agricultural sector was also planned. Propagators of liberalisation argued that increase in the price of agricultural produce would result in increase in income of rural poor. Advocates of liberalising economic reforms often argue that there will be net gains to the poor from the higher relative prices of agricultural goods, including food, consequent to devaluation, the removal of restrictions on external trade, and cuts to subsidies on agricultural inputs (Ravllion, 1998). But, in India, poorest households in rural areas are net consumers of food, as sufficient land for excess production of food products is not available with the farmers in most of the regions. Role of mediators in selling rural produce is also very strong in India. Therefore, gains from rise in food prices will be insignificant. There has been a long-standing concern in India; it is plausible that the poorest households tend to be net consumers of food, since in most regions they are unlikely to have sufficient land for their own consumption needs. They may benefit as agriculture workers, depending on the dynamics of wage adjustment and income shares from this source. But it remains that some of the poorest households in rural areas could lose initially from higher food prices, with the initial gains being concentrated amongst the rural non-poor (Ravllion, 1998).

Survey-based estimates show that the correlation co-efficient between India's national poverty rate (percentage below poverty line, on the vertical axis) and index of the relative price of food in the period 1958-94 is highly significant, i.e., 0.76 (Ravllion, 1998). Performance of Indian economy after the reforms was mixed. Moderate change was seen in performances of many sectors. On an average, Indian economy grew at 5.3 percent per annum during the first five years since the reforms (1992-96), which was 0.6 percent lower than that of 1986-91. The annual growth rate of primary and secondary sectors since 1991-92 was lower at 2.5 percent and 6.3 percent compared to 3.7 and 7.4 percent respectively during 1986-91. Tertiary sector, with about two-fifth share in the GDP, grew fastest in the 1990s (6.8% per year). Within this sector, trade, hotel and restaurants witnessed a sizeable rise (1.7%) in its annual growth rate, from 6.5 percent (Nagraj, 1997).

Critically examining the investment pattern of the post-reforms years, Nagraj (1997) comments that sectors witnessing bulk of spending cuts are defence and economic services. Governmental final consumption expenditure on defence has come down from 4.1 percent of GDP during 1986-91 to 3.3 percent during 1992-95. In the same period, current expenditure of administrative departments on economic services fell from 6 percent to 5.2 percent of GDP. However, he again specifies another important aspect. The sum of spending on health, education, housing and social services has remained constant at 2.9 percent of GDP during 1992-95. The same measure as a proportion of total government final expenditure rose from 26.2 to 28.1. Finally, he describes that, contrary to earlier apprehensions, social spending, averaged over four years since the reforms, did not suffer, as defence and economic services bore bulk of the adjustment burden. However, in the 2000-01 budget of the central government, allocation for defence was increased after the Kargil episode. Now, it is to be seen how the new policy is going to affect the common man and the social services.

There was a deep cut in public investment level in the first five years since the reforms, which often make the researchers anxious about the results associated with it. Questions of the sector, which bore the burden of these adjustments and of sustainability of economy, often arise. Allocation on social spending remained constant, but it remains to be seen whether it can be equivalent to social spending as in the pre-reforms period. Public sector expenditures in many sectors are going down (and may go down further) with the increasing flow of money from the private enterprises in these sectors. The government should realise this and attempt to increase public investment in the social sector because the sustainability of economic development is dependent on the successful nature of human development.

There is also an increasing gap between the rich and the poor even in potential mega-cities, where the benefits of liberalisation are more. Lack of public investment can cut down the level of basic amenities in the poorer areas in a city and private services may be costlier to afford affecting the utilisation rate as well as increasing cost of living of the poor. Researchers are more critical in monitoring structural adjustment with an apprehension that the investments in social sector/facilities will go down, as direct returns from this sector are not very high. It will not be favourable for the private investors and, on the contrary, government will cut investment in the expectation of it from the private enterprises. It was expected that private sector would be able to fill up the gap created by withdrawal of public agencies.

In the Economic Survey 2000-01, it was claimed that "India has the distinction of being one of the fastest growing economies in the world". This ecstasy is now somewhat subdued, after the release by the Central Statistical Organisation (CSO) of its revised estimate of GDP growth in 2000-01.

According to the latest estimate, the GDP growth in 2000-01, instead of being 6 percent as anticipated, was only 5.2 percent. One may still argue, and perhaps rightly so, that even 5.2 percent growth rate is higher than what has been achieved by most other countries. The reality, however, emerges when one looks at the GDP growth rate of agriculture, during the first four years of the Ninth Plan. It has been only 1.4 percent per annum. During these four years, the population of the country, and of agriculturists, has increased by no less than 1.9 percent.

From these, it is evident that during the last four years, agriculturists have become poorer, not only in comparison with non-agriculturists, but also in absolute terms. Per capita availability of foodgrains has also declined, as reported by the Planning Commission in its Mid-Term Appraisal of the Ninth Plan. One may ask, "If 60 percent of our population, dependant on agriculture for their livelihood, have become poorer and more undernourished, then what is there to rejoice about?" The industrial sector too, during these years, has not performed well than in the past. Only, the service sector maintained its tempo. No less than 70 percent of the benefit of growth in GDP has accrued to less than 20 percent of our population engaged in the service sector.

GDP growth rates can be raised and sustained beyond 6 to 6.5 percent, if certain critical reforms be implemented soon. India's economic reforms have played a critical role in the performance of the economy since 1991. It is important to note that despite the slowdown in 1997-98, the average growth rate in the four years, from 1994-95 to 1997-98, was 6.9 percent, significantly higher than the growth rate of 5.6 percent achieved in the 1980s. Moreover, the growth in the 1980s was not sustainable without further reforms, as the lack of export dynamism contributed to a balance of payments crisis at the end of the decade. In 1998-99, the GDP was estimated to have grown at 5.9 percent.

A few of the Indian states such as Andhra Pradesh, Gujarat, Karnataka, Maharashtra and Tamil Nadu have been more reform-oriented, while states like Haryana, Kerala, Orissa, Madhya Pradesh, Punjab, Rajasthan and West Bengal have lagged in carrying out state-level reforms. Bihar and Uttar Pradesh are even further behind. States that move against the populist policies and set up regular markets for services, such as power and water, are going to be ahead of the rest in the game. They are likely to garner faster state-level economic growth and job creation, from both domestic and foreign investments.

Broadly speaking, there are currently rather significant differences in reform interest and economic performance between a large part of northern India and southern India. Karnataka, Tamil Nadu and Andhra Pradesh are quite dynamic now in trying to improve the physical and legal infrastructure, in order to attract large-scale foreign investment. In the north, especially in Bihar and Uttar Pradesh, one does not see the same kind of reform dynamism and the results are therefore poor in terms of economic growth. We believe that these differences will be noticed politically sooner rather than later, as inequalities between states in their economic performance become glaring. The states that are ahead will be rewarded with better performance while the states that are behind will find that there is the demand to catch up with the states that are growing. This kind of inter-state competition will spur the overall reform process, as has the inter-regional competition in China.

Swamy (2002) conducted a study on the success of the structural reforms and the road to which India is now headed. According to him, the two decades since 1980-81 have been easily the best in India's economic performance in the last century. After averaging about 3.6 percent a year in GDP growth rate during the thirty years between 1950-51 and 1980-81 and less than 1 percent a year in the half century before that, GDP growth accelerated to 5.6 percent in the 1980s (5.3 if 1991-92 is included) and averaged even higher at 6 percent in the final decade up to 2000-01. Indeed, if the crisis-affected year of 1991-92 is omitted, GDP growth in the past nine years (1992-93 to 2000-01) averaged an unprecedented 6.3 percent. And, between 1992-93 and 1995-96, the growth rate averaged even higher at over 7 percent a year.

This vindicates the stand that economic liberalisation, deregulation and market principles were essential for raising the growth rate in the economy that required eschewing the then current command economy ideology copied from the USSR, and which failed there too. In his book, *Indian Economic Planning: An Alternative Approach* (1971), Subramaniam Swamy had predicted that such a transformation in policy towards market economy would raise the growth rate to 10 percent a year, but alas had then found little acceptance because of Indian economists: that India was bound by the "Hindu rate of growth" of 3.5 percent a year.

The past trend in decadal growth rates looks increasingly better, partly because of the declining population growth rate over the years. When we look at per capita GDP growth, we find that it has accelerated from 0.8 percent in the 1970s to 4.6 percent in the nine years following 1991. Furthermore, while the growth performance in the 1980s was bedevilled by unsustainable fiscal deficits and increasing drain in external reserves, which led to the balance of payments crisis of 1990-91, in the nine years after 1991, the external sector has been manageable despite the fiscal imbalances deteriorating.

What is significant is that in an international perspective India's growth performance of the last two decades ranked amongst the top six in the world growth league, along with China, Korea, Thailand, Singapore and Vietnam. Moreover, since the 1997 East Asia meltdown, India's rank is now second only to China in growth rates. In PPP (purchasing power parity) terms, the 1990s growth has also put India among the top four in the world. In fact, on corrected data, the growth rates of China and India in the 1990s have been about equal, and unless the present dispensation in power makes an even bigger mess than it managed to do since 1998, the Indian growth rate can exceed China's during the first two decades of the 21st century.

Much of this growth has been due to macro-economic policy changes since 1991, but also due in part to fortuitous international circumstances and to the global environment. Sadly, it is now quite clear, however, that reforms in India have run out of steam. What is more alarming is that since 1996-97, even the relatively high growth rates are not sourced to agricultural and industrial growth but to the services sector.

If we sub-divide the nine years following the 1991 crisis into an initial period of five years (corresponding to the Eighth Plan) and the subsequent four years up to 2000-01, the following points are worth nothing: *First*, the acceleration of GDP growth to -6.7 percent from the pre-crisis decadal (1980-89) average of 5.6 percent is remarkable and attributable to reforms. *Second*, it is noteworthy that in the post-crisis quinquennium, all the major sectors (agriculture, industry, services) grew at a noticeably faster pace than in the pre-crisis decade. *Third*, the average growth performance in the four most recent years is, in sharp contrast, disappointing. Overall GDP growth drops to 5.8 percent. Of much more concern is the collapse of agricultural growth to 1.4 percent and the significant fall in industrial growth to 4.9 percent. In 2000-01, the rate only dropped to 2.1 percent. Indeed, the drop in GDP growth in these four years would have been much steeper but for the extraordinary buoyancy of services, which averaged a growth of 8.8 percent. This growth in services was much faster than in the case of industry – a pattern that raises questions of sustainability. No economy can continue to grow this way for long.

A part of the services sector growth in the last four years was, furthermore, bogus in the sense that it simply reflected the revaluation of the value-added in the sub-sector "Public Administration and Defence" because of higher pay scales resulting from decisions based on the Fifth Pay Commission Report. National income accounting practice requires that value added in non-marketed services be estimated on the basis of 'cost' and in current prices. These Pay Commission effects, including in states, were spread mainly over three financial years 1997-98, 1998-99, 1999-2000, when growth of "Public Administration and Defence" soared to 14.5 percent, 10.3 percent and 13.2 percent, respectively, compared with an average growth in the previous five years of less than 4 percent.

Thus, the nation needs to launch on a second generation of reforms after an in-depth analysis as to where we have gone wrong. There are four major areas of the Indian economy summarised below, which require urgent attention:

(i) Fiscal Deficit

There has not been too much progress in cutting the fiscal deficit. Whatever little the central government has managed up to 1999 has been cancelled out by the deteriorating fiscal position of the state governments. Since 1999, even the Centre has failed to curb fiscal deficit. The combined fiscal deficit is now near 10 percent of GDP. High fiscal deficit crowds out private investment and banks' capacity to lend, since the government corners the lion's share of the bank's funds. Fiscal measures to encourage domestic saving and foreign direct investment (FDI) are essential now.

(ii) Poverty

There is no consensus yet on the key question: have the reforms helped the poor? The data put out by the National Sample Survey Organisation suggest that poverty rates have remained static, but National Council for Applied Economic Research (NCAER) data show that poverty rates have fallen. However, since the rent-losers from economic reforms are entrenched and organised, and the gainers are not, the legitimacy of reforms is being eroded every day. This needs to be set right.

(iii) Growth Distribution

Growth has been unevenly distributed, especially in terms of regions. Some dynamic states like Maharashtra are sprinting ahead, while the likes of Bihar have stagnated. This could put pressure on the federal system, since the bulk of the poor and rapidly growing population lives in the already populous northern states. The North-South divide (as it is seen globally) is reversed in India, and could upset the polity in the future.

(iv) Growth Impulses

The economy's growth impulses are getting weaker, while domestic industry, with exceptions like TVS, is caving in to foreign companies in hostile take-overs. While the government still talks about pushing GDP growth rate to 8 percent, the harsh reality is that India seems stuck in the 5-6 percent range during the last four years. Talk cannot be a substitute for action.

While growth is the ultimate target of macro-economic policy, low fiscal deficit, high savings and investment are intermediate targets. Controlled inflation, increasing employment and decreasing poverty are immediate targets of macro-economic policy. Macro-economic policy needs to be designed keeping all three types of targets in mind.

If growth is the key measure of macro-economic performance, inflation (or rather its absence) is the generally preferred indicator of macro-economic stability. In the 1980s, India's average inflation rate of 7.2 percent was close to the average rate for Asian developing countries as a group (7.1%), a little above the average rate for the developed countries (5.6%) and much lower than the average for all developing countries (39%), which was driven high by Latin American inflation (145.4%). In the 1990s, the conspicuous difference was that inflation in developed countries dropped to a low 2.6 percent, or one-third the average rate for India. And, in the last three years, inflation in the Latin American countries came down to single-digit figures.

Thus, inflation was contained worldwide, and India was a beneficiary. It is therefore not merely because of India's macro-economic policy that inflation was contained, but because of the global environment of price stability.

In the next wave of reforms, what is going to be crucial is the launching of what India's representative at the IMF, Vijay Kelkar, calls meso-economic reforms, otherwise known as 'second-generation reforms': that is, major infrastructure sector reforms in energy, irrigation works, transportation, telecommunications, universities and other higher institutions of learning and housing construction. In a growing economy, these sectors will require enormous amounts of new investment. That is easier said than done in India, because no country in the world has achieved a sustained growth rate or high rate of investment with such high interest rates as in India (of 6-8% in real terms). Bringing the real interest rates in the neighbourhood of 3-4 percent is therefore essential. It can trigger a spectacular investment boom throughout the economy.

Such a reduction in the long-term interest rates will also be essential to maintain an exchange rate regime that is supportive of trade liberalisation, that is, avoid the overvaluation of the rupee. Thus, the reduced interest rate and competitive exchange rate can become the 'Archimedean' lever to propel the economy on the high growth path.

Currently, by and large, all infrastructural sectors are in the public sector and in some cases they are monopolies. If in these sectors we introduce both privatisation of public sector enterprises and the entry of the private sector, the gains to the economy are likely to be quite spectacular. In the Indian economy, the benefits of these meso-economic reforms could add 3-4 percent of GDP per annum, which can accrue with little capital, and provide the springboard for further gains, particularly by inspiring new private investment and productivity growth. In this list of meso-economic reforms, emphasis needs to be laid on reforms in higher education, that is, colleges and universities, to dismantle, for example, the severe entry barriers to start a private university in India, to permit collaboration or alliance of Indian educational institutions to be outsourced for academic research and even teachers by cost-strapped academic institutions of the United States and other developed countries.

A major implication thus of these meso-economic reforms is a need to create a new institutional and financial architecture for the management of the Indian economy to sustain a full-fledged modern market economy, where stability, predictability and transparency of policies are seen to be of fundamental importance by foreign investors.

The new institutional architecture will also imply the strengthening of independent regulatory agencies such as the Securities and Exchange Board of India (SEBI), the Telecom Regulatory Authority of India (TRAI) and the Central Electricity Regulatory Commission (CERC), and to their independence being treated on a par with the independent judiciary. Such a new institutional architecture will have an independent monetary authority. This will be achieved by giving greater independence to the RBI on the lines of the autonomy enjoyed by the Federal Reserve in the United States and the Bank of England. This will inspire confidence amongst both investors and consumers and promote competition in these sectors since it would end the crony capitalism that plagues India and inundates the economy with mega scandals involving insider trading and plain fraud.

In the reforms initiated in 1991, the emphasis was on reforms of product markets by abolishing industrial licensing and import barriers. These reforms, however, left the factor markets such as labour markets, land markets and capital markets, the natural resources market such as water, and institutions mostly untouched.

However, now, among the necessary factor market reforms, two are crucial: first, of the labour markets, and second, of the financial sector. India's present laws of bankruptcy (exit policy) and corporate control require reforms so that the market for corporate control becomes competitive. The financial sector reforms would involve reforms of the banking sector, equity markets, debt markets and foreign exchange markets. In this, privatisation of state-owned banks is perhaps the most essential, but preceded by strengthening of the regulation and supervision of financial institutions and of capital markets, which are really non-existent at present. The recent developments in the Indian stock market vividly show how the actions of one private bank, one cooperative bank, one major stock exchange management and a giant mutual fund of 20 million subscribers can have a deleterious impact on national equity markets and particularly on small shareholders, because of a lack of strong supervision.

3

Liberalisation in India

Reforms in the States

Fiscal conditions of most states in India have deteriorated over last several years. The gross fiscal deficit of 25 states has increased from Rs 37,120 million in 1980-81 to Rs 2,36,950 million in 1993-94, which is more than 700 percent. Similarly, the revenue deficits of the states have increased from Rs 10,880 million to Rs 45,120 million during the period between 1987-88 and 1993-94. In this context, it was felt necessary to carry out economic reforms in all the states. Many states have initiated the reform process from 1992 onwards. But, in some states, it was introduced in a very comprehensive and logical fashion while in some cases it was ad hoc and short-term in nature. Following the process of the national government, some state governments have undertaken procedural and policy reforms for promoting foreign investment, private participation in infrastructure development, etc.

States like Gujarat, located on western coast, have become popular for industrial and urban development. The successive state governments of Gujarat have taken the initiative for economic reforms by constituting the State Finance Commission and prepared the agenda for reforms. All leading political parties of the state have accepted the agenda for reforms. The fiscal reforms were initiated to reduce the fiscal deficit from 4 percent of the Net State Domestic Product (NSDP) to 2 percent over a period of two years. For state-owned enterprises, reforms were introduced through privatisation, disinvestments, restructuring, merger and closure, as many such units were not performing well. Infrastructure development was identified as a necessary step for the overall development of the state. But, the present situation shows that the state has not been able to reduce the fiscal deficit. It indicates that reforms at the state level are going to be little more difficult and social services are going to be more affected as these services are included in the State List. Backward states like Bihar, Orissa and many others will find it difficult to introduce reform measures in their respective states and eventually demand more from the central government.

Reforms and Agriculture

Agricultural sector is the mainstay of the rural Indian economy round which socio-economic privileges and deprivations revolve, and any change in its structure is likely to have a corresponding impact on the existing pattern of social equality. The Indian agricultural sector provides employment to about 65 percent of the labour force, accounts for 27 percent of GDP, contributes 21 percent of total exports, and of raw materials to several industries. The livestock sector contributes an estimated 8.4 percent to the country GDP and 35.85 percent of the agricultural output. India is the seventh largest producer of fish in the world and ranks second in the production of inland fish. Thus, no strategy of economic reform can succeed without sustained and broad-based agricultural development, which is critical for

- raising living standards,
- alleviating poverty,
- assuring food security,

- generating buoyant market for expansion of industry and services, and
- making substantial contribution to the national economic growth.

Studies also show that the economic liberalisation and reforms process have impacted on agricultural and rural sectors very much (Madaswamy, 2002). Also, the reforms will have an impact on agricultural trade, technology, rural infrastructure, productivity and employment and food security (Bhalla, 1993).

In most developing countries, the rural areas are characterised by low income and poverty. The small farmers represent the bulk of the poor. Studies by FAO have shown that small farms constitute between 60 and 70 percent of total farms in developing countries and contribute around 30 to 35 percent to total agricultural output (Randhawa and Sundaram, 1990). Although they represent the largest group owning the total land collectively, their sphere of influence is very limited considering their individual positions. It is the large landowners, comprising only 1 percent of the population, who own almost 14 percent of the total land in India and exercise their powerful interests in matters of agricultural development. The bulk of the small farmers has been increasing steadily over the decades and this shows the increasing trend towards casualisation (erratic and low-paid work) and marginalisation. A just cause for concern and worry, planners and policy makers are worried that with the policy-cum-market trend of liberalisation, this will further increase. The stress on agricultural development after the New Economic Policy (NEP) is towards incorporation of new technology and scientific methodology and for the largely small farmers in the Indian agricultural sector, this is not an immediate possibility.

In the 1990s India was blessed with normal monsoons without interruptions. Despite this, there are clear indications that the growth of foodgrain output had declined in the 1990s, and there was some slowdown even in the growth of total crop output when compared to the 1980s. This is corroborated by slowdown in the growth of irrigated area and a sharp decline in the rate of growth of fertiliser consumption (Rao, 1998). This decline in the foodgrain output during the 1990s is explained by economic reforms related factors, i.e., insufficient reforms as well as improper sequencing of reforms. Reforms have been insufficient in so far as export of superior cereals like wheat and rice, in which the country has a comparative advantage, continues to be restricted. The rate of disproportion for these crops in 1996-97 was as severe as in the immediate pre-reforms period. On the other hand, oilseeds, in which the country does not have a comparative advantage to the margin, are still protected, causing a shift of resources, at the margin, away from foodgrains to oilseeds (Gulati and Sharma, 1997).

But, the basic explanation for the recent slowdown in agricultural output, especially foodgrain output, is the improper sequencing of reforms bearing on the supply-side factors, such as irrigation and fertilisers. Reforms in management of irrigation system for recovering user charges will take time to yield results. As such, resources need to be raised in the intervening period to protect capital and maintenance expenditures. However, the emphasis so far has been on containing fiscal deficit by reducing these essential expenditures that has led to a slowdown in the expansion of irrigated area (Rao, 1998). The decline in the foodgrain output in the 1990s is also related to declining contribution of total factor of productivity. The growth rate in output, which was about 40 percent in the 1960s and 1970s, declined to around 30 percent in the late 1980s (Desai and Namboodri, 1997). The ongoing drought condition in states like Gujarat and Rajasthan will slowdown the agricultural growth in these states and put pressure on the economy. However, it is expected that the central government should give a lot of relaxations and subsidy for agricultural development.

Reforms and Manufacturing

The key elements of India's economic liberalisation programme initiated in 1991 were the abolition of the industrial licensing system, substantial liberalisation of foreign trade and foreign direct investment (FDI) regimes, removal of ceilings on interest rates and associated reforms in the financial sector. This section assesses the impact of the reforms on methods of financing investment and productive efficiency of the major industries in India's manufacturing sector.

The 1991 reforms have been analysed extensively (Joshi and Little, 1998; Forbes, 1999). The principal reform measures included the abolition of licensing procedures for manufacturing investment, reduction in import tariffs on most goods other than consumer goods, liberal terms of entry for foreign investors, liberalisation of the capital market, the abolition of ceilings on interest rates and laying down of the Capital Issues Control Act (Table 3.1). The consensus appears to be that these reforms were substantial though not radical. They were substantial insofar as they reduced bureaucratic control over economic activity, enhanced the role of the private sector and the price mechanism. But, they hardly addressed the perennial problems posed by the inefficient public enterprises, and labour legislation and company laws, which hamper efficiency and flexibility of operations. Even so, what has been achieved constitutes a major departure from the centrally controlled and protectionist regime that prevailed prior to 1991.

In some respects, the 1991 reforms are no more than a culmination of the attempts at liberalisation initiated in the mid-1980s by Rajiv Gandhi, the then Prime Minister of India. The 1985 reforms, however, were piecemeal; they exempted firms with assets of a pre-designated amount from licensing requirements, but did not do away with industrial licensing entirely; they increased the range of capital goods and raw materials which could be imported without licenses, but did not abolish import licenses in total, nor did they reduce the level of import tariffs. The fairly stringent foreign investment regime was not also relaxed. The 1991 reforms in contrast were much broader both in scope and scale, and initiated a departure from the earlier regime of controls and permits towards a market-oriented regime.

Table 3.1
Major Reforms Influencing the Indian Manufacturing Sector

Prior to 1991	Reforms
Industrial licensing, reserved several industries for the public sector.	Abolished with a few exceptions.
MRTP act restricting corporate investment.	Relaxed.
Imports subject to quotas and tariffs.	Removal of quotas except for consumer goods, substantial lowering of tariffs.
Restrictions on FDI, foreign equity discouraged.	Many sectors opened up to FDI, automatic approval of foreign equity up to 51 percent in many sectors.
Control over foreign exchange.	Largely liberalised current account, though restrictions on capital account remain.
Ban on foreign portfolio investment	Relaxed rules.
Severe restrictions on the timing and pricing of capital issues.	Substantial capital market reforms.
Interest rate ceilings, subsidised lending.	Ceilings largely removed, subsidised lending reduced.
Access to foreign technology restricted.	Policies relating to technology relaxed.

Although the Rajiv Gandhi reforms were piecemeal, they do appear to have promoted growth and productive efficiency of the manufacturing sector. Growth rate of manufacturing output was around 8.5 percent per annum during the second half of the 1980s, substantially high by historical standards. Statistical studies (Ahluwalia, 1991; Srivastava, 1996), though subject to several limitations, suggest that many of the industry groups in the manufacturing sector experienced technical change and growth during this period. Estimated growth in total factor productivity (TFP) is put at around 2.7 percent per annum during 1981-89 compared to a trend decline of 0.5 percent per annum during 1960-80. Another study estimates TFP growth of manufacturing firms between 1987-88 and 1991-92 to be 2 percent per annum compared to -1.0 percent between 1982-83 and 1986-87 (ICICI, 1994).

There is, therefore, reason to believe that the manufacturing sector does respond to liberalisation and the impact of the relatively large-scale 1991 reforms on growth and productive efficiency should be much more robust than that of the earlier limited attempts at liberalisation. These hopes were not entirely belied. The growth rate of manufacturing which had declined to -3.7 percent in 1991-92, recovered to 4.2 percent during the very next year. During the next four-year period, from 1993-94 to 1996-97, manufacturing output grew at an appreciably high rate of around 10.4 percent per annum. This improved performance, however, appears to have ended abruptly when the economy slid into a recession in early 1997. There are a number of reasons for the decline in growth rates in the post-1997 period. Market forces set in train by the reforms appear to have worked with a vengeance. Removal of ceilings on interest rates led to the expected increase in interest rates that reduced investment and production. In addition, banks, which sought to strengthen their balance sheets, curtailed credit to risky ventures. The decline in production may, in fact, be due to the demise of firms which were unable to function in the new competitive environment. In addition, infrastructure bottlenecks appear to have held back investment.

The years since 1996-97 may be one of turbulence in product and financial markets with weak and inefficient firms struggling to cope with increased competition and new firms trying to establish themselves in the new-found competitive market environment. In this respect, Indian experience appears to mirror that of other developing countries such as Chile, which embarked on a programme of liberalisation. This aggregate picture, however, conceals developments at the micro level of the manufacturing sector. The objective of this paper is to analyse developments at the level of individual sectors and industries.

Reforms and Poverty and Employment

Since the launching of economic reforms, the question of their impact on the poor has received much attention from researchers and policy makers. Economic reforms are part of the broader strategy assigning distinctive roles to the government, market and people's organisations in promoting growth and in eradicating poverty. In this scheme, economic reforms are expected to play major role in stepping up growth with the government and people's organisations looking after the people.

There is now substantial evidence that India's success at reducing the incidence of poverty during the 1970s and 1980s was halted, if not reversed, during the 1990s. Estimates made at the World Bank (Datt, 1999) show that the incidence of poverty, which between 1972-73 and 1989-90 fell from 55.4 percent to 34.3 percent in rural India and from 54.3 percent to 34.1 percent nationally, has in subsequent National Sample Survey (NSS) rounds up to 1997 (when the incidence was 34.2% national and 35.8% rural) never gone below the 1989-90 level and has in fact risen to much higher levels in individual years. Other estimates suggest an even greater increase in rural poverty during the 1990s. The estimates for the head count ratios of rural population living in absolute poverty are provided in Table 3.2. All these estimates indicate, moreover, that the gap between rural and urban areas, which had decreased during the 1980s and the 1970s, increased considerably during the 1990s.

Food items have a large weight in the indices of consumer prices for industrial workers and agricultural labourers, especially the latter. The faster rise in these indices is, therefore, likely to result in faster increase in the prices of various food items, particularly cereals, than of other items consumed by the rich. Thus, what emerges is that one of the reasons for the stagnation in real per capita consumption and thereafter of the incidence of rural poverty during the 1990s is the adverse consequence that rising food prices have had for the poorer sections of India's population. Clearly, the rise in the relative food prices during the 1990s has hit the poor hard, even at a time of relatively high income growth which itself was accompanied by some increase in the inequalities in nominal consumption expenditures.

Table 3.2

Estimates for the Rural Head Count Poverty Ratios

(in%)

NSS Round	Year	Rural Poverty Ratio World Bank	Rural Poverty Ratio S.P. Gupta	Real Per Capita Consumption (1973-74 prices)	Gini-Index
46	Jul 90-Jun 91	36.43	35.00	66.73	27.72
48	Jan 92-Dec 92	43.47	41.70	63.80	29.88
50	Jul 93 Jun 94	36.66	37.30	67.45	28.58
51	Jul 94-Jun 95	41.02	38.00	66.39	30.17
52	Jul 95-Jun 96	37.15	38.30	67.37	28.43

Source: Datt, 1999 and *Sarvekshana*, various issues.

But, in addition to this decline in the purchasing power of the incomes of the rural poor, the rate of growth of per capita rural income in real terms has sharply decelerated. This fall in rural incomes is, however, not just because the share of agricultural income in national income has fallen. The share of non-agricultural incomes in total rural incomes, which rose sharply between 1977-78 and 1990-91, has stagnated since then. One reason why rural poverty declined during the 1970s and the 1980s was that income-earning opportunities in the rural non-agricultural sector expanded substantially, driven mainly by a large expansion of government expenditure in the rural areas. The reduction in such expenditure during the years of reforms has affected that expansion adversely.

In terms of rural employment patterns, Table 3.3 presents the workforce participation rates (number of all workers as a ratio of total population) for men and women in rural India from the early 1970s to the late 1990s. It is evident that the male workforce participation rates have remained broadly stable over this entire period. The overall picture of female workforce participation in the rural areas is one of fluctuations around a declining trend. Female workforce participation rates were, on average, significantly higher in the 1970s until the mid-1980s. The latest year in fact shows the lowest rate over the entire period.

Table 3.3
Workforce Participation Rates for Rural Men and Women

(in%)

Year	Male	Female
1972-73	54.5	31.8
1977-78	55.2	33.1
1987-88	53.9	32.3
1989-90	54.8	31.9
1990-91	55.3	29.2
1993-94	55.3	32.8
1994-95	56.0	31.7
1995-96	55.1	29.5
1997	55.0	29.1
1998	53.9	26.3

Source: Sarvekshana, various issues.

There is now significant evidence that the main dynamic source of rural employment generation over the period from the mid-1970s to the late 1980s was the external agency of the state rather than forces internal to the rural economy or other extra-rural forces including modern industry and commerce. In fact, in most areas, the pivotal role in the expansion of rural non-agricultural employment appears to have been played by the expansion of government expenditure.

The pattern of structural adjustment and government macro-economic strategy since 1991 involved the following measures which specifically related to the rural areas:

(i) Actual declines in central government revenue expenditure on rural development (including agricultural programmes and rural employment and anti-poverty schemes), resulting in an overall decline in per capita rural government expenditure.

(ii) Substantial declines in public infrastructure and energy investments, which affect the rural areas. These have related not only to matters like irrigation but also to transport and communications, which indirectly contribute significantly, even to agricultural productivity, besides being an important source of rural non-agricultural employment.

(iii) Reduced transfers to state governments which have been facing a major financial crunch and have, therefore, been forced to cut back their own spending, particularly on social sectors such as education and health and sanitation, which had provided an important source of public employment over the 1980s.

(iv) Reduced spread and rising prices of the public distribution system for food.

(v) Financial liberalisation measures which effectively reduced the availability of rural credit.

Thus, in the 1990s, several of the public policies, which contributed to more employment and less poverty in the rural areas in the earlier decade, have been reversed.

In the last few years (when India's economy has begun to take-off, though not fly), some good numbers on poverty are beginning to come in. Enough to make one think, how swiftly things can change overall, if one were to focus on more investments in the social sector. In the Economic Survey 2000-2001, published by the Ministry of Finance, 26.1 percent of Indians are reported to be impoverished. For the country as a whole, the poverty numbers since 1973-74 have been diminishing (Table 3.4).

Table 3.4
Poverty Numbers in India, 1973-1999

(in%)

Year	All India	Rural	Urban
1973	54.9	56.4	49.0
1978	51.3	53.1	45.2
1983	44.5	45.7	40,8
1988	38.9	39.1	38.2
1994	36.0	37.3	32.4
1999	26.1	27.1	23.6

How the rate of decline in poverty numbers has accelerated since economic reforms began in 1990 is shown below in Table 3.5:

Table 3.5
Rate of Decline in Poverty Numbers, 1973-1999

(in%)

Between	All India	Rural	Urban
1973 & 78	3.6	3.1	4.2
1978 & 83	6.8	7.4	4.4
1983 & 88	5.6	6.6	2.6
1988 & 93	2.9	1.8	5.8
1993 & 99	9.9	9.4	8.8

Dr. Surjit Bhalla of Oxus Research, in a draft paper called "FAQ's on Poverty in India" (July 20, 2000) concludes: "No matter what the data source, survey or national accounts, growth is shown to lead to poverty decline, almost one for one. No growth, no poverty reduction is the only conclusion." "It cannot be concluded that there was economic growth in India in the nineties, and that there was an increase in absolute poverty. There is no evidence for this joint conclusion." and "...economic reforms initiated in 1991 have led to a radical transformation in the well-being of the bottom half of the population. From an approximate level of 38 percent in 1987, poverty level in India in 1998 was close to 12 percent." The distribution of poverty too is not uniform across the country as shown below in Table 3.6:

Table 3.6

Distribution of Poverty Across States

Poverty Level below	States
10%	Goa, Haryana, Himachal, J&K, Punjab, Daman/Diu, Delhi
20%	Andhra, Gujarat, Karnataka, Kerala, Mizoram, Rajasthan, Lakshadweep, Dadra/Nagar Haveli, Andaman
30%	Maharashtra, Manipur, Tamil Nadu, Bengal, Pondicherry
40%	Arunachal, Assam, MP, Meghalaya, Nagaland, Sikkim, Tripura, UP
50%	Bihar, Orissa

The poverty estimates for 1993-94 shows that the incidence of poverty or the proportion of people below the poverty line was lower than 1987-88. However, the rate of decline in the incidence of poverty over the 1990s was much more than in the preceding decade when there was a series of good monsoons and green revolution spread to the poorer states in eastern India, leading to a rise in employment elasticity in agriculture (Rao, 1998).

In the post-reforms period of early 1990s, however, the growth rate in GDP had come down significantly; the rate of inflation was high (persisting around 10% consequently for four years) and the expenditure on social sectors including poverty alleviation programme slowed down. The consumer price index for agricultural labourers increased by 50 percent over five years, ending in 1993-94. This is because, among other things, the drive to reduce food subsidies led to a steep increase in the issue prices of foodgrains supplied under the Public Distribution System (PDS). The difference between the free market and PDS prices narrowed down significantly leading to the reduced off take from the PDS and the decline in the per capita availability of foodgrains (Rao and Radhakrishanan, 1997). These factors may explain the slow pace of reduction in poverty in this period when compared to the 1980s.

On the other hand, impact of economic reforms so far seems to have been favourable on the urban poor as the rate of reduction in urban poverty is greater than in the previous decade. In the last three decades ending 1996-97, growth rate in GDP rose close to 7 percent, the rate of inflation came down to 5 percent and the expenditure on social sector has been picking up. It is, therefore, very likely that the pace of poverty reduction both in rural and urban areas would have improved significantly.

V.M. Rao (1998) commented that the poor will remain too weak and vulnerable to move upwards with their own initiative and efforts. The system helps them in distress but does little to nurture them as productive and creative beings. There are many question marks on the capacity of economic reforms to bring about sustained growth accessible to the poor. However, it is difficult to foresee clearly the course taken by this process, its impact on the system and consequences for the poor. But, the common feeling among many social scientists is that in the long run all the structural adjustment may give negative result, more people will remain poor and the gap between the rich and the poor will increase.

On Labour Market

The economic reforms, as already stated, had the objective of replacing a centrally controlled, protectionist economic regime with a competitive environment where free interaction of market forces would ensure efficient allocation and use of resources, thereby enabling Indian industry to become globally competitive and export-oriented. The reform process started with a series of policy initiatives to stabilise the economy that had been unhinged by mounting fiscal and current account imbalances. These policies had a contractionary impact on the economy, particularly on the industrial sector. Into this situation were introduced measures designed to restructure industry: progressive dismantling of state control and regulatory mechanisms, freeing of entry into industry, clearing of blocks in the way of foreign capital inflows, opening of areas for private investment in pockets hitherto reserved for the pubic sector, reduction in customs duties, tax reforms, moves towards full convertibility of the currency and capital market reforms.

These reforms threatened to create substantial additional unemployment in a situation already burdened with the contractionary impact of stabilisation policies, particularly since a sizeable quantity of surplus labour had been carried over from pre-reform days. This, in the absence of a social security system of any kind, involved social costs that could not be ignored. The government, therefore, decided to create a 'safety net' for the workers who might find themselves out of jobs in the process of restructuring. This eventually took the form of the National Renewal Fund (NRF).

Unemployment due to restructuring is expected to arise from three sources: closure of some of the economically non-viable enterprises, downsizing of the workforce in other weak units and adjustments in labour force in perfectly healthy enterprises necessitated by changes in market conditions and/or technological innovations. The NRF is designed to deal with redundancy arising from the first two sources. The redundancy arising from the third source is in the nature of frictional unemployment that is a normal feature of any dynamic economy.

The number of non-viable enterprises had been growing over the years. These enterprises, referred to as 'sick industries', are found in the private as well as the public sector. Under the prevailing laws, no private enterprise employing 100 or more workers could wind up, without the permission of the government – a permission that was rarely granted. And, of course, there was no question of closing down any public enterprise. However, the growing problem of industrial sickness did not go unnoticed and, while freedom to exit was not considered, the Sick Industrial Companies Act (SICA) was passed by the parliament in 1985. Under the SICA, the Board of Industrial and Financial Reconstruction (BIFR), the operational arm of the Act, was constituted. According to the SICA, an enterprise was sick if it had been registered for seven years, had eroded its entire net worth and had made losses consecutively over the past two years. Such an enterprise had to apply to the BIFR within a stipulated time. The BIFR, after scrutiny, could sanction a rehabilitation package for the enterprise, or, finding it beyond repair, order its closure. The SICA also defined an enterprise weak or potentially sick if it had been registered for five years and had eroded its peak net worth by half. Such an enterprise was obliged to make a reference to the BIFR which, however, could only insist that the erosion of net worth be reported to the shareholders and discussed in a specially convened general body meeting.

The definition of sick enterprise under the SICA was clearly restrictive. It was not aimed at catching companies in early stages of sickness, so that rehabilitation packages turned out to be considerably more costly than they need have been. Sickness was allowed to continue for much longer, with accompanying loss and waste, than was necessary. The functioning of the BIFR was also found to be slow which again meant unnecessary locking up of capital or accumulation of losses.

The BIFR itself responded to these weaknesses in the system and recommended amendments to the SICA. Among the amendments later incorporated in the Act was a change in the definition of sick enterprise. The stipulation of loss over two consecutive years was dropped and the period of registration was reduced from seven to five years. Some other changes of note were better protection of the BIFR from litigation, right of the BIFR to directly wind up an enterprise on the recommendation of a financial institution or the government to the effect that it could not be rehabilitated and the adoption of a single window concept for the implementation of rehabilitation packages by designated lead financial institutions.

A recent study of industrial sickness in India presents a detailed analysis of the phenomenon. The study pinpoints the role of the Reserve Bank of India (RBI) guidelines in creating or perpetuating industrial sickness. Briefly, the main points are: (i) under the guidelines, a loss-making sick enterprise can get loanable funds at substantially lower rates of interest than a healthy one; (ii) the guidelines frown on write off of bad debts and this leads banks and financial institutions to prepare overly optimistic viability reports to justify further funding, which only increases the stock of bad debts; and (iii) sick units are encouraged to remain sick by allowing them a generous equity-to-debt leverage along with incremental debt at a highly subsidised rate which makes remaining sick more advantageous than making profit.

Originally, the SICA did not cover financial and public sector enterprises. Subsequently, its coverage was extended to central and state public sector undertakings (PSUs). Currently, 54 central and 66 state PSUs are registered with the BIFR. Prior to the economic reforms, funds were indiscriminately made available to support loss-making PSUs. It is not so any more; PSUs are now expected to apply to the BIFR. However, in case the government can come up with a rehabilitation scheme of its own before the BIFR has organised the first hearing for a registered PSU, the unit is taken out of the purview of the BIFR. This then has been the government's response to the problem of industrial sickness. The response, however, remained incomplete until recently since a response to the problem of redundant labour was missing. The NRF seeks to address this latter problem.

This following section examines the nature and extent of potential labour redundancy and, against this backdrop, considers the adequacy and effectiveness of the NRF as a response to the problem.

It is reported that the demand for labour increased after liberalisation but the increase was not shared evenly in rural and urban India between men and women, and regular and casual workers. By and large, the demand for casual and intermittent work increased faster than durable and regular work. The structure of employment moved away from the primary sector for rural men, but rural women lost in employment. Real wages and the share of primary sector in their employment increased. Gender base reduced but that in the earnings of regular workers increased. Liberalisation has affected casual workers, particularly women casual workers, more than regular workers (Deshpande and Deshpande, 1998).

M.S. Dev (2000), in an article, reported that the growth of employment has not declined in 1990s as it has happened in Pakistan. However, employment in the organised sector has been declining over time. Employment growth in unorganised sector has been increasing. Thus, the hypothesis of shifting of workers from the formal to the informal sector during the initial years of liberalisation seems to be correct empirically.

Infrastructures and Urban Governance

The demographic growth in urban India has been projected to be very high because of natural growth of population and in-migration. Population projection across the country by the international agencies like World Bank and by several researchers shows that India is poised for rapid urbanisation in next twenty years. It is also argued that structural reforms and the associated development strategy would accelerate rural-urban migration and give boost to the pace of urbanisation. The proponents of this strategy believe that linking of India with the global economy will increase the inflow of foreign capital as also facilitate indigenous investment, resulting in rapid development of infrastructure and industries. This is likely to give impetus to the process of urbanisation since much of the industrial growth and consequent increase in employment would be within or around the exiting urban centres.

Liberalisation's impacts on urban infrastructure and basic services are also not very clear. Recent efforts have been made to change the set-up of local government by empowering them for planning and execution of projects. But, as the capacity building process is limited to mega-cities only, the gap between the mega-cities and small and medium towns is increasing gradually. Increases in administrative and financial power do not help the small and medium towns, as these towns are not attractive enough for foreign private investment (as well as from inside the country). On the other hand, after liberalisation, public investments in these towns are decreasing gradually in expectation of private investment. Due to lack of both private and public investment, small and medium towns may face severe problem of service inadequacies.

Rapid population growth and low investment in urban development have created a serious deficiency in the availability of infrastructure and basic amenities in the towns and cities of the country. The rate of capital formation for this purpose has been extremely low during the 1980s. The same is true for investment in basic services.

When we analyse the inter-state disparity for different size-classes of urban centres, it works out as low in case of larger cities. This is because in the latter, the differences in socio-cultural factors are less important as these would have high literacy levels, modern values, etc. Most of the class I cities have high per capita income, large percentage of manufacturing activities and, correspondingly, a high level of investment in basic amenities across the states. Small towns, on the other hand, are different, both in terms of economic as also cultural factors in different regions, as discussed above. These would affect their level of basic services resulting in high disparity across the states.

Understandably, the variations in the percentage of households having the amenities across size-class of urban centres within the states are not as high as those across the states. The size-class disparity is, however, relatively high in the less developed states like Bihar, Orissa, Kerala, Madhya Pradesh and Uttar Pradesh (Kundu et al, 1996). The developed states, on the other hand, report a low variation, the small and medium towns here reporting a reasonable level of coverage. The states of Punjab and Haryana, for example, record very low percentage of households not having any of the facilities in smaller size-class of towns -- with less than 20,000 population. The corresponding figures for other developed states like Gujarat, Karnataka, Maharashtra, Tamil Nadu and West Bengal are also low, viz., less than 10 percent. One would, therefore, infer that the average level of amenities are reasonably satisfactory in the developed states in all size-classes, although the metropolises and class I cities have an edge over the others. In the backward states, however, the level of amenities in larger towns is high (although less than satisfactory) while the smaller towns exhibit a very high level of deficiency and deprivation.

About a fifth of the population in these smaller towns live in totally dehumanised conditions, as they have to do without safe drinking water, electricity and toilet facility.

There have been improvements in the availability of basic amenities across the states and size-classes of urban centres during 1981-91. The increase, however, is much more in case of class I cities compared to the lower order towns. The percentage of households having electricity, for example, has gone up from 62 to 81 in these cities during 1981-91. Similarly, the figures have improved from 75 to 84 in case of drinking water and from 58 to 74 in case of toilet facilities. The corresponding increase for other size-class of urban centres is much less. The fact that in the less developed states of Kerala, Madhya Pradesh, Bihar and Orissa, the percentage of households covered by toilet facilities in towns with less than 50,000 population has remained stable or registered a decline must be viewed with concern. In case of Orissa, a significant fall in the figure is noted even in class II towns (Kundu et al, 1996). It can be argued that a larger incidence of secondary and high valued tertiary activities in large cities gives the people residing there a high level of income. In the small and medium towns, on the other hand, the earnings of the people turn out as low, due to the poor economic base and lack of employment opportunities in the organised sector. These towns have a weak base of manufacturing activities and a high percentage of workforce dependent on agriculture. Instability in their economy is reflected in high fluctuation/variation in their demographic growth over time as also across regions within the states. One would argue that very many among the small and medium towns are not in a position to generate funds to provide civic services to all sections of population and stabilise their economic base. These towns, particularly those located in less developed states, should be the major concern of government policy in the context of provision of basic amenities.

It would be worthwhile to look at the changes in the system of urban governance linked with structural adjustment and analyse their possible impact on availability of basic amenities and their access to the poor. Indeed, there have been dramatic changes in urban governance in the 1990s. The responsibility of urban development, including provision of infrastructure and basic services like water supply, sanitation etc., is being shifted systematically from Centre to states and to local bodies. This is being done with the expectation that the governments at lower levels would mobilise a large part of required resources internally by improving managerial efficiency or externally from the capital market. Involvement of voluntary and community-based organisations is expected to contribute in the implementation of infrastructure projects. With such restructuring policies and reorganisation of responsibilities at the national and state level, the funds available for urban development, directly and indirectly, have gone down in backward regions and small towns (Kundu, 1999).

There is also an increasing gap between the rich and the poor, even in potential mega-cities, where benefits from liberalisation are more. Lack of public investment can cut down the level of basic amenities in the poorer areas in a city and private services may be costlier to afford affecting the utilisation rate as well as increasing cost of living of the poor. Researchers are more critical in monitoring structural adjustment with an apprehension that the investments in social sector/facilities will go down, as direct returns from this sector are not very high. It will not be favourable for the private investors and on the contrary, government will cut investment in the expectation of the private enterprises. There is a deep cut in public investment level in the first five years since the reforms, which often make the researchers anxious about the results, associated with it. Questions of the sector, which bore the burden of these adjustments and of sustainability of economy, often arise.

The External Sector

One of the failures of structural adjustment in India has been its inability to stimulate India's exports to a degree that would counteract any tendency towards stagnation in the domestic market. In the recent period, as well as in the 1990s overall, Indian exports have performed much worse than world exports, and India's share of total world trade has fallen.

Over the fiscal year 1999-2000, the main features of the external trade and balance of payments of India included the following: a recovery in exports after three years in stagnation/decline; an even sharper increase in imports which consequently meant a substantial enlargement of the trade deficit; the continued positive role played by inward remittances in keeping the current account deficit in check; and an increase in portfolio inflows which became the most important form of capital inflow over the year. These processes occurred in a period that was marked by significant policy changes in the external front as well. There was a substantial liberalisation of imports, with the removal of hundreds of items from the list covered by quantitative restrictions, and progressive reduction in import tariffs. The inability to provide export subsidies meant that commodity exporters faced problems in a depressed world market. Meanwhile, there have been substantial changes in the capital account as well. Some of these features can be easily observed in Table 3.7.

Table 3.7
Key Indicators of the Balance of Payments (as percent of GDP)

	1990-91	1996-97	1997-98	1998-99	1999-2000
Exports	6.2	8.9	8.8	8.2	8.5
Imports	9.4	12.8	12.6	11.3	12.3
Net invisibles	-0.1	2.7	2.4	2.2	2.9
Current account deficit	-3.2	-1.2	-1.4	-1	-0.9
Foreign investment	0.03	1.6	1.3	0.6	1.1

Source: RBI Annual Report 1999-2000.

Exports increased by 13.2 percent in US dollar terms, in positive contrast to the decline of more than 5 percent of the previous year. As a result, the value of exports amounted to $37.6 billion. The turnaround was evident mainly for all categories of manufactured goods except leather and leather manufactures. The exports of primary goods, especially of a product, fell by nearly 9 percent, with sharp falls evident for rice, tea and coffee. Software exports, which are classified under service exports rather than commodity exports, are estimated to have increased by 53 percent to reach the level of more than $4 billion. Imports also accelerated over the year, with total dollar imports increasing by 11.4 percent to reach $47.2 billion, after only 2.2 percent increase in the previous year. Much of this was due to the increase in international oil prices. However, non-oil imports also increased.

The invisibles account remained the source of strength for the balance of payments. The net surplus on invisibles amounted to nearly $13 billion, up from just above $9 billion in the previous year. This was essentially due to the continued strength of remittance income, which amounted to $12.26 billion and was able to counteract the increase in outflows of investment income (profits and interest) that was as high as $3.6 billion. One healthy sign is that the geographical base of such remittance income has expanded beyond the Middle East.

It is significant that in 1999-2000, as indeed in almost every other year since 1991, total net invisibles (led essentially by remittance income) have been greater than all forms of capital inflow taken together (Table 3.8).

Portfolio investment recovered from the net outflow recorded in 1998-99, and in fact grew so rapidly as to outstrip FDI as it had earlier in 1995-97. The difficulty with excessive reliance on such inflows is well known after the experience of several emerging markets over the 1990s. Thus, the rediscovery of India as a desirable destination by international portfolio investors is at best a mixed blessing.

Table 3.8
Capital Inflows

(in US dollar million)

Percent of total	1990-91	1997-98	1998-99	1999-2000
Foreign direct investment	1.4	36.2	29	21.2
Portfolio investment	0.1	18.6	-0.8	29.5
External assistance	31.3	9.2	9.6	8.8
External commercial borrowing	31.9	40.6	50.9	3.1
Short-term credits	15.2	-1	-8.7	3.7
NRI deposits	21.8	-7.8	-9.4	-6.9
Rupee debt service	-16.9	-7.8	-9.4	-6.9
Other capital	15.2	-7.2	9.1	19.8
Total (US$ million)	7,506	9,844	8,565	10,242

Source: RBI Annual Report 1999-2000.

Over the years, the capital account has been progressively liberalised. There have been measures to further liberalise ease of entry and exit of foreign capital, as well as access of domestic firms to foreign borrowing. Thus, Indian companies have been permitted to issue rights/bonus shares and non-convertible debentures to non-residents, as well as to issue units to FIIs with repatriation benefits. Policies for both external commercial borrowing and foreign direct investment have been very substantially liberalised. Similarly, rules for capital export have also been liberalised for Indian companies in sectors like IT, pharmaceuticals and biotechnology.

4

Health in India: An Overview

Health Situation in India

India is entering a health transition characterised by shifting demographics, altered health behaviours, and changes in disease patterns, with increasing degenerative and man-made diseases and further polarisation of health conditions. A high proportion of the population continues to suffer and die from preventable infections, pregnancy and childbirth-related complications and undernutrition. These are the so-called "unfinished agenda" of the health transition. There are large disparities across India, which places the bulk of the burden of these conditions upon the poor, women, and scheduled castes and tribes. Further improving the health, fertility and nutritional status of India's poor is essential if the poor are to participate in development, and is an important societal goal in itself.

Overall health conditions have been improving in India, but today's challenges are enormous. Life expectancy at birth rose from 49 years in 1970 to 63 years in 1998. The infant mortality rate (IMR), a sensitive indicator of both socio-economic development and use of health services, came down from 146 deaths per 1,000 births in the 1950s to 70 in

1999. Yet reductions in the IMR stagnated in the 1990s, and the nutritional status of children under five years improved only very slowly over the last twenty years. Nearly half of all children under five are malnourished, and anemia remains a problem for about three-fourths of children under three and for half of all women in the reproductive ages. India was one of the first countries in the world to intervene in population control as a national programme in 1951. Although the total fertility rate fell from 6 in the 1960s to 3.3 in 1999, it remains higher than in most other Asian countries (Ministry of Health and Family Welfare, 2000).

New health threats are stretching the capacity of the health system to respond. India's health system is at a crossroads. Since independence, there have been significant changes in health conditions and the composition of the health sector, while major transformations have occurred in knowledge and technology, as well as in the political and economic environment. An estimated 3.5 million Indians are living with HIV, and the virus has now spread beyond highly susceptible groups to the general population in some states. Historically, epidemics, famines and other health disasters have had a dominant role in shaping societies and nations. The current situation is no different for India. The HIV epidemic threatens to erase much of the social, economic and health gains since its independence, much as it is already doing in Sub-Saharan Africa. An important part of the response to this and future threats is to build a viable health system.

The government has built a vast infrastructure of public health services, and is implementing health programmes in priority areas of reproductive and child health and the control of major communicable diseases such as tuberculosis, HIV/AIDS, malaria and leprosy. These interventions have met with considerable success, but the government could be doing much more. The effectiveness of public programmes has been limited in part because overall public investment in health remains low, and because constraints in the structure of the health system have made it inefficient. At the same time, private provision and financing of health care have grown to dominate the health sector in India, largely because of the private sector's involvement in curative care. Yet, the private health sector has been away from public scrutiny, and grown in an undirected manner.

The public remains badly informed about much of the health system. It knows little about whether health services are appropriate, who is benefiting from them, whether quality is sufficient, or whether people are getting good value from public and private spending on health. The analysis in this report shows that there are major problems with equity, vulnerability to financial catastrophe, quality and accountability in both the public and private health sectors. The time has come to reassess how the Indian health system should function, and retool it for the new millennium.

Current Structure of the Public Sector

As outlined by the Indian Constitution, the provision of health care by the public sector is a responsibility shared by the state, central and local governments, although it is effectively a state responsibility in terms of delivery. State and local governments account for about three-fourths and the Centre for about one-fourth of public spending on health, though there are large variations between states. Local governments have no significant financial authority in India except in large cities. In some states, however, local bodies have a significant responsibility for managing services and implementing national or state government programmes. The degree and pattern of decentralisation in state-local relations exhibits wide inter-state variation.

The public sector has been organised largely to finance and deliver curative care, as well as implement a number of centrally sponsored family welfare and disease control programmes.

These programmes are almost exclusively delivered through public institutions. As a result, India has amassed an enormous but underfunded public delivery infrastructure and staff, that in 1999 included about 137,000 sub-centres, 28,000 dispensaries, 23,000 primary health centres (PHCs), 3,500 urban family welfare facilities, 3,000 community health centres (CHCs) and an additional 12,000 secondary and tertiary hospitals (CHCs are 30 bed secondary hospitals). In rural areas, public sector manpower included 29,000 doctors, 18,000 nurse midwives, 1,34,000 auxiliary nurse midwives (ANMs), 73,000 male multipurpose workers, 21,000 pharmacists, and another 60,000 paramedical staff, in addition to non-technical staff.

Although the amount of staff and infrastructure in India's public sector appears large, but by international comparisons, the ratios per population are rather modest. Internationally comparable data on workers and facilities are very weak, but what is available indicates that India's public sector is well below comparable ratios of workers and hospital beds in other low-income countries. Adding the private sector figures to the public sector numbers in India shows that the number of physicians per 1,000 population is about average for low-income countries, though the ratio of nurses and midwives are well below average, as is the ratio of hospital beds per 1,000 population. However, the number of hospital beds in the private sector in India is likely more than double the number recorded in government estimates, so that India is likely near average for low-income countries.

Structural Constraints of the Public Sector

Previous sector work (World Bank, 1995; 1997b), numerous projects documents (e.g., State Health Systems Development Project II, Immunisation Strengthening Project, etc.), and an Independent Commission on Health have identified a wide variety of problems facing public sector health delivery. There are general problems of high levels of poverty that lead to and are exacerbated by poor health conditions, and poor governance that creates a weak environment for reform. There are also specific issues affecting the health sector that are often identified. In the public sector, these problems include: (a) weak health management; (b) poor quality of health services; and (c) limited financial resources. Weak management and low quality of services are related problems, and include structural and institutional issues, as well as process and skills constraints.

Public health management is affected by structural problems such as overly centralised planning and control of resources, high levels of political interference over staff postings and transfers in some of the larger states, the segmentation of family welfare, nutrition, disease control programmes and different levels of care, and the neglect of approaches that would encourage the private sector to meet public policy objectives. Public sector management relies on inflexible input-based planning and expenditure controls that are centrally determined, and do not adequately account for differences in needs or demands. For example, staffing norms for ANMs are based on standard population coverage, although birth rates vary widely across the country. As a result, the workload to deliver immunisations to children in high fertility states like Uttar Pradesh and Bihar is more than double that in a low fertility state like Tamil Nadu (Satia, 1999).

Managers have neither the authority nor timely information to make decisions in an accountable way. Human resource systems are particularly underdeveloped, and offer little by way of monitoring, staff incentives, or in-service training, leading to indiscipline and poor performance. Inappropriate skills mix is one of the most critical issues, as there are large numbers of vacancies of key posts, particularly in rural areas. According to the staffing norms established for existing sub-centres, PHCs and CHCs, there is a shortfall of about 28,000 ANMs (17% of all posts), 65,000 male multipurpose workers (47%), 21,000 nurse midwives (47%) and 10,000 doctors (28%).

The problems are not simply that the staff norms are too ambitious, the selection of staff is inappropriate, or that there are not enough health workers being trained. The problems extend to insufficient pay in the public sector, particularly in comparison to the private sector, unsatisfactory living conditions in rural areas, and limited professional opportunities. However, questions of staff motivation and incentives have not been well studied in the health sector and need a more systematic assessment.

Quality of health services is not well monitored in either the public or private sector, as there is a lack of meaningful standards and quality assurance systems. Little is known about clinical outcomes or quality assurance processes, as there are a lack of standards and quality assurance institutions and systems to ensure quality in the health sector in any of the dimensions of clinical quality, management quality, or quality from the perspective of the user. Public sector health services are largely underutilised at the lower levels of the health system in rural areas (in Uttar Pradesh, bed occupancy rates of rural inpatient facilities are around 30%), though the large urban public hospitals are frequently overcrowded. One reason for low utilisation in rural areas is that the quality of services is poor. The public sector is further constrained by staffing limitations, particularly in poor and remote areas that are also not served by the formal private sector, and is more hampered by weaknesses in supervision, maintenance, drugs and supplies.

Despite the establishment of a large public network of health providers, public spending on health is relatively low, and has stagnated at levels of around 1 percent of GDP. This is far below what is needed to provide basic health care to the population (World Bank, 1997b; Mahal, Srivastava and Sanan, 2000). Though the bulk of public spending on primary health care has been spread out too thinly for these services to be

effective, the referral linkages to secondary care have also
suffered (Mukhopadhyay, 1997). As in other countries,
preventive and promotive health services take a back seat to
curative care. Yet preventive care is almost exclusively provided
through the public sector: about 90 percent of immunisations
and 60 percent of antenatal care is estimated to be provided
through the public sector. The states, which bear between 75 to
90 percent of the burden of public health spending, have their
funds largely tied up in "non-plan" salary expenditures (Duggal,
1997; Reddy and Selvaraju, 1994). It appears that the disparity
between the rich and the poor states is increasing, while the
funds that are spent are not reaching the implementing bodies,
particularly the more remote they are.

Structure of the Private Sector

In India, the private health sector is commonly understood to
refer to private, for-profit, medically trained providers. Their
range of practice varies from solo practice, small nursing homes
(inpatient facilities with usually less than 30 beds) to large
corporate hospitals. However, a much broader set of
non-government actors is involved, that can be categorised
according to organisational type (profit or non-profit), size and
scope of service (solo practice, small nursing home, large
specialised hospital), or system of care (Indian systems of
medicine – ayurvedic, unani; or western medicine – allopathy).
Many untrained providers offer a combination of systems of
medicine, though allopathy tends to dominate. The private
sector also offers ancillary services such as diagnostic centres,
ambulance services and pharmacies. In addition, there is a large
number of private actors providing services or managing other
inputs to the sector (construction companies, consultancy
firms). However, there has been a limited formal role for
private sector agents involved in health financing, though a few
private companies and community organisations finance health
services for their members.

Although there has been an increase in the number of studies concerning the private sector in recent years, until this sector work, there had not been a systematic attempt to synthesise the literature on the private health sector. Three Indian institutions have created a single database on private health sector studies in India pointing towards the rapid growth of private sector health provision, particularly by for-profit and non-qualified providers. Despite this growth, there are relatively few studies conducted on the for-profit private sector in India. Studies on the non-profit sector tend to have small coverage, with many having weak methodologies. There is also a lack of documentation on some key innovations that have been taking place in India in the last few years, including areas such as contracting of services in the public sector, partnerships between public and private sectors, payment systems, and use of subsidies. The data on health financing is also limited, but points to a situation where throughout the country, health financing is predominantly private, and paid out of pocket from individual consumers in a fragmentary way to many different types of service providers. The lack of a clear health policy framework and implementation mechanisms at national, state and local levels towards private sector health is cited as a major reason why the research and information base for planning and evaluation of the private sector in India is very limited.

The most recent data suggest that the private provision of health is growing rapidly, and is the major source of outpatient and inpatient health care across India. However, the data to demonstrate this is quite weak. At the time of independence, the private sector involved in allopathic medicine was quite small. Only about 8 percent of all medical institutions in the provinces were estimated to be operated by private agencies, with another 5 percent in the non-governmental sector receiving grant-in-aid from the government. By 1995, government publications estimate that there are 10,300 private hospitals in all of India, and about 225,000 private hospital beds, comprising over two-thirds of the all hospitals and nearly 40 percent of the hospital beds. This is an increase from an estimated 3,000 private hospitals and 1,33,000 private hospital beds estimated to exist in 1981. However, when a census of private facilities was undertaken in Andhra Pradesh in 1993, it was found that the official numbers undercounted hospitals by 3.8 times, and the number of hospital beds by 10.5 times. More recent estimates put 67,000 private hospitals in all of India, comprising 93 percent of all hospitals and 64 percent of the hospital beds nationwide. In addition to these allopathic facilities, it is estimated that there are another 2,800 hospitals (and 46,000 hospital beds) under the Indian systems of medicine, the vast majority of which are in the private sector.

Health workforce data in the private sector are hard to come by in any state. Overall, it is estimated that 75 percent of 3,30,000 allopathic doctors in 1986 were working in the private sector. Current estimates are that there are between 4,00,000 and 4,70,000 allopathic doctors (Planning Commission, 1998), with about 80-85 percent of them in the private sector (Duggal, 2000). However, it should be noted that many doctors employed in the public sector also work in the private sector, with one study in Delhi showing 85 percent of public sector doctors also practising in the private sector. Overall, about 60 percent of allopathic doctors are presumed to be working in urban areas. Of the 1,20,000 doctors estimated to be practising Indian systems of medicine in 1981, about 85 percent are in the private sector. While information on the numbers of private doctors is limited, estimates about the numbers of other medical and para-medical professions in the private sector are not available.

Estimating the number of informal providers is even more problematic, since they are not registered, and many work part-time. Conservative estimates put the number of non-qualified rural medical practitioners at 1.25 million; almost all are solo practitioners located in outpatient settings (Rohde and Viswanathan, 1995). A census in three districts in Andhra Pradesh found that there was about one non-MBBS doctor per 2,000 population, which would extrapolate to about 5,00,000 non-qualified medical practitioners. A number of other studies have examined the role of traditional practitioners in its various. Broadly, these studies reveal that majority of the qualified solo practitioners practise in urban areas. Untrained practitioners, faith healers, traditional birth attendants, priests and local medicine women and men largely cater to the rural areas. In both areas, the allopathic treatment is the dominant type of care provided. Population surveys on the use of health services indicate an increasing use of health services through the private sector. Between the 42nd Round of the NSSO survey in 1986-87 and the 52nd Round in 1995-96, there was an increase in the proportions of people using care outside the public sector.

The vast majority of people (over 80%) use the private sector for outpatient curative services as a first line of treatment in both urban and rural areas. As mentioned previously, there is much heterogeneity in qualifications and systems of medicine used for outpatient care. Indigenous and folk practitioners, along with traditional providers, are particularly used as a first line of outpatient treatment in rural areas (Rohde and Viswanathan, 1995). For inpatient care, the majority of people are now using the private sector for hospitalisation. There are large differences in the use of private services between states, and according to level of poverty and type of service provided. The majority of private hospitals are small (less than 30 beds), and are owned by one person, usually a practising doctor. Despite some well-known private hospitals, very few of the private hospitals and private hospital beds are in the tertiary sector, comprising roughly 1 percent of the total number of institutions, whereas charitable hospitals cater to about 4 percent of hospitalised patients (NSSO, 1998). Although a number of hospitals are owned through partnerships, relatively few are corporate, public limited, or trust hospitals. Most of the nursing homes are owned by a doctor entrepreneur, and provide general curative medical and maternity services.

The large private hospitals are either owned by trusts, or are corporate enterprises, and have a more specialised nature. A typical staffing pattern for small hospitals has less than four physicians working at the hospital, with dependence on visiting consultants. For example, in Muraleedharan's study of private hospitals in Chennai, the consultant physician averages just over three hours per day in a hospital, and visits at least two different practice localities. He also found that about two-thirds of private hospitals had government doctors on their panel of consultants, averaging about two government doctors per private hospital. This is commonly reported in other parts of the country as well, even in states where private practice by government doctors is not permitted.

Liberalisation and Health

Since mid-1991 a wide range of economic and policy reforms in India have been initiated with the broad objective of attaining a higher and sustainable growth rate coupled with equity and human development. The economic reforms process included two major components: (a) stabilisation of the macro-economy aimed at controlling the fiscal and balance of payment deficits and lowering the rate of inflation, and (b) opening up the economy to international trade and investment through structural adjustments including internal and external deregulations, leading to a shift towards a neutral foreign trade regime. More recently, in the Union Budget of 2001-02, the second-generation economic reforms have been announced by the Union Finance Minister by focusing, amongst other things, on human development, specifically on demand creation, investment generation, strengthening rural infrastructure, government downsizing, employment and labour flexibility and social security.

In the light of these reforms this chapter attempts to raise some critical issues: (a) How much progress the country has made in various health outcomes? (b) What is the status of health provision and financing? (c) Are the health equity issues in terms of accessibility and use are adequately addressed?

During the period of macro-economic adjustments and structural changes, some of the critical health parameters and their determinants are affecting the people. For instance, these are: growing incidence of lifestyle diseases due to changes in the demographic structure, emerging new public health threats (spreading of HIV infection and injury) and increasing health risks due to high prevalence of alcohol and tobacco consumption. While these are not directly the result of policy initiatives, they are certainly susceptible to policy impact and raise important equity concerns. It is well understood that there are no straightforward impacts of economic reforms on the health status of people. However, certain important parameters which affect the purchasing power of people in turns exhibit significant impact on the health outcomes. In fact, there is a strong association between poverty and health and any policy changes influencing poverty (such as employment generation, income growth, income distribution, prices, income transfers and safety nets) would also impinge on health, of course with a lagged effect. The impact of reform measures initiated in 1991 at the macro level appears to be satisfactory. However, its impact at the micro level has become a subject of debate among scholars and policy makers. Evidence from Latin America and other countries shows that faster growth has brought about a corresponding widening of the set of available economic opportunities and increase in poverty. In India, the relative increase in the level of poverty in the initial period of reform appears to be marginal.

Health Care System

According to the World Bank estimates for 1990, India spent about 6 percent of GDP on health care, which amounts to Rs

320 per capita. By 1993 per capita health spending in India had increased further to Rs 334. This is a very high proportion when compared to OECD and Asian countries. For instance, OECD countries including Canada are spending between 7 and 8 percent of GDP and some of Asian countries such as China, Sri Lanka, Indonesia, Philippines and Thailand are spending between 2 and 5 percent of GDP. However, the quality of life (measured in terms of life expectancy, infant and child mortality, maternal mortality, child malnutrition, etc.) in these countries is much better.

The question therefore arises as to why India's health sector seems to perform relatively poorly? One has to really gauge various health outcomes in relation to health spending pattern in the Indian economy. One issue that emerges when we closely look into the nature and pattern of health spending is that the government's share in the total health spending is just 25.1 percent with wide inter-state differentials (it ranged from 13.6% in Andhra Pradesh to 42.3% in Jammu & Kashmir). This indicates that the household out-of-pocket expenditures on health care are enormous. In contrast, the government health spending ranges between 70 and 90 percent in OECD countries (including Canada) and between 50 and 65 percent in several South-East Asian countries.

A cross-country analysis suggests that as countries get richer, they spend more of their income on health care, and the government's share grows larger (World Bank, 1993). However, among Indian states, this does not seem to hold true. In spite of the fact that Indian economy has grown at around 6 percent during the post-reforms period, in real terms the per capita government spending on health (as percentage of GDP/NSDP as well as in relation to other sectors) has actually declined in the initial years of reforms. This clearly reflects that the health is yet to be considered as a priority sector. The same is true for access to health services.

Table 4.1

Health Expenditure, Services and Use

Name of the Economy/Country	Health Expenditure			Physicians (per 1000 pop.)		Hospital Beds (per 1000 pop.)	
	Public % of GDP 1990-95[a]	Private % of GDP 1990-95[a]	Total % of GDP 1990-95[a,b]	1980	1994	1980	1994
World	3.2	2.8	5.4	1.0	1.4	3.5	3.8
Low income	1.5	2.7	4.2	0.6	1.0	1.5	1.6
Middle income	4.3	2.4	5.1	1.4	1.6	-	4.6
High income	6.9	3.7	9.6	1.8	2.5	-	7.4
SAARC countries							
Bangladesh	1.2	1.3	2.4	0.1	0.2	0.2	0.3
India	0.7	4.4	5.6	0.4	0.4	0.8	0.8
Nepal	1.2	3.8	5.0	0.0	0.1	0.2	0.2
Pakistan	0.8	2.7	3.5	0.3	0.5	0.6	0.7
Sri Lanka	1.4	0.4	1.9	0.1	0.1	2.9	2.7

Notes: a. Data are for most recent year available.

b. Data may not sum to totals because of rounding.

Source: World Bank, World Development Indicators, 1998, Washington D.C., USA.

Both health provision and financing are considered to be a state's subject. On an average, out of the total government health spending, the state's share is about 80 percent. There is a clear demarcation between central and state provision and financing of various health services. While the states fully finance hospital services, primary health care facilities and ESIS (Employees' State Insurance Scheme), the family welfare programmes are fully financed by the central government. Most of the national disease control programmes are funded on 50:50 share arrangements with the states. (However, in terms of total expenditure on these programmes the state's contribution turns out to be about three-fourths, i.e., only basic inputs are shared equally, and the state has to bear all the administrative cost including salaries of the staff). Centre and states share capital investment equally. Out of the total expenditure on medical education and research, the central government's share is little over 40 percent. Thus, by and large, the states fully finance all the curative care services. It implies that the states' economic conditions and financial and human resources have direct bearing on the health outcomes, especially during the post-reforms period.

Table 4.2
Access to Health Services

(in%)

Name of the Economy/ Country	Health Care Population with Access		Safe Water Population with Access		Sanitation Population with Access		Sanitation in Urban Areas
	1980	1993	1980	1995	1980	1995	1995
World	-	-	-	78	-	47	-
Low income	-	-	-	76	-	28	65
Middle income	-	-	-	-	-	60	67
High income	-	-	-	-	-	92	-
SAARC countries							
Bangladesh	-	74	-	79	-	35	77
India	50	-	-	81	-	29	70
Nepal	10	-	11	48	0	20	51
Pakistan	65	85	38	60	16	30	53
Sri Lanka	90	90	-	-	-	-	-

Source: World Bank, World Development Indicators, 1998, Washington D.C., USA.

The other major difference in the nature of Indian health care spending with respect to South-East Asian countries is that both central and state governments are spending far less on preventive and promotive care. India spends only one-third on preventive and promotive health care whereas the proportion is as high as two-thirds in China and Sri Lanka. Preventive and promotive health care services include immunisation, antenatal,

Table 4.3

Health Spending for Major States in India, 1993

State Ranked by Col. 6	Per Capita Annual Health Expenditure			Share of House-hold Health Expendi-ture (2 as % of 3)	House-hold Health Expendi-ture as % of House-hold Income	Total Health Expendi-ture as % of NSDP/ NNP
	Government	House-hold	Total			
	1	2	3	4	5	6
Jammu & Kashmir*	238	325	563	57.7	NE	10.7
Kerala	111	482	593	81.3	11.9	9.5
Himachal Pradesh	209	370	579	63.9	6.7	8.9
Bihar	51	223	274	81.4	6.1	7.5
Orissa	74	276	350	78.9	8.2	7.4
Andhra Pradesh	66	421	487	86.4	7.8	7.4
Karnataka	93	360	453	79.5	8.8	6.5
Rajasthan	83	196	279	70.3	4.2	5.4
Uttar Pradesh	55	175	230	76.1	4.5	4.9
Gujarat	78	259	337	76.9	4.7	4.4
Madhya Pradesh	63	168	231	72.7	6.9	4.3
Tamil Nadu	100	202	302	66.9	6.5	4.2
West Bengal	73	154	227	67.8	3.4	3.8
Haryana	83	267	350	76.3	4.1	3.4
Punjab	110	282	392	71.9	6.2	3.2
Maharashtra	85	259	344	75.3	5.4	3.2
Assam	66	96	162	59.3	2.4	2.8
All-India	84	250	334	74.9	6.0	5.5

NSDP – Net State Domestic Product, NNP – Net National Product.

Note: Estimates for Jammu & Kashmir are based on the previous NCAER survey of 1990.
Source: Shariff et al. (1999:56).

maternity and postnatal care, contraceptives and other family planning measures; community-based services such as spraying for malaria, and health education. Further, out of the total curative care spending, nearly three-fourths is spent on secondary and tertiary hospitals (which are primarily located in urban areas). In this country, where a majority of population resides in rural areas, government is spending very little on their day-to-day health care needs. The important issue remains how the state can strengthen the primary health care services both in terms of resources and accessibility.

There are close relationships between per capita state domestic product, per capita state health expenditure and the health status of the population. In other words, richer states are spending higher on health care, resulting in raising the health status of people. Conversely, the per capita health care spending is very low in poorer states; they are unable to raise the matching funds for implementation of several centrally executed public health programmes and thus have not succeeded much in improving the health status of the people. In the light of this argument one have to examine the achievements of various state governments in the post-reforms period.

The World Development Report, 1993; and 'Investing in Health' prepared by the IMF is propagating privatisation of the health care. At first sight, the Report appears very reasonable, wanting the underdeveloped countries to concentrate public effort in the sphere of health to certain 'essential' clinical services, to be conscious of the cost-effectiveness of such efforts in terms of the Disability-Adjusted Life Years (DALYs) saved, and to leave the 'discretionary' clinical services to the private sector (Patnaik, 1999). This shift to privatisation appears reasonable in view of the fact that government resources are limited and choices have to be made and that, under the Bank's proposal, these meagre resources, supplemented by 'aid' from abroad, can apparently go far in terms of public health achievement.

The basic assumption behind the Bank's proposal is that the government's resources for spending on health are limited. Consequently, what we are talking about is not the optimal use of social resources, but the most cost-effective manner of using limited government funds available for health expenditure. This, it may appear merely being pragmatic. But, when we remember that the Fund-Bank prescriptions themselves seek to reduce the funds available to the government, we are clearly not facing some innocent variety of pragmatism.

First of all, for the sake of 'trade liberalisation', import tariffs are to be reduced according to these prescriptions, which in turn entails limits upon the rates of excise duties. Second, for the sake of providing 'incentives' to foreign capital, direct tax rates upon such capital have to be lowered, which in turn entails a general lowering of direct tax rates (the lowering of income tax rates is often recommended by invoking the vacuous conceptual entity called the 'Laffer Curve'). In short, structural adjustment seeks to bring about a general lowering of tax rates of all descriptions (which is in keeping after all, with the basic tenets of 'supply-side economics' so avidly espoused by Reagan and Thatcher). The profile of the government revenue could still increase despite the reduction in tax rates if the growth rate in the economy could be raised compared to what it otherwise would have been, but the structural adjustment package not only does not ensure this, on the contrary, actually lowers the growth rate because of deflation and privatisation.

Privatisation also means loss of substantial actual as well as potential non-tax revenue for the government. In fact, the very health document of the World Bank can be used to illustrate this point. If it believed that non-essential clinical services should be charged higher tax rates, then this constitutes a particularly strong reason for keeping them within the public health sector, so that the revenue earned from such services could be used to sustain an expansion in the essential health services. But, if the government itself keeps away from such services entirely and has also relinquished tax instruments, then the possibilities of any revenues accruing to the government from this source, either directly or indirectly (by taxing away a part of the high profits arising in the non-essential services), disappear. In short, by keeping what by its own admission is potentially the most lucrative part of the health services exclusively for the private sector (and for that matter all potentially lucrative production) and simultaneously insisting upon a reduction in tax rates, the Fund-Bank package brings about the very condition that is assumed in this analysis as a constraint. The government is first starved of funds; and then this very shortage is used as an argument to cut down on the range of services it provides to the people. If the Bank's health plan is adopted, then the ordinary people would get only a limited number of services from the public health system: family planning and pregnancy-related services, TB and STD control, and care for some serious illnesses for small children. For other requirements, including even hospital-based emergence care, whose public provision is to become optional, they would have to pay exorbitant prices to the private sector. Health insurance as suggested by the Bank does not negate this; it only staggers this payment.

From 1999 the second generation of reforms have started by the present government headed by the BJP. At present, all the national political parties except the Left Front are broadly supporting the structural adjustment and privatisation of services. International agencies are also influencing the policy framework in favour of new polices at macro as well as micro level. It appears that the process is going to continue for a longer time and several changes are expected in next few years.

There is no gainsaying that our health status is intimately linked to the condition of our lives and the livelihoods that we pursue. And, this is even truer as one goes down the scale of economic categories. Common sense would dictate that it is at these levels -- condition of living and livelihoods -- that any intervention to improve health status would have the most permanent effect. However, over the decades, it has been pointed out repeatedly that that road to health is a long-term one and, in the immediate future, what is needed is good accessible, affordable medicare and disease prevention and control. If these are effective then, it is argued, the upscaling of the condition and quality of people's lives would become that much easier. That long road to health, however, seems to be growing longer and more difficult to traverse each year. In the last few years there has been much focus on the fact that the wide-ranging changes in the economy will inevitably affect some sections of society in the interim.

The solution has been to create social safety nets which would prop these sections until presumably the outcomes of the new economic programmes filter down. This it has been envisaged would mean that the state, even as it pulls out of certain sectors, will enhance its investment in these areas, creating resources and security measures for the possible victims of change. These new demands should, one imagines, be reflected in the budgetary allocations of the central government, giving a sense of direction to the states.

Even if we take a broad definition and include allocations made to the ministries of health and family welfare, human resources development which includes the department of education, rural development, urban development and poverty alleviation, social justice and empowerment, tribal affairs, labour and the department of youth affairs and sports, the government deems about 10 percent of the total central budget sufficient for the creation of support and relief. Even more importantly, it is also an indication of how small is the government's concern for the creation of resources, say, for education. And worse, these ministries are in charge of areas which directly affect the condition of living and therefore the health status of people -- the newly created departments of drinking water, of rural sanitation and water supply, and of housing and nutrition supplementation.

However, these are areas that have seen long neglect and require far greater resources. That a country, stepping into the IT era cannot provide drinking water to such a large proportion of its citizens is perhaps the most telling comment on the distorted developmental perspective followed in the last fifty years. It is against this background that the central health budget comes into focus. The government health sector has been shrinking rapidly over the last decade. This has been a consequence of the falling state inputs into health care, as well as the rapidly expanding private and corporate medicare infrastructure. As has been well documented, the shrinking transfers to the states from the Centre have imposed austerity in the state budgets which has translated itself as smaller health care budgets.

Health is a state subject and as such most of the funding for medicare infrastructure and its upkeep comes from the state budgets. However, the Centre is responsible for the national programmes of disease control. Incredibly though, the disease control budgets of the government have hardly undergone any change over the years. What change has come about has been entirely because of the inputs of international agencies. For instance, the tuberculosis control programme has received massive funding from the WHO and the World Bank. Other than this, malaria continues to account for 29.5 percent of the entire public health allocation. There is reason to believe, however, that the disease control programmes need a radical revamping. It is interesting that the revised estimates for 1999-2000 for all the national programmes (except *kalaazar* which accounts for Rs 10 crore) are lower than the budget allocations for the year, indicating administrative lapses or lack of financial management and proper budgeting. These are huge programmes, and critical to the health of the people. The fairly static nature of the public health budget in a country, where the health scenario may be undergoing large changes, is indicative of a lack of monitoring which will affect much more than the nation's finances.

Cost and Burden of Treatment

Undoubtedly, price is the most important consideration in choosing the public over the private facility, especially for the treatment of chronic and catastrophic illnesses. According to the NSS data, the average cost of treatment in the private sector for rural inpatients was 1.6 times and for urban inpatients 2.4 times higher than in the public sector during 1986-87. The gap got widened further to 2.1 for rural patients in 1995-96 and remained same for the urban patients. The difference in the cost of treatment between private and public sector was much higher in Tamil Nadu, West Bengal and to some extent in Andhra Pradesh and lower in Bihar, Haryana, Punjab, Rajasthan and Uttar Pradesh (Table 4.3). Interestingly, as compared to the public sector, the cost of treatment for outpatient care was lower in the private sector during 1986-87. However, over time, the private sector has become costlier by 40 percent for rural and by 20 percent for urban patients.

The inter-state variations continue to exist and here once again (as observed for inpatient care) the private-public cost ratio was the highest in Tamil Nadu and in Uttar Pradesh the private sector turned out to be cheaper than the public sector. This clearly reflects on the public delivery system in Tamil Nadu to be managed better and run efficiently than several other states including Uttar Pradesh. The average expenditure on treatment (such as fees, medicines, clinical and diagnostic tests, surgery, and hospital bed charges) per hospitalisation episode in 1995-96 was Rs. 3,202 for rural and Rs. 3,921 for urban patients for the country as a whole. As expected, the cost of treatment was higher for urban than rural patients due to cost of living and the nature of care sought. The inpatient care was much cheaper in Orissa, Assam and West Bengal and costlier in Andhra Pradesh, Punjab and Uttar Pradesh for both rural and urban patients and was also costlier in Haryana for urban patients.

Although the cost of treatment depends upon the type of disease, insurance coverage and the type of services availed of, the inter-state differentials in costs also reflect on the affordability, level of income and the purchasing power the people. The cost of outpatient care was much lower than the inpatient care and on the average rural and urban patients were spending between Rs 176 and Rs 194 for treatment during 1995-96. The care was costlier in those states where the public delivery was also poor (e.g., in Bihar and Uttar Pradesh) and other way rounds in the case of Tamil Nadu, West Bengal and Kerala. The cost of care was also found to be higher in urban areas of Haryana and Madhya Pradesh. The comparison of cost of care with the previous NSS data for 1986-87 shows an alarming increase in the health care prices. On an average, the cost of health care has grown enormously with an annual arithmetic growth rate of 26-31 percent for inpatient care and of 15-16 percent for outpatient care. For inpatient care the increase in cost of care over time was much faster for rural patients of Andhra Pradesh, Tamil Nadu, Kerala and West Bengal and for urban patients of Haryana, Andhra Pradesh, Tamil Nadu, Jammu & Kashmir and Orissa. These states have also reported faster growth in the cost of outpatient care as well. Only Himachal Pradesh and Gujarat have reported a slow increase in the costs of both inpatient and outpatient care. The expenditure on treatment as a percentage of MPCE constitutes the burden of treatment. Overall, the burden for inpatient treatment ranged between 351 and 476 percent for the country as a whole during 1986-87. The burden was relatively lower for outpatient care, which ranged between 45 and 63 percent for the country as a whole during the same period. However, in both inpatient and outpatient care, the burden was found to be higher among rural than urban populations. This could be due to the difference in the cost of living between rural and urban areas than the cost of treatment itself because most of the rural patients have to avail of hospital facilities located in urban centres. Further, poor households are spending relatively higher proportion of their income on health care than the better off section of the society.

Equity in Benefits Received from Government Health Spending

The NCAER has recently completed a World Bank commissioned study assessing the extent to which health expenditure benefits the poor throughout India (Mahal and Gumber, 2000). The study looks at utilisation of health services (inpatient admissions, short hospitalisations, inpatient admissions for childbirth, outpatient visits, immunisation, antenatal and postnatal visits) according to socio-economic attributes of the population in terms of scheduled and non-scheduled population, below and above poverty line and MPCE quintile groups. Data is broken down by state, urban/rural location, sex, type of facility (hospitals, PHCs and others), and type of provider (public, private). It also assesses the extent to which the burden of user fees is shared between income groups. It further estimates total net subsidies by MPCE groups from public health expenditure. The key findings are stated as under:

- The better off utilise health services more than the poor: the top quintile are hospitalised over seven times more frequently than the lowest quintile and almost 10 times more often in rural areas. In terms of outpatient visits the top quintile made 65 percent more outpatient visits than the bottom quintile in urban areas and 125 percent more in rural areas. In terms of immunisation a child in the top quintile has on average 4.6 immunisation shots whilst a child from the lowest quintile has 3.8. The top quintile account for 27 percent of all inpatient days associated with childbirth (despite the fact that they only account for 10.9% of children aged less than one year).

- The rich are the main users of public sector facilities: the top quintile account for almost 40 percent of inpatient days in public hospitals whereas the bottom quintile just over 10 percent. At PHCs and other facilities middle-income groups account for the majority of inpatient days. For short stay hospitalisations the picture is less extreme. An exception is childbirth where the poorer groups make far greater use of public facilities accounting for almost five times more inpatient days than the top quintile.

- The poor make relatively more use of the public sector but still make significant use of the private sector: for the poorest quintile 61.9 percent of inpatient days were spent in public facilities compared to 28.5 percent for the top quintile. The private sector dominates the provision of outpatient services although the poorest quintile are slightly more likely to use the public sector with 20.8 percent of treatments being made in the public sector compared to only 7.9 percent for the private sector. As a result, utilisation of public facilities is shared relatively evenly between income groups. Immunisation is mainly carried out in public facilities. In rural areas, 96.6 percent of shots for the lowest quintile are provided in the public sector; for the top quintile the figure is 85.7 percent. In urban areas, where the private sector is more developed, the figures are 88.9 percent and 31.6 percent respectively. A total of 57.7 percent of inpatient days related to childbirth for the lowest quintile are spent in the public sector compared to only 13.3 percent in the top quintile. The lower quintile groups benefit predominantly from prenatal/postnatal visits and childbirth conducted by ANMs and LHVs. In urban areas, 78.2 percent of such prenatal/postnatal visits are to those in the lowest quintile. For childbirth 40.7 percent are to those in the lowest quintile. In rural areas, ANMs and LHVs serve a broader clientele though the lower income groups predominate.

- Formal user fees are primarily paid by the better off: 89.2 percent of hospital charges in rural areas are paid by those in the top income quintile. Also, 92.9 percent of charges at PHC level and below are paid by those in the top two income quintile.

- Public sector subsidies benefit the better off more than the poor. This reflects the trends outlined above. Whilst public sector subsidies for PHC and immunisations tend to benefit the poor, this is more than offset by the concentration of public subsidies for inpatient care on middle and higher income groups. Estimates for distribution of public subsidies are also provided for major states. As hospital care accounts for a majority of share in the total subsidies (86% at all India level), it would be interesting to analyse inter-state variation on this aspect. The distribution of public subsidies in Bihar, Haryana, Himachal Pradesh, Madhya Pradesh, north-eastern states, Orissa, Rajasthan and Uttar Pradesh is less equitable than for India as a whole. On the other hand, it is more equitable in Gujarat, Tamil Nadu, Kerala and, to some extent, Punjab, because the poor tend to have relatively more access at all levels of facilities in these states.

Policy Options

To address equity in distribution of public health subsidies, the government must adopt better targeting mechanisms. These could be achieved through (i) focusing more on resources in areas where the poor already get significant benefits, (ii) improving the targeting of resources in areas where the poor do not make currently benefit, (iii) shift resources from areas where the poor do not benefit to those where they do, and (iv) enabling measures to improve targeting of public resources. Given the fact that the bulk of current subsidies go to the hospital sector, this is where initial emphasis might be placed on shifting of resources from hospital to PHC which could be achieved through holding overall allocation to hospitals constant in nominal (real terms); greater self-financing of hospital services (e.g., pay beds for the better off, in the longer term looking at insurance); shifting resources from tertiary to district hospitals; and allocating resources according to workload and good performance of the facility. Increasing the share of hospital subsidies going to the poor through investigating the potential for better targeting, better monitoring of performance of autonomous hospitals in providing services for the poor, learning from experiences of few states (such as Kerala and Tamil Nadu) which have been extremely successful in focusing public hospital subsidies on the poor and replicating these to other states. Strengthening network amongst public, private and NGO sectors in poor and underserved areas. Encourage the private sector to establish a bigger presence in rural areas so that the better off rural section, which enjoys major share in public subsidies, can seek care from non-public facilities. Regulate this private sector to ensure it at least delivers an acceptable quality of care at reasonable cost and provides at least some essential services.

The foregoing analysis and articulation has clearly demonstrated that the economic reforms initiated in the country since the 1990s have had little (if any) impact on the health sector. This is so whether we consider the trends in the allocations made for the health sector or in the health outcomes since the initiation of reforms in the country. The central budgetary allocation to health sector was 1.2 percent of the total allocation in 1991-92 and during 1993-94 to 1998-99 it was around 1.4 percent and marginally stepped up to 1.7 percent during 1999-2000 and 2000-01 and further to 1.8 percent in 2001-02. Although, in nominal terms, the allocation to health sector increased from Rs 1,734 crore in 1991-92 to Rs. 6,752 crore in 2001-02, in real terms, the increase could be marginal. One possible reason for this behaviour may be our belief that economic reforms would necessarily be accompanied by all-round improved outcomes in the health sectors on its own. However, since health is a state subject and almost all decisions are taken by the state governments in the areas of their domain, economic reforms which are initiated by the union government may not thus have much impact on health sector (and that too indirectly) unless the state governments on their own undertake such reforms in their respective states in the health sector. Indeed, the World Bank, under the State Health Systems Project operating in seven major states in the country, has attempted to influence the health outcomes in these states through specifically focusing on reforms at the secondary level health care facilities. However, certain deficiencies have been pointed out in this approach, and it is in this context we may cite the example of Andhra Pradesh where, apart from the State Health Systems Project, recently under the A.P. Economic Reform Project, primary health care has been emphasised and resourceful links with the state health systems are being attempted.

A word of caution in regard to the aspect of equity is in order. Most of the recent health projects have underlined the need to promote user charges/cost sharing mechanisms as a means to overcome the financial problems experienced by the hospitals. Clearly, the levy of user charges is likely to hurt the cause of equity, as a large section of hospital beneficiaries is the poor who are generally exempted from payment of user charges. Also, at the same time, the well-to-do people are shifting away from public health care system to the private one. This situation has resulted in a dismal performance of the user charges as is evident from rather small collections on this account. Thus, user charges apart from hurting equity have also put a question mark on the sustainability aspect, as well. Thus, if we have to ensure both equity and sustainability of projects in the health sector, we have to seek other options of raising funds (e.g., health insurance and providing additional resources). In addition, a good deal of attention needs to be paid to the aspect of improving allocative efficiency within the health sector. This exercise should be in the nature of a stand-alone exercise largely independent of economic reforms, but within its broader framework.

5

Education in India: An Overview

The Constitution of India envisaged fulfilling the promise of all states to provide "free and compulsory education for all children until they complete the age of 14 years" by 1960. Yet, if present trends continue, India is still fifty years away from reaching the goal. Meanwhile, the absolute number of illiterate people in the population is steadily rising year after year. At about 50 crore, the number of illiterates in today's India is larger than the total population of the country thirty years ago. Even in the younger age groups, illiteracy remains endemic. About half of all adolescent girls, for instance, are unable to read and write.

The low priority given to education by this nation is apparent from the mean years of schooling – the average period spent in school by a citizen. Indians spend a little over two years in the classroom. Chinese spend five, Sri Lankans over seven and South Koreans nine.

Census 2001: Literacy in the Present Scenario
The Census 2001 provisional reports indicate that India has made a significant progress in the field of literacy during the decade since the previous census in 1991. The literacy rate in 2001 has been recorded at 65.38 percent as against 52.21 percent

in 1991. The 13.17 percentage points' increase in the literacy rate during the period is the highest increase in any decade. Also, for the first time, there is a decline in the absolute number of non-literates during the past ten years. The total number of non-literates has come down from 320 million in 1991 to 296 million in 2001. During 1991-2000, the population in 7+ age group increased by 171.6 millions, while 203.6 million additional persons became literate during that period. Out of 858 million people above the age of seven years, 562 million are now literates. Three-fourths of our male population and more than half of the female population are literate. This indeed is an encouraging indicator for us to speed up our march towards the goal of achieving a sustainable threshold literacy rate of 75 percent by 2005.

The Census 2001 provisional figures also indicate that the efforts of the nation during the past decade to remove the scourge of illiteracy have not gone in vain. The eradication of illiteracy from a vast country like India beset by several social and economic hurdles is not an easy task. Realising this, the National Literacy Mission (NLM) was set up on 5th May, 1988 to impart a new sense of urgency and seriousness to adult education. After the success of the areas-specific, time-bound and voluntary-based campaign approach, first in Kottayam city and then in Ernakulum district in Kerala in 1990, the NLM had accepted the literacy campaigns as the dominant strategy for eradication of illiteracy.

During the last ten years 574 districts out of 597 districts in the country have already been covered by the literacy campaigns, of which 272 districts have entered the post-literacy phase and 112 are in the continuing education phase.

The NLM was revitalised with the approval of the union government on 30th September, 1999. The Mission's goal is to attain total literacy, i.e., a sustainable threshold literacy rate of 75 percent by 2005. The NLM seeks to achieve this by imparting functional literacy to non-literates in the 15-35 age group.

Table 5.1

Literacy Rate of India, Census 2001

India/States/ Union Territories	Literacy Rate 2001		
	Persons	Males	Females
INDIA	65.38	75.85	54.16
Jammu & Kashmir	54.46	65.75	41.82
Himachal Pradesh	77.13	86.02	68.08
Punjab	69.95	75.63	63.55
Chandigarh	81.76	85.65	76.65
Uttaranchal	72.28	84.01	60.26
Haryana	68.59	79.25	56.31
Delhi	81.82	87.37	75.00
Rajasthan	61.03	76.46	44.34
Uttar Pradesh	57.36	70.23	42.98
Bihar	47.53	60.32	33.57
Sikkim	69.68	76.73	61.46
Arunachal Pradesh	54.74	64.07	44.24
Nagaland	67.11	71.77	61.92
Manipur	68.87	77.87	59.70
Mizoram	88.49	90.69	86.13
Tripura	73.66	81.47	65.41
Meghalaya	63.31	66.14	60.41
Assam	64.28	71.93	56.03
West Bengal	69.22	77.58	60.22
Jharkhand	54.13	67.94	39.38
Orissa	63.61	75.95	50.97
Chhattisgarh	65.18	77.86	52.40
Madhya Pradesh	64.11	76.80	50.28
Gujarat	69.97	80.50	58.60
Daman & Diu	81.09	88.40	70.37
Dadra & Nagar Haveli	60.03	73.32	42.99
Maharashtra	77.27	86.27	67.51
Andhra Pradesh	61.11	70.85	51.17
Karnataka	67.04	76.29	57.45
Goa	82.32	88.88	75.51
Lakshadweep	87.52	93.15	81.56

Contd...

Contd...			
Kerala	90.92	94.20	87.86
Tamil Nadu	73.47	82.33	64.55
Pondicherry	81.49	88.89	74.13
Andaman & Nicobar Island	81.18	86.07	75.29

Note: The population of India includes the estimated population of entire Kachchh
district, Morvi, Maliya-Miyana and Wankaner talukas of Rajkot district, Jodiya
taluka of Jamnagar district of Gujarat and entire Kinnaur district of Himachal
Pradesh where population enumeration of Census of India, 2001 could not be
conducted due to natural calamities. The literacy rates for India have been worked
out by excluding the population and number of literates of areas affected by natural
calamities of Gujarat and Himachal Pradesh as per details given.

Literacy rates shown against Himachal Pradesh and Gujarat do not include areas
affected by natural calamities, the details of which are given in the note above.

Source: Census of India, 2001.

To tackle the problem of residual illiteracy, now it has been
decided to adopt an integrated approach to literacy campaigns
and post-literacy programme. This means the basic literacy
campaigns and post-literacy programmes will be implemented
under one literacy project called 'Literacy Campaigns and
Operation Restoration' to achieve continuity, efficiency and
convergence and to minimise unnecessary time lag between the
two. Post-literacy programmes are treated only as a preparatory
phase for launching continuing education with the ultimate aim
of creating a learning society.

In order to promote decentralisation, the State Literacy
Mission Authorities have been given the authority to sanction
continuing education projects to districts and literacy-related
projects to voluntary agencies in their respective states.

The scheme of 'Jan Shikshan Sansthan' or Institutes of
People's Education, previously known as the Scheme of
Shramik Vidyapeeth, was initially evolved as a non-formal
continuing education programme to respond to the educational
and vocational training needs of adults and young people living
in urban and industrial areas as well as for persons who had
migrated from rural to urban settings. Now, their activities
have been enlarged and infrastructure strengthened to enable

them to function as district level repositories of vocational and technical skills in both urban and rural areas. At present, there are 92 Jan Shikshan Sansthan in the country.

The NLM is laying great stress on vigorous monitoring and systematic evaluation of adult education programmes launched under its aegis in the country. It has developed and circulated guidelines for concurrent and final evaluation of the literacy campaigns and post-literacy programmes. A comprehensive set of guidelines on continuing education has also been prepared. So far final evaluation of literacy campaigns has been undertaken in more than 210 districts. It is hoped that the new approach of evaluating literacy campaigns and continuing education schemes will ensure complete transparency and enhance the credibility of the results and impact assessments.

Literacy Across States

In 1991, nine out of the 32 states fall in the high literacy category. The range is from Kerala with a literacy rate of 89.8 percent to Daman and Diu with 71.2 percent. These states could clearly be said to be confronting the issue of residual illiteracy within a band where literacy rates vary over a wide range of 18.6 percent. The category of high literacy states/districts might be termed as the "zone of residual illiteracy". The range of variation is high as compared to that of the 25 medium literacy rate states (15.8%) and especially the range of the eight low literacy rate ones (5.7%). The latter eight states – Madhya Pradesh, Andhra Pradesh, Arunachal Pradesh, Uttar Pradesh, Dadra and Nagar Haveli, Rajasthan, Bihar and Jammu & Kashmir, in that descending order of literacy rate – are faced with the daunting context of mass illiteracy and stand clustered towards the upper end of a category which might be described as the "zone of mass illiteracy". Given the literacy trends over the last census decade, however, they could well enter the medium category by the year 2001, just as the states of Haryana, Assam, Meghalaya and Orissa did in 1981. As regards the category of medium literacy rate states, one could expect about half the number of these states with literacy rates of 60 percent and above in 1991 to move into the high category in the near future. With the additional efforts of the literacy campaigns and primary education initiatives, even those states with literacy rate of 55 percent and above are likely to do so. States/districts falling within this medium literacy category are characterised by the phenomenon of 'transitional illiteracy', given the highest growth rates of literacy within this category and the movement of states/districts into and out of it.

The probable scenario by the year 2001 is that two-thirds of the states in the country would fall within the category of high literacy rate with residual illiteracy, resulting in a polarisation with the states characterised by large population size and mass illiteracy; the latter states being additionally burdened with gender, regional and communal disparities in literacy. This tentative sketch will be more clearly manifest from the following analysis.

Some conclusions stand out from the Census 1991 data for the country as a whole: the very low mean female literacy rate (39.3%) varying over a wide range (65.8%); the comparatively high urban literacy rate (73.1%) varying over a low range of state differences (32.5%); and the extremely low rates for scheduled castes (SC: 37.4%) and scheduled tribes (ST: 29.6%), as compared to that of the general population of non-SC/ST (57.7%). In the category of high literacy rate states, the mean literacy rate for rural areas is surprisingly slightly higher (86.8%) than that for urban areas (83.8%), the mean data being skewed to the higher side by the comparatively large rural population of Kerala. The mean literacy rate for this belt of states is also slightly higher for the ST population (73.6%) as compared to the SC (70.9%). In contrast, the low literacy states are confronted with the problems of gender, region and SC/ST community, which are mutually reinforcing in a deprivational sense, the literacy rates being as low as: female 26.2 percent, rural 35.1 percent, SC 27.4 percent and ST 22.1 percent. The mean literacy rate for the high category of states was as high as 85.5 percent in 1991, as compared to 59.1 percent in the medium and only 41.5 percent in the low category. It may be pointed out that while there were only about 5.2 million non-literates in the nine states falling in the high literacy category, there were about 134 million and 190 million non-literates in the medium and low literacy states, respectively. The massive task ahead is clearly that of enabling access to literacy in the latter two categories of states and enhancing learning while confronting residual illiteracy in the relatively urbanised areas of the high literacy states and partly in the medium literacy ones.

At the national level, the highest growth rate in literacy from 1981 to 1991 was among women (9.5%), even higher than the national mean (8.6%) for the period. Even though it is largely attributable to female growth rates in literacy in the medium category of states, this phenomenon is a positive sign for the future, given that women are the largest absolute category with the greatest need. However, the rest of the data suggest that the growth rates favour the non-SC/ST and the urban areas as against the rural areas and the SC/ST, thus acting as a drag on the possibilities for change. Examining the categories of states classified according to literacy rate in greater detail, one finds that the high literacy states demonstrate a reversal of the above-mentioned trend with the ST/SC population, the females and the rural areas having the highest growth rates in that order.

Clearly, these states have reached what might be termed as a 'saturation' point with respect to literacy within the opposite sections of society and are addressing themselves to sections that are in the greatest need of literacy. The contrasting gender, regional and communitarian characteristics of literacy are brought sharply into focus when one considers that in the low literacy states precisely the reverse is true: comparative growth rates in literacy favour urban areas, non-SC/ST and males in that order. Both the polarisation trends in national level literacy as well as the saturation effects in high literacy areas, referred to earlier in the analysis of the previous table, are revealed by the literacy growth rate data. The literacy growth rate of 6.7 percent for the high literacy states indicates a tapering off into a plateau as compared to 9.1 percent for the medium and 8.3 percent for the low literacy states. Incidentally, Chandigarh in the high belt had the lowest growth rate in literacy (3%) as compared to Arunachal Pradesh, with the highest overall growth rate (16.1%), but in the low belt.

In case of the inter-sex, region and community differentials in literacy rates for 1981 and 1991 for the different states at the mean national level, the differentials are greatest for region (28.4%), sex (24.8%) and community (18.8%), in that descending order for 1991. While there is a decrease in the differences with respect to the former two categories, there is a slight but disturbing increase in inequalities as regards access to literacy between the SC/ST and others for the period 1981-91. The range of increase or decrease in differences is also sharpest in the community category, from a healthy --40.8 percent in Lakshadweep to an alarming +13 percent increase in the tribal pocket of Dadra & Nagar Haveli. The impending polarisation and disparities in literacy become all the more evident when one considers that the belt of high literacy states has shown an overall decrease in mean differentials over the ten year period, with the sharpest decrease being that between SC/ST and others; while the low literacy rate states have in contrast performed poorly, with a slight increase in mean differentials with respect to sex (+0.3%), an increase in urban-rural disparities (+2.7%), and an even sharper increase in disparities between SC/ST and the general population (+5%). Even, the data for medium-literacy states suggest an increase in the differentials for community (+1.1%). All the 15 states in the medium literacy category have shown an increase in the differentials between the SC/ST and the others as regards literacy rate for the period 1981-91, except Himachal Pradesh and Sikkim. In the low literacy belt the states of Madhya Pradesh, Uttar Pradesh, Dadra & Nagar Haveli and Rajasthan demonstrate an increase in literacy differentials as regards all the three categories of gender, region, and community; whereas in Bihar the increase in differentials is with respect to the last two categories.

Literacy and Development in India

The national level decadal growth rate of population was 23.6 percent for 1981-91. The high literacy states have the highest mean decadal growth rate (33.3%), thanks to their highest mean rate of urbanisation (43.1%) and their highest mean density of population (570) as compared to the medium and low literacy states. Kerala and Goa appear to be the only states within the high literacy category that go consistently against the trend of population growth accompanied by high urbanisation. Delhi, in contrast with a 50.6 percent decadal growth rate, 89.9 percent urbanisation and an index of population density of 6,352, is consistently the highest as regards these indicators within this belt. It is noteworthy that Nagaland in the medium literacy category and Arunachal Pradesh in the low stand out as states within the north-eastern region of the country with relatively high decadal growth rates of population but with low ratios of urbanisation and population density. This phenomenon cannot be explained by birth rates, but perhaps by the process of in-migration. The low literacy states have a higher mean decadal growth rate of population than the medium literacy ones, despite a lower degree of urbanisation and density of population, apparently because of less success with family health care measures.

The sex ratio in the low literacy states is the least (913), in sharp contrast to that in the high literacy states (975), indicating that literacy interventions need to be highly sensitive to the

status of women, especially in these regions, both for reasons of
equity and pragmatic organisation. In contrast stands Kerala
with the highest sex ratio of 1,040 and the highest literacy rate
of 89.8 percent. The states with a tribal concentration in the
north-east generally fall in the medium literacy rate category
except for Mizoram and Arunachal Pradesh which are in the
high and low literacy categories, respectively. Punjab, Himachal
Pradesh, West Bengal and Haryana are major states in the
medium literacy category with high concentrations of SCs, but
with relatively high SC literacy rates (41.1%, 53.2%, 42.2% and
39.2%, respectively) as compared to the national mean literacy
rate for SCs (37.4%). In contrast, in the low literacy states of
Madhya Pradesh, Andhra Pradesh, Uttar Pradesh, Rajasthan
and Bihar -- with concentrations of SC ranging from 21 percent
to 14.5 percent and their literacy rates ranging from 35.1
percent to 19.5 percent – the socio-economically deprived status
of the SCs has reinforced educational disadvantage. On an
average, a quarter of the population in the low literacy states
belongs to the deprived community of SC and ST, as compared
to 14.2 percent in the high literacy ones.

A relation also exists between literacy and health
characteristics. Kerala and the high literacy states in general, are
better endowed with access to health facilities, going by the
number of beds and doctors per lakh of population, as
compared to the medium and low literacy states. The
exceptions to this general trend with respect to the low
availability of doctors are the states of Karnataka, Maharashtra
and West Bengal in the medium literacy category, and Andhra
Pradesh in the low one. Uttar Pradesh is the most deprived as
regards health personnel on the basis of available data. The
consequences of the lack of infrastructure on other health
indicators are evident: the low literacy states have the highest
mean infant mortality rate of 86, the highest overall crude death
rate of 11.4, as well as the highest mean birth rate of 32.2, as
compared to the national averages of 80, 9.8 and 29.5,

respectively. As regards the last two indicators, where adequate data for states and union territories in the high literacy category are available, the situation here appears to be the healthiest. As compared to the 70.8 expectation of life at birth in Kerala, the mean expectation in the medium and low literacy states is 60.4 and 55.8, respectively. The tragic situation of the low literacy states is indicated by the fact that all these states, with the exception of Andhra Pradesh, have birth and death rates higher than the national average and expectations of life at birth lower than that of the country. Uttar Pradesh has, on the basis of available evidence, the lowest (52) expectation of life at birth and the least number of doctors per lakh of population in the country; and ironically, close to the highest birth rate as compared to other states. When one considers that this state has a literacy rate of 41.6 percent that is the fourth lowest and about one-fifth of the non-literates of the country, then the close relation between basic education and health status within a context of underdevelopment becomes evident. The situation of Orissa, at the lowest end of the medium literacy states, and of the other states in the low literacy northern belt -- Madhya Pradesh, Rajasthan and Bihar -- is not far different, except for minor inconsistencies in rank order.

One of the sharpest indicators of uneven development in the country is perhaps the "relative index of development" formulated by the Centre for Monitoring Indian Economy. The relationship between this and other socio-economic indicators with literacy can also be considered. With 100 as the mean and 470 index points as a national level range of variation, one observes a sharp decrease in mean indices of development from 167 for the high literacy states, to 96 for the medium and only 73 for the low literacy states. The mean literacy rates for these categories of states are 85.5 percent, 59.1 percent and 41.5 percent, respectively. Chandigarh (513) in the zone of residual illiteracy and Bihar (43) at the bottom of the mass illiteracy zone provide the extremes of variation. Punjab demonstrates the highest index of development (199) within the zone of transitional illiteracy. Kerala, in a manner comparable with its per capita income (5,065), has a depressed index of 117. A significant feature of this relative index is the consistently low indices of development for all the seven 'peripheral' north-eastern states, a region of extraction of natural resources and exploitation of economic surplus for the dominant 'central' states, irrespective of the fact that except for Arunachal Pradesh all these states may be found in the medium or high literacy categories. The spread of education through Christian influence explains the latter phenomenon. Per capita incomes at current prices in 1992-93 closely follow the contours of the foregoing economic scenario, with Rs 8,581 being the mean for the high, and Rs 6,525 and Rs 4,913 being the means for the medium and low literacy states, respectively. The national mean was Rs 6,249. All the states in the low literacy zone fall below this level, with the exception of Arunachal Pradesh in the north-east.

The percentage of landless agricultural labourers to total main workers provides some indication of the pressure on land resulting from dependence on agriculture and of the inequity of production relations resulting from land distribution. The low literacy states have the highest proportion of the landless (26.9%), with Andhra Pradesh and Bihar in the forefront of skewed land distribution. In addition, Pondicherry in the high literacy belt, and Karnataka, Orissa and Maharashtra in the medium are states that have proportions of the landless agricultural labourers to main workers that are higher than the mean for the country (26.1%). That the underdevelopment of the north-eastern states has less to do with internal production relations in agriculture than with an external siphoning off of surplus is suggested by the generally low proportion of the landless in a region highly dependent on agriculture and forestry. In contrast with Kerala in the high literacy belt with 17 percent of its population reported to fall below the poverty line in 1987-88, the medium literacy states in general have 23.6 percent and the low literacy ones as high as 33.7 percent of their population on the average in the category of the impoverished. The national mean for those below the poverty line was 29.9 percent. On the basis of available data one finds that all the states in the low literacy category, with the exception of Rajasthan, have proportions of their population below the poverty line that are higher than the national average. Orissa (44.7%), Tamil Nadu (32.8%) and Karnataka (32.1%) in the medium literacy category are other states that face high levels of stark poverty. A contrasting positive scenario is found in Punjab (7.2%), Himachal Pradesh (9.2%) and Haryana (11.6%), which are regions of agricultural and agro-industrial prosperity falling in the medium literacy category of states. It appears that it would be near impossible to confront mass illiteracy in the low literacy states without at the same time engaging in land reforms and income generation measures, just as functionality towards productive employment would greatly facilitate basic educational interventions in regions of residual illiteracy within medium and high literacy states.

Literacy, in particular adult literacy, and primary education have what might be called a symbiotic relation within the sphere of basic education. When seen in terms of primary schools per 1,000 population, it is not surprising that the high literacy states – generally the most urbanised, densely populated and having the highest decadal growth rates of population – should also have the lowest mean ratio (0.3), even lower than the low literacy states and the medium literacy ones (0.7). In fact, the sparsely populated north-eastern states have generally a high ratio of schools per 1,000 population, in all cases higher than the national mean with Meghalaya (2.3) heading the ranking of states. However, these schools are highly dispersed when seen as a ratio of geographical area. Delhi has the highest such proportion (5.6 per 5 sq kms) within the country. The high literacy states are the best endowed with respect to percentage of trained teachers (91.3%) and the mean percentage of budgetary expenditure on education in 1989-90 on revenue account (21.8%). Chandigarh and Delhi in the high literacy belt, and Tamil Nadu, Gujarat, Haryana and surprisingly Orissa in the medium literacy zone report a total coverage of trained teachers. The states of the north-east are more modest in this claim and perhaps more accurate.

That the basic educational problems of the low literacy states might have less to do with the availability of schooling facilities but rather the quality of these assets -- in terms of material and human resources and the nature of pedagogical practices -- is suggested by the fact that at least as regards the first two of the above-mentioned indicators (schools per given area and trained teachers), they fare as well as or better than the medium literacy states. A schooling push factor reinforced by survival strategies of households in the face of depressed socio-economic conditions appear to explain the situation of basic education in the low literacy states. Consider, for example, that these states are reported to have the highest mean number of students in primary school per teacher (48). Andhra Pradesh with 53 students per teacher and Uttar Pradesh with 51 head the list. The result is crowded classrooms and multigrade teaching; the lowest mean enrolments in primary schools per 1,000 population (105.9); the lowest average gross enrolment ratio for the age group corresponding to classes I-V (93.7%); and the highest dropout (drive out) ratio for these classes (53.6%), more than half the initial enrolment at class I.

In matters of enrolment per 1,000 population (130.1) and as a gross ratio for the age group of the primary classes (113.9%), the medium literacy states do even better than the high literacy ones. However, the latter states are able to retain their wards to a far greater degree as seen from the lowest mean dropout ratio of 9.9 percent. In fact, some states like Kerala (--4.2%), Pondicherry (--4.6%) and Chandigarh (--6.9%) are reported to have a negative dropout ratio.

The high literacy states, regions of residual illiteracy, and even more so perhaps the high literacy districts (if such detailed data were readily available) do have a problem of providing quality access to basic education to their burgeoning populations. These cases of relative prosperity within a desertified nation are able to draw in flows of humanity as indicated by the highest decadal population growth rate, percentage of urbanisation and density. But they also generate an informal sector at a rate that is faster than their industrialisation, commercialisation and organised employment generation capacities. Thus, these uprooted from the hinterland throng the 'peripheries' within the metropolis and add to the number of slum and pavement dwellers. For these persons, the value of investment of time for education is weighed against survival. The price is paid in terms of having foregone basic education for the adults, especially for women and the aged, and present child labour for the young.

Some index of this basic educational phenomenon in the high literacy states/districts is provided by the following data: while these states have the highest percentage of trained teachers, the greatest investment in education and retention rates, and the best teacher-student ratios, as we have discussed earlier, they are also constrained to provide universal basic education as seen from the lowest index of primary schools as a ratio of population and area, and from the fact that enrolment rates as a proportion of population and of the relevant age group are lower than the medium literacy states. For example, when one considers enrolments in primary education as a proportion of 1,000 population, the urbanised centres of Chandigarh (77.3) and Delhi (97.7) are among the lowest in rank order, close to the union territory of Daman and Diu (96.3) in the high literacy belt and Bihar (99.2) in the low literacy one. Their gross enrolment ratios for primary education also follow a broadly similar pattern, with Chandigarh (60.6) and Delhi (90.2) being among the lowest in performance. In fact, the mean for the former index (107.6) for the high literacy states is brought down by the areas of urbanisation to a level lower than the national mean (125.6). In the case of the latter index, the regions of high literacy have a mean slightly higher than that of the country, for similar reasons. It is clear that universal enrolment in basic education is far from a reality in high density urban areas and that the developmental trajectory of capital intensive industrialisation and restricted market commercialisation in select metropolitan regions is constrained in its capacity to meet further basic education needs even within those regions.

For such persons in the underpaid informal sector the real demand for socio-economic mobility through education, initially sparked off by survival migration, can only be met by attractive and accessible basic formal education, which is presently largely conducted by municipalities, and by non-formal educational complementarities that are specific to occupational group and have high components of functional linkages with open certification and employment generation. The heavy price attached to education by those who struggle at barely subsistence levels in larger contexts of urban prosperity can only be made valuable enough to offset their immediate economic needs and to facilitate their long-term basic human entitlements.

Issues and Trends in Literacy Campaigns

A major attempt to address the issue of illiteracy was the literacy campaign strategy initiated in 1989 under the auspices of the National Literacy Mission (NLM). Started in Ernakulam, Kottayam and then in the entire high literacy state of Kerala at the initiative of a major voluntary organisation, the Kerala Shastra Sahitya Parishad. Thanks to the enterprise of some administrative officials, the campaign approach was also adopted in selected districts of the country, generally high literacy ones. A strategy evolved in a context of residual illiteracy with a history of social reform movements and labouring class organisation and struggle was then implemented across the board throughout the country in generally an undifferentiated manner and without much care for contextualisation. Even certain basic preconditions during the preparatory phase of the campaigns, such as the generation of widespread voluntarism within diverse institutional and informal resources, its organisation and the creation of an environment conducive to literacy through the use of folk media, came to be neglected as the campaigns gradually came to be both finance-driven and drawn by the needs of low literacy states. While the gains in the initial phase, both in terms of absolute numbers made literate and the social impact of the approach, have been significant, the strategy has reached a point of relative stagnation seeking a tactical breakthrough in regions of mass illiteracy and underdevelopment such as in the Hindi heartland and ironically also in districts of residual illiteracy and high urbanisation. The strategy is sound and anyhow is all that exists, without a large-scale alternative in sight. The problem lies in its tactical contextualisation according to the political economy of uneven development.

The status of the literacy campaigns in March 1996 in terms of enrolment and the achievement of learners having completed all the three prescribed primers as a proportion of the targeted non-literates, i.e., those identified through preliminary surveys, is explained in the following paragraphs in this section.

The national level data indicate that a total of about 87 million non-literates have been identified through surveys within 22 states by March 1996. About 77.1 percent of them, numbering in all about 67 million, have been enrolled in the teaching-learning process within their respective state campaigns. About 55.3 percent of the enrolled forming 42.7 percent of the initially identified and targeted are reported to achieve completion of the three primers. The states of Kerala and Pondicherry in the high literacy category, and

Maharashtra, Tamil Nadu, Gujarat and West Bengal in the medium literacy category stand out as having achievement rates that are more than 50 percent of their targeted non-literates. Andhra Pradesh and Rajasthan among the low literacy category are the only states that come close to this success rate. Kerala's achievement rate of 55.6 percent of the target is outdone by Pondicherry's 87.8 percent. Delhi, the capital city falling in the high literacy category, fares the worst with a 1.3 percent achievement rate, even lower than Haryana (13.6%) in the medium, and Uttar Pradesh (19.8%) and Bihar (18.7%) in the low categories.

This is an important illustration of the problems in addressing residual illiteracy in urban, high density areas. The state level aggregated data tend to reinforce this conclusion. The medium literacy states with 50.2 percent of achievement fare better than the high literacy ones (45.5%), with the low literacy states bringing up the rear (33.2%). The heightened performance of some high literacy states, e.g., Kerala and Pondicherry, which had the backing of major voluntary organised initiatives, tends to statistically raise the level of the mean performance of the high literacy states.

Punjab and Haryana, additional states in the medium literacy category and ironically states with high indices of economic development, have the lowest achievement rates of 36.5 percent and 13.6 percent, respectively, in this group. All the states in the low literacy Hindi belt where data is available have achievement rates well below the national mean of 42.7 percent, with the exception of Rajasthan. These are also the states which have the largest concentration of illiteracy in the country. Clearly, the campaign approach as presently practised requires major modifications when it comes to these states where gender, community and class relations present major obstacles to literacy interventions. The low literacy states have the lowest mean achievement rate as compared to the medium and high literacy ones, but an enrolment rate that is higher than that of the high literacy states. The desire for literacy appears to be present, but not adequate means of achieving it.

Constraints and Strategies

In 1990, accompanying the experience of the literacy campaigns in Ernakulam, Kottayam and the Kerala state, literacy campaigns were initiated in Sindhudurg and Wardha districts in Maharashtra as also in a few selected districts within other states of the country. Three other campaigns in Maharashtra followed, viz., Latur in 1991 and Ratnagiri and Nanded in 1992. The Goa literacy campaign started later in 1992. Between 1989 and 1993, the Committee of Resource Organisation (CORO), with an organisational base in the M ward – a major concentration of non-literates in Bombay (now Mumbai) city – worked on a literacy drive in the metropolis. The CORO literacy drive has in common with the other literacy campaigns the aspects of social mobilisation and the spirit of voluntarism, but differs in that it was a voluntary organisational effort in an urban metropolis, relying mainly on literacy activists drawn from local communities with some support from individuals from educational institutions and with little or no coordination with the official educational machinery. The CORO effort, despite the shortcoming of inadequate literacy outcomes in an urban context, has been a major contributor to creating a climate for literacy and basic education in the city which has presently emerged as the SAHAS literacy campaign and the PRATHAM primary education initiative for Bombay.

Goa, Bombay and Sindhudurg along the Konkan coast, together with Wardha in the north-eastern Vidarbha region of Maharashtra, are clearly areas of high literacy rate according to the Census 1991. The literacy rates range from 82.5 percent in Bombay to 70 percent in Wardha. With the exception of Sindhudurg district – which, however, has a close connection to the urban areas of Goa through commuting and seasonal migration – lying to the north of Goa, these regions are also ones of comparatively greater urbanisation: Bombay 100 percent, Goa 41 percent and Wardha 26.6 percent. These indicators are in contrast to those of Ratnagiri district lying north of Sindhudurg, and Latur and Nanded districts in the semi-arid and comparatively underdeveloped region of Marathawada. Literacy rates range from 62.7 percent in Ratnagiri district to 48.2 percent in Nanded. The latter districts also have a lower degree of urbanisation with a greater concentration of scheduled castes (SCs) with low literacy rates; the exception as regards SCs is Ratnagiri district. Data on the relative index of development for these districts/states indicate that Greater Bombay (704), Goa (222), Wardha (99) and Sindhudurg (68) while falling in the high literacy category, contrast sharply with Nanded (53), Ratnagiri and Latur (both 51) which are in the medium literacy group.

The indicators of depressed literacy rates, generally lower degrees of urbanisation and development and higher proportions of SCs are relevant especially when one finds that these latter districts were also the better performing districts with respect to literacy outcomes in their respective campaigns. Sections of society traditionally deprived of formal education within these districts appeared to have responded better to the campaign approach than those in the former districts, generally more urbanised and having to address the problem of residual illiteracy.

Literacy campaigns are located in a historical context and are built into contemporary situations. The selected literacy campaigns in Maharashtra, while drawing inspiration from earlier social reform movements especially among the dalits and more recent efforts at mass literacy, lacked the intensive involvement of trade unions, peasant associations and voluntary organisations with their cadre of activists, as for example in Kerala and West Bengal. The political economy of Maharashtra is, at the same time, by and large different from the contexts faced by literacy campaigns in semi-feudal regions of the country, like parts of Madhya Pradesh, Andhra Pradesh, Uttar Pradesh, Rajasthan and Bihar, the low literacy states of the country. The midway position of Maharashtra could thus provide a useful index of what to expect from literacy campaigns at the national level.

Some other characteristics of interventions in regions of residual illiteracy stand out. In Goa, for example, while the primary focus of the campaign was the younger age group of 15-35 years, and in fact a higher percentage (91.5%) of the non-literate in this age group was enrolled as compared to the same for the older age group of 36-60 years (71.5%), yet the latter formed a higher proportion (58.5%) of those enrolled. This suggests that the problem of illiteracy is essentially residual; among the older generation left out from restricted schooling during the pre-independence period till 1961 and primarily among women who formed 73 percent of the enrolled. The medium of instruction poses a major problem in a multilingual, high urban context like Goa. Of the total, 81.6 percent were instructed through Marathi, while only 8.1 percent and 5.4 percent were instructed in Konkani through the Devnagari and Roman scripts, respectively. Another 4.9 percent were taught in the languages of migrants from the surrounding states. This is in a state where approximately 90 percent were reported to be using Konkani as the mother tongue and the language of the domestic sphere. Apart from the cultural alienation resulting from learning a script in what is not one's mother tongue, literacy interventions in regions of high literacy tend to further marginalise interior blocks such as Sattari and Canacona which were both initially low in literacy and later low in performance in the campaign.

Regions of high literacy do have the human and cultural resources to address their illiteracy issues. This is demonstrated by the intervention of the CORO – a voluntary organisation in the city of Bombay. During the period 1989-93, about 40 percent of the learners were taught by instructors who were school students resident in the same slum communities as the learners and often related to them. In addition, in a highly community-centred and participatory manner, about 50 percent of the learners were covered by literate adults from these communities and the rest by either the literacy activist youth or literate adults from outside the communities. An analysis of a survey conducted in April 1991 provides a profile of the learners. The vast majority of them (80%) were women. About 76 percent were aged 26-45 years while the targeted age group was 15-45 years. Most of the learners were post-1970 neo-migrants to the city for marriage and/or employment escaping the drought that hit the countryside in the early 1970s and were first generation learners in their families of origin. However, an encouraging fact was that 98 percent of the learners had no present family member of the school-going age who was non-literate and non-school going. The CORO literacy drive had in effect concentrated on the dalit neo-Buddhists (67%) and the SCs (16%).

An important feature of the SAHAS campaign in the nine wards of Bombay was the involvement of the secondary education system and the school children as instructors. Primary school teachers also participated as full-timers against great odds. However, our observations suggest that a major weakness was the general absence of the participation of slum communities in an organised manner. Negligible attempts were made to secure community participation through the appointment of local coordinators who later could serve as the activists of the post-literacy phase, i.e., nuclei around whom post-literacy could attain sustainability as an educational and cultural movement. Ongoing cultural, environment-building programmes to sustain motivation for literacy were generally neglected. The dichotomy between literacy and a post-literacy phase, especially in an urban context where an 'instrumental orientation' to literacy predominates, becomes highly artificial. The functional awareness and organisational aspects of post-literacy need to be initiated right from the start so as to sustain motivation for literacy. Voluntary organisations, a major resource in urban contexts, were generally ignored or chose to keep away because of their own priorities. The general lack of community and voluntary organisational support resulted in a heavy burden being placed on the adult, primary and secondary educational administration. Monitoring the programme thus becomes largely a process of information gathering and bureaucratic meetings to take reviews of progress.

These problems do not seem to be reflected in the high literacy outcomes that are reported. The internal monitoring data of the SAHAS campaign suggest that about 53,401 learners forming 63.8 percent of the identified non-literates in the nine wards have completed the three primers and have become neo-literate. These success rates range from 96.5 percent in the F southward to 30 percent in the M eastward. About 17.7 percent of the identified and enrolled had dropped out at various stages. Based on field visits, observations, attendance at meetings and discussions, one considers the reported achievement rate of 63.8 percent to be an overstatement, contradicting the general trend of poor performance in urban literacy campaigns. The learner achievement rates emerging from the literacy intervention of the Tata Institute of Social Sciences, Bombay, in a neighbouring slum pocket -- Panjrapole -- as part of the SAHAS efforts in M eastward, appear to be a more realistic reflection of the problems of literacy intervention in an urban, residually illiterate area. By April 1996, out of 131 non-literate learners who initially attended instruction by about 80 students over a period of about a year and a half (1994-1996), 25 dropped out, 31 became literate to the level of the NLM norms, and 75 learners were at various intermediate levels. The many problems faced by the programme could be reduced to: (i) the problem of time of both learners and student instructors/ faculty coordinators, reflecting levels of motivation and conflicting priorities in a metropolis; and (ii) the problem of coordinated, consistent faculty involvement, reflective of constraints to institutional (a university) involvement in a co-curricular activity for the marginalised/residual within the relatively unstructured setting of an urban slum, despite considerable community developmental activities. It appears clear that a major constraining factor in urban areas is that both the literate as well as the residually non-literate adults have very little time for literacy, and for different reasons which will be discussed in greater detail in the following section.

Literacy and Social Space

The condensation of literacy in the present follows a spatial distribution that closely approximates the uneven development within the country. States and districts demonstrate literacy rates according to a pattern. The literacy rates in the nine high literacy states suggest a 'saturation effect' with the mean growth rate in the last decadal period being the lowest for all the three categories of states and reaching a low of 6.7 percent. For example, the urban areas in the high literacy districts of Maharashtra show the least growth rates in literacy when compared to all categories of disaggregated data in the state. The deprived communities and the rural areas in the high literacy states have a higher growth rate than the respective national means, suggesting a catching up on a backlog. The reverse is true for the low literacy states, regions of 'mass illiteracy' as different from the former regions of the 'residual illiteracy', with the added factor of neglect of female literacy.

The high literacy districts, generally islands of urbanisation and commercialisation, are to be found predominantly in the high and medium literacy states. Literacy trends suggest a spread of literacy over the medium literacy states, regions of a 'transitional illiteracy', most of which will have a residual illiteracy by the turn of the century; but a sharp polarisation with regions of mass illiteracy where gender, community, class and rural location tend to reinforce each other in a vortex of deprivation.

Literacy interventions, especially in low literacy districts, would have to directly address the question of the status of women. In the 163 low literacy districts of the country gender differences in literacy rates in 1991 were not only the highest, but had also increased over the decade. The increase in literacy rate differentials is also seen for region and community.

In states like Maharashtra which tops the medium literacy states, the tribal stands marginalised and deprived of literacy within the developmental trajectory of the state. The two sectors that show the least growth rates in literacy within this state are the urban and the tribal, ironically at the two extremes of a developmental continuum where commerce, heavy industrialisation and urbanisation have a high premium. The stagnation in literation within the urban areas reflects both the inability of educational infrastructure to absorb the neo-migrants from regions of deprivation, as well as the creation of such regions through the exploitation of human and natural resources of the periphery. The wider significance of this polarisation is that it is a close reflection of the distribution of literacy in states/districts of the country, with the added element of gender insensitivity.

The tragic situation of the low literacy states is illustrated by Uttar Pradesh -- a state with the lowest expectation of life at birth, the least number of doctors per lakh of population, one of the lowest sex ratios in the country, and ironically close to the highest birth rate. With a literacy rate in 1991 of 41.6 percent, the state held about a fifth of the non-literates in the country. In the 'peripheral' north-eastern states, however, the low indices of development contrast sharply with relatively high literacy rates which were largely the result of religious influence. The seven states in this region of concentration of STs fall in the category of high or medium literacy rate with the exception of Arunachal Pradesh. All the seven states in the low literacy category have relative indices of development that are below the national mean and all the states, except Rajasthan, have proportions of their population falling below the poverty line that are higher than the national average. It appears impossible to confront mass illiteracy in low literacy states/districts without major interventions on the socio-economic front such as land reforms, income generation measures and mobilisations on issues of caste and the status of women.

Formal elementary education has been and will have to be strengthened to be the main contributor to literacy. However, it is clear that universal enrolment in basic formal education is far from a reality even in high-density urban areas. The developmental trajectory of capital-intensive, and now globalised, industrialisation and restricted-market commercialisation in select metropolitan regions is stretched in its capacity to provide elementary education even within regions of concentration of resources. These centres of relative prosperity draw in flows of humanity as indicated by the highest decadal population growth rates, percentage of urbanisation and density. But, they also generate an informal economic sector at a rate that is faster than their organised employment generation capacities. The high literacy states/districts have the highest percentage of trained teachers, the greatest investment in education and retention rates, and the best teacher-student ratios. But, the number of primary schools per thousand population and enrolment rates as a proportion of population and of the relevant age group are lower than the medium literacy states. For example, Chandigarh and Delhi are among the lowest in rank order with respect to these indices as compared to other states/union territories.

Female literacy rate, urbanisation and the relative index of development are major positive co-variants of the literacy rate, and highly statistically significant. This is true for the then 452 districts of the country and the 30 districts of Maharashtra, which heads the medium literacy category of states. The map of distribution of literacy and urbanisation/development in Maharashtra broadly represents the disparities and contradictions at the national level. High density, urban, highly literate, centres like Greater Bombay whose commercialisation and industrialisation result in high indices of development, attracts migrants in a proportion that their infrastructures for basic needs are unable to support. At the other end of the contradiction lies an underdeveloped rural hinterland like the Konkan belt, with medium levels of literacy, which serves as the terrain for the extraction of human, agricultural and natural resources. Lastly, one finds regions of neglect like Marathwada and Vidarbha with concentrations of deprived communities confronted with semi-aridity, drought, underemployment and mass illiteracy.

Literacy in India after the Reforms: Concepts and Problems

The account of contemporary literacy campaigns in India since 1989 is partly a story of voluntary people's participation and cultural awakening. It is in part a narrative of the resistance of two regions to the literacy campaign approach – the urban areas of relatively high literacy and the rural areas within underdeveloped regions, especially in the northern belt. The analysis of residual illiteracy cannot remain unrelated to the latter regions of mass illiteracy.

It is ironical that literacy campaigns encountered a contextualised resistance from the areas that, on the surface, required them the least; as well as from parts of the country where the objective need for literacy was the most – at two ends of a spectrum of intervention, as it were. This suggests a need for a readjustment of the campaign style in a manner that is far more sensitive to the contexts of intervention. The particular characteristics of the Kerala model of literacy campaign were never intended to be applied across the board throughout the nation. Yet there has been inadequate reflection on those aspects of a campaign that needs to be finely tuned to contexts of uneven development.

There are several reports of problems faced by literacy campaigns in high literacy, urban areas. The case of Pondicherry, a high literacy region with four districts, serves as an illustration. Reports suggest that the degree of participation in village committees was in inverse proportion to their geographical distance from the seat of government. In Mahe, Yanam and Karaikal, both administrative and community supports were forthcoming. In the outer low literacy blocks of Pondicherry the response was less, but in the nearer semi-urban areas and in urban Pondicherry proper it was the least. Political/administrative counter pressures at a later stage, the lower degree of a sense of community and consequent difficulties in evolving decentralised organisational forms with acceptable local leadership are stated as reasons for this phenomenon. Sustained outreach to sub-groups through college students is suggested as a solution, especially in urban areas.

In a survey of three districts in West Bengal, namely, Burdwan, Birbhum and Bankura, a lack of response was identified and sometimes a resistance to the literacy campaigns in the urban areas of these districts. Officials attributed this to a lack of interest and time among casual labourers, the indifference of the municipal councillors and the lumpenisation of sections of slum-dwelling workers. In addition, the surveyor draws attention to the comparative lack of social cohesion among migrants to cities and towns, organisational difficulties with respect to workers in the informal sector and the alienation of the urban middle class from the issues that affect the poor.

In addition to these problems, the literacy situation in regions of residual illiteracy suggests an urgency to look beyond basic literacy. With the 1991 national literacy rate standing at

52.2 percent and the probability of at least a 10 percent increase in literacy over the decadal period by the turn of the century, several states and districts are likely to enter the high literacy bracket. What is the quality of this literacy? How functional is it in terms of economic entitlements? What are the means to sustain and enhance this level of basic education? These are major concerns. There is also the real possibility of a 'neo-illiteracy' being generated among the marginalised in the informal sector during the process of rapid urbanisation that is underway, contributed by a relapse from semi-literacy, inadequate access to a stretched primary education system and for lack of continuing educational facilities linked to employment generation.

Centres of urbanisation have become increasingly important nodal units mediating between their rural hinterland and unrestrained globalisation processes brought about by a revolution in technology, information and communication, and by the power of dominant economic systems. The marginalised require the enabling skills of literacy to cope with these hegemonic systems and to be able to offer a critique in favour of more equitable and democratic entitlements.

Defining the residual with reference to illiteracy and identifying regions of mass illiteracy calls for a process of categorisation of states/districts within the country. Categorisation is itself relative to context and has necessarily been specific to country situation and the stage of development of literacy. Absolute cross-national norms, while perhaps being necessary for reasons of comparison, have a major limitation as regards interventional relevance.

Financing Education

The issue of financing education has been central to educational development in India. Expenditure on education comes from two major sources. The first is the expenditure borne by the union government and state governments. The second is the expenditure incurred by the households on the payment of fees, purchase of books, stationery and uniforms, conveyance, private coaching and maintenance in schools. Besides such direct household expenditure on education, there is indirect expenditure in the form of earnings forgone by an individual who opts for schooling instead of engaging in gainful wage or self-employment (Shariff and Ghosh, 2000).

Despite expert advocacy of an increase in the share of public expenditure on education in India's GNP, the share declined from 4.1 to 3.8 percent between 1990-91 and 1991-96. Of this expenditure elementary education accounts for less than half as against the two-thirds plus deemed necessary. Although both the central and state governments have been responsible for education in India since 1976, the Centre accounts for a relatively small proportion of the total expenditure, though its share has been increasing over the years. It increased to 11.1 percent in 1995-96 from a low 6.8 percent in 1980-81. This may be due to higher outlay on education in the five-year plans.

In India budgetary resources flow into education from the department of education (in the main) and other ministries/departments, at both the central and state levels. Over the years, the contribution of these ministries to overall education has increased from 4.4 percent of the total education budget in 1950-51 to 16.8 percent in 1995-96. These expenditures are basically meant for higher and professional education. An increase in the share of plan expenditure in the total government expenditure on education is essential for the further development of education.

The annual rate of growth of expenditure on education as a whole was 10.2 percent between 1980-81 and 1990-91. After this period it has been declining and was 3.4 percent between 1990-91 and 1995-96. This trend is more or less similar for all levels of education. The relative share of elementary education in the total education budget has declined over time in most s_ates. This decline is particularly conspicuous because structural adjustment and stabilisation policies have accorded low priority to social sectors like education. This has had quantitative and qualitative impact on education.

State governments provide most educational funding, although since independence the central government has increasingly assumed the cost of educational development as outlined under the five-year plans. India spends an average 3 percent of its GNP on education. Spending for education ranged between 4.6 and 7.7 percent of total central government expenditures from the 1950s through the 1970s. In the early 1980s, about 10 percent of central and state funds went to education, a proportion well below the average of 79 other developing countries. More than 90 percent of the expenditure was for teachers' salaries and administration. Per capita budget expenditures increased from Rs 36.5 in 1977 to Rs 112.7 in 1986, with highest expenditures found in the union territories. Nevertheless, total expenditure per student per year by the central and state governments declined in real terms.

Share of Education in National Income: Six Percent of GNP?

The second issue relates to financing of education. The Economic Survey states: "Financing of education -- increase in government and non-government spending on education, and bringing this up to 6 percent GDP level" (1998-99, p. 150). This is also not altogether new, though few expected that it would find a place finally in the Economic Survey and in the draft Ninth Five-Year Plan. The National Agenda for Governance has promised to "formulate and implement plans to gradually increase the governmental and non-governmental spending on education up to 6 percent of the GDP" (p 5; emphasis added). The Economic Survey (p. 150) repeats this goal verbatim; so does the draft Ninth Five-Year Plan. This is not in conformity with the widely accepted view and the resolve made by the Government of India repeatedly earlier that the government expenditure on education would be raised to the level of 6 percent of GNP or GDP.

The origin of this resolution is the recommendation of the Education (Kothari) Commission (1966). The Commission had recommended that the public expenditure on education in India should be increased to at least 6 percent of national income by 1986. The recommendation was based, *inter alia*, on (a) the projected requirements of education sector in India, and (b) on international comparisons. This goal was reiterated in the National Policy on Education, 1968. Since the goal could not be achieved, the goal was again reiterated in the National Policy on Education, 1986 (including the revised policy in 1992). The review committee on National Policy on Education (Acharya Ramamurthy Committee), and the several reports of the CABE, have repeatedly made it clear that 6 percent of national income should be devoted to education from the government exchequer by the central and state governments. The then Prime Minister of India also promised in 1993 from the ramparts of the Red Fort to the same extent.

When some doubts were expressed on this clause in the National Policy on Education, 1986, Anand Sarup, former Education Secretary, who was involved in the formulation of the policy made it abundantly clear. Sarup (1988:253) observed: "Since it is public policy on education that is the crucial determinant of available educational places and opportunities in our country, *it (6%) is the Centre and State expenditure on education* that is used for policy planning and implementation. This includes both plan and non-plan outlays."

Secondly, the Education Commission observed: "Economically advanced countries like Japan, US and USSR were spending more than 6 percent of their GNP on education. These countries spent no more than a small fraction of their GNP on education at the beginning of the century. Further, these countries might be spending about 10 percent of GNP by 1986, and in fact more than 10 percent, if comprehensive disarmament takes place. The gap between India and other rich countries needs to be reduced" and accordingly recommended that India should allocate 6 percent of national income to education.

Since international comparisons formed an important basis for the recommendation of the Kothari Commission, it is important to note that most international statistics and national level statistics on education expenditures in other countries refer to public expenditures only. These statistics rarely include private expenditures on education.

One can also safely conclude that the recommendations of the Delors Commission (International Commission on Education for the Twenty- first Century 1996), UNDP and other intentional organisations are at least partly influenced by the policy goal of the Government of India that it would allocate 6 percent of national income from the public exchequer.

Thus inclusion of non-governmental spending on education for the purpose of reaching the goal of 6 percent of GDP (and to show that we have over or nearly achieved) is thus against the letter and spirit of the resolution of the Government of India (1968) and later official papers. It may also be noted that when the Planning Commission made earlier during the Janata government period a similar attempt formally or informally in 1988 (Kolhatkar, 1988), reinterpreting the 6 percent to be consisting of public and private expenditures, it backfired, with an uproar in the parliament and finally the government sticking to the earlier position of allocating 6 percent from the government sources.

Of course, there is no sanctity of the 6 percent norm, as actual requirements of financial (and physical) resources for education have to be periodically worked out, as has been stated in many policy documents. According to the recent estimates (Tilak, 1994), the government expenditure on education has to be raised to above 8 percent of national income to fulfil the modest goals of the education system. Instead of planning to raise the level of public expenditure from the current level of 3.7 percent of GDP to at least 6 percent, if not higher, the government seems to be arguing that the goal has already been achieved, as it is argued that the 6 percent should compose of not only government expenditure, but also household and private sector, including household expenditures on education. This is attempted in the Economic Survey as well.

Allocation of Financial Resources

Now, a few specific issues on allocation of resources to education. First, the draft Ninth Plan does not give any details regarding allocation of resources to education, not to speak of allocation within education to various sub-sectors. The only financial allocation referred to in the draft *Ninth Five-Year Plan* (vol. I, p. 183) is under the special action plan of the Prime Minister: Rs 20.4 thousand crore is allocated, as a part of the central outlay. For the Centre and the states/union territories as a whole, allocation to social services is made as a lump sum, Rs 1,82,000 crore.

In the absence of any more details on the allocation of resources to education in the Ninth Plan, let us briefly look at the allocations made in current year's annual budget of the union government. In the last year's and also in the current year's annual budgets, there has been a reasonable, though not a very significant, increase in the allocation of resources to education. In the 1999-2000 budget allocation there was a significant increase in the allocation to education -- both plan and non-plan, over the preceding year's revised estimates -- all by about Rs 1,500 crore, though the revised estimates for 1998-99 are much less than the budgetary outlays for the same year. But, the percentage of increase in the plan expenditure is only about half the increase in non-plan expenditure. Compared to the increase between 1997-98 and 1998-99, the increase in 1999-2000 over 1998-99 revised estimates, is rather modest, e.g., the total allocation to education in 1997-98 was Rs 4,983 crore, which increased to Rs 6,733 crore in 1998-99. More importantly, the relative share of plan expenditure on education increased from 5.9 percent in 1997-98 to 6.4 percent in 1998-99. The latter figure could increase to 6.6 percent only in 1999-2000.

The general need for tightening of the budget perhaps resulted in reduction in plan expenditure on general education, as non-plan expenditure could not be reduced; in fact, the non-plan expenditure on general education was Rs 500 crore higher as per the revised estimates compared to the budget estimates in 1998-99. However, in case of higher education, there has been big shortfall by about Rs 600 in non-plan expenditure. This seems to have been done mainly by deferring the improvement in salary scale of university/college teachers.

On the whole, the revised estimates for 1998-99 are less by Rs 200 crore in plan expenditure on education, and Rs 450 crore in non-plan expenditure, compared to the budget allocations for the same year. It would be useful to find out the reasons for shortfall in the expenditures, i.e., budget outlays minus the revised estimates. Though there has been a shortfall in case of both overall plan and non-plan expenditure on education, and the shortfall is higher in case of non-plan expenditure, it is also important to note that a larger number of plan programmes suffered severely in terms of shortfall in budget expenditures. They include non-formal education, district primary education programme (DPEP), vocational education, adult education and technical education (regional engineering colleges and community polytechnics).

Intra-sectoral allocation of budgetary resources, i.e., by different sectors and by different items within education, reveals certain important dimensions of changing priorities of the government. The growth in plan outlays for elementary education is important, but the increase is very modest. Important items of the budget for elementary education include operation blackboard, non-formal education, and free education for girls, mid-day meals and the DPEP. There is an increase in the total outlay for elementary education to the extent of just Rs 300 crore in the current year, over the preceding year's revised estimates. It is interesting to note that at the same time, there is a decline in the outlay for mid-day meals by as much as Rs 400 crore.

A substantial part of the increase in the outlay for elementary education -- to the extent of Rs 220 crore -- in the budget for 1999-2000 compared to the revised estimates for 1998-99, is also accounted by external aid. Among the several externally-aided projects, DPEP is the most important one in terms of the amount of money involved. The contribution of the DPEP amounts to Rs 750 crore in the current year's budget. Other externally aided projects include Mahila Samakhya (funded by Dutch government) and Shiksha Karmi and Lok Jumbish (both funded by SIDA). In all, externally aided projects amounted to Rs 827 crore in 1999-2000. It forms 27 percent of total central plan outlay for elementary education. The increase in the contributions of the externally aided projects is by 36 percent between the revised estimates of the last year and the current year's budget estimates. This may be compared to the overall increase in the expenditure on elementary education of only 10.7 percent. All this may lead many to warn that the growth in public expenditure on elementary education is largely 'borrowed growth'.

In case of secondary education, 85 percent of the budget outlays are accounted by Kendriya Vidyalayas and Navodaya Vidyalayas. All other programmes including vocational education, education technology and computers in schools receive petty amounts. The programme of vocational education aims at diverting 25 percent of the students at +2 level to vocational studies, but currently less than 5 percent of the students opt for these courses. Many believe that the programme did not take off due to, *inter alia*, scant attention paid, including financial resources allocated, to vocational education. The goals, the programme and the persistent neglect continue.

Generally, and also constitutionally, the union government is expected to take care more of higher education and less of school education. But, in the recent years, the union government has been increasingly concentrating on school education, particularly elementary education, through a variety of centrally sponsored schemes. In the current annual budget, 65 percent of the total plan budget outlay for education is allocated to elementary education and less than 10 percent for higher education. There is an impressive increase in the budget allocation for higher education, but the substantial part of the increase is in non-plan expenditure, which might have become necessary with the revision of pay scales of university teachers and other staff.

Now, let us note priorities given to a few important specific programmes. The mid-day meals programme launched in 1995 is to gradually expand to cover all children in primary classes in all government and local body schools. The number of students benefiting from the programme was estimated to be 9.75 crore. Generally, it is felt that the programme is very important in not only improving enrolments of children in schools, but also in improvement of nutritional and health status of children. But, the priority seems to be changing. In the budget for 1998-99, Rs 1,092 crore were allocated. The revised estimates are 28.2 percent higher than the allocation, suggesting the need to further scale up the budgetary allocations. But, the provision made in the current year's budget is only Rs 1,031 crore, 5.6 percent less than the outlay made in the last year's budget, and 26 percent less than the revised estimates for 1998-99.

The Prime Minister has promised to provide free education to all girls up to the college level. As a measure of improvement of girls' enrolment in schools and colleges, this is an important step. Accordingly, this has been given a priority in the union budget. Allocation for girls' education was hiked from Rs 100 crore in 1998-99 to Rs 160 crore in 1999-2000. But, this amount is not enough to provide really free education to all girls enrolled in schools and colleges. While the scheme announced by the Prime Minister is to cover school and college levels, including professional level higher education, in the budget, allocation is made only under elementary education! Further, lest there is any confusion on the concept of 'free' education, the draft *Ninth Five-Year Plan* (vol. II, p. 130) defines it to be free of tuition fees, inclusion of provision of basic textbooks, maintenance expenditure in hostels and library books. There can be several types of fees other than tuition fees. Many a time it is found that the other fees are much higher than the tuition fees -- both at school and college levels. So it is not all that free, though the term 'free' is wider in scope than free primary education, as it provides for maintenance expenditures of the girl students in hostels.

The programme of residential upper primary/secondary schools in rural areas to take care of the special needs of migration population and scattered habitations, which was allocated Rs 24 crore last year, could not take off. As a result, it seems to have been dropped out altogether. In case of adult education, the rural functional literacy project seems to have been closed, with no allocation at all being made in the current budget. The overall allocation to adult education has, however, been increased by about 40 percent.

Much of the budget outlay for the national scholarships meant for the poor but meritorious students could not be used. As per the revised estimates, only 46 percent of Rs 3.26 crore allocated could be utilised in 1998-99. However, in the current budget the allocation has been stepped up to Rs 10.9 crore.

How to raise more public resources for education? Recently, the Minister for Human Resource Development has announced that an education cess would be levied for raising resources for elementary education. There is no proposal of this kind in the budget. However, in the budget, there is a hike in the price of diesel by Re 1 per litre. It is also promised that half of additional resources generated through hike in diesel price would be allocated to rural development and social sectors, including education. What fraction of the revenue would go to education is yet to be seen. Earlier also, the union government has promised that the some of the savings made through public sector disinvestment programme, and the voluntary disclosure of income scheme (VDIS) would be allocated to human development sectors like education and health. One can only hope that a substantial proportion of the revenue now generated would be allocated to education.

Summary and Conclusions

As far as education is concerned, the union budget is an extremely partial one to give any comprehensive picture of public expenditure on education in the country, as the state governments incur sizeable expenditure on education. For example, according to the budget estimates in 1996-97, states met 85 percent, the union government meeting the remaining 15 percent of the total government expenditure on education, which is a 'concurrent subject'. In case of plan expenditure, however, the share of the union government was above 40 percent (MHRD 1998). Nevertheless, the union budget does indicate the direction in which the priorities of the union government are being shaped; and it obviously has considerable influence on the development of education in the states. With this in view, a brief attempt is made in this article to examine the education priorities of the union government as reflected in the union budget, 1999-2000, the Economic Survey, 1998-99 and the draft Ninth Five-Year Plan (1997-2002).

The union government promises to accord a high priority to education, making it an important component of 'NHDI' and also the Prime Minister's 'Special Action Plan.' In a situation, when the need for strong political commitment to education is being increasingly felt, these proclaimed intentions of the union government are certainly welcome. But, these high sentiments expressed in favour of education are not well reflected in the programmes, plans and other initiatives proposed in the Ninth Five-Year Plan, the Economic Survey, and also the resource allocations proposed in the union budget, 1999-2000. The only major initiative proposed in the union budget is the Education Guarantee Scheme for the poor, which may have major internal contradictions, particularly when it is aimed as a strategy of providing education to the rural poor, SCs, STs and OBCs.

Further, the urgency to check the growth of out-of-school children is not being felt. The need for making elementary education a fundamental right and the need for allocation of resources for the same is also not clearly recognised. Further delay would only accentuate the problem. Further, it is clear that attempts are being made to interpret universal elementary education to mean only primary education up to fifth standard; and the long promised goal of allocating 6 percent of GDP to education is being diluted so as to include in it not only government expenditure but also private expenditure including household and other private sector expenditures on education. These do not seem to be good auguries of according a high priority to education.

6

The State of Gujarat

The state of Gujarat was formed in 1960 when the erstwhile bilingual Bombay State was split into two separate states. So far, the state has done well in terms of overall economic growth. It has progressed to acquire the fourth rank in per capita income among the major 16 states in India and has maintained this rank for approximately the last two decades. In March 2001, the population of Gujarat was 48.4 million against 41.3 million in 1991, excluding the earthquake-affected areas of the state.

Social and Cultural Background

Gujarat, within a broad framework of the national Indian culture, is a regional cultural area having its own language, lifestyle and literature. Gujarat is generally known as a prosperous and progressive state and the Gujaratis as a peaceful people ('shantibhai') (Joshi, 2000). Gujaratis are also known as the best entrepreneurs in India, and next only to Jews in the world. Gujarat and Gujaratis are also known as more westernised and modernised than the rest of India and Indians, respectively. This sort of stereotype of Gujarat and Gujaratis is not true for the whole of Gujarat and Gujaratis. For the purpose of understanding Gujarat better, the region can be divided into three sub-cultural areas as follows:

1. The Plain Belt of Central Gujarat,
2. The Western Peninsular Zone of Saurashtra and Kachchh, and
3. The Eastern Belt of Hills and Forests.

All the three areas have been different land systems in the past and it is these differences that have shaped the different sub-cultures, within a broader framework of the regional culture of Gujarat, while the sub-cultural traits have facilitated or restricted the development potential of the people.

The central or the plains belt of Gujarat stretches from Palanpur in the north to Bardoli in the south. They not only developed a democratic ethos, but also became a dominant pressure group to turn development plans to their benefits. The locations of Ukai, Kadana and other dams gave them the benefits of the green revolution and the resultant shift of farmers to business and industry. In fact, all the major industries of Gujarat are located in the 4,02,450 sq km strip between Mehsana in northern Gujarat and Umergaon in southern Gujarat. This belt has come to be known as the "Golden Corridor of Industrial Development". The over-concentration of industries in this area has reached the point of saturation and it is becoming economically unviable for big new enterprises to be located here. This belt of central and southern Gujarat attracted more than 92 percent of the industrial investments in large and medium industries in the 1980s. Even after saturation in the post-reforms (1991) period, it has received 70 percent of the total industrial investment.

The three biggest cities of Gujarat (Ahmedabad, Surat and Vadodara) are located in this belt. This belt has also witnessed the highest level of urbanisation. This corridor is also known as the "rail and road corridor" as the National Highway 8 and the Mumbai-Ahmedabad and Mumbai-Delhi lines are located in this corridor. Banaskantha, in the north, is the only undeveloped part in this belt. This, however, is not because of the lack of entrepreneurship. Prior to the green revolution, all merchants dealing in precious items like diamond, jewellery and precious stones, were settled in and around Palanpur, the headquarters of Banaskantha district. But, because of the paucity of irrigation, the green revolution was not successful in this district and most of the enterprising traders migrated to Mumbai and Surat.

The landholding system in this belt has been *ryotwari* since the Mughal period, where the cultivator was the owner and paid the revenue directly to the state. There was no intermediate authority between him and the state. There was no authority above him in the village and he was an independent decision-maker as far as his land and agriculture were concerned. This autonomy provided him a chance to take decisions for his own development interest. This autonomy, aided by facilitating external factors, led to their agricultural development. Not only did it lead to an individual's development, it also provided the ground for people of similar interests to come together and form interest groups. Anand Milk Union (AMUL) is an example of farmers coming together, in the form of milk cooperatives, to further their interests. This sort of forming of milk cooperatives has taken place in the entire belt. It was the spirit of cooperation among the farmers of this belt that has unfolded in the form of successful cooperative ventures and this was possible due to the existence of the right type of political climate. Except for one (CSMCRI of Bhavnagar), all the research institutes are located in this belt. There is also the presence of many NGOs in this belt, most of who are development-oriented NGOs. The specific term used for them is 'rachnatmak' (constructive) institutions.

Most parts of Saurashtra and Kachchh had the *zamindari* system. There were three different forms of the *zamindari* system: Girasdari, Barkhalidari and Inamdari. In the Girasdari system, land or villages were given to the relatives who were generally the younger brothers of the kings. These 'Garasiyas' became feudal lords in the Girasdari villages. In the Inamdari system, land or villages were given for showing valour in battles or for maintaining religious organisations. In the Barkhalidari system, land was given to Brahmins or administrators as a reward for the service rendered to the kingdom. In 1956, land reforms on the line of land to the tillers were brought in Saurashtra and Kachchh and all these three systems were legally abolished.

For a long time, the semi-feudal culture and relations persisted in Saurashtra and Kachchh. The eulogisation of these cultural traditions by folklorists and pseudo folklorists facilitated this. Even eminent writers like Meghani could not avoid this. In many populist ways, these feudal values still survive in Saurashtra and Kachchh. The dominant caste in central belt is Patidar, popularly known as Patel. The Kshatriyas are lower to the Patels in the caste hierarchy in the central belt, whereas in Saurashtra and Kachchh, the reverse is true. The tiller was a tenant, who was generally a Patel, under a feudal lord in a village where the lord was dictating terms to all tenants in a village. The tenants had to give to the feudal lord half of whatever portion of the produce as decided by the lord. This did not allow autonomy on part of tenants to take their development decisions.

The eastern belt, running right from the north to the south and cutting across the boundary of three Indian states, viz., Rajasthan, Madhya Pradesh and Maharashtra, is mountainous and covered with forests of varying dimensions. The entire belt is inhabited by various tribal communities. There are 32 talukas in this belt where all the major tribal communities have resided since generations. The historical records prove that the Bhils (not 'tribe' in modern parlance) were either subjugated or driven away in the interior forests by the invading Rajputs. The subjugation or life in forests brought changes in their lifestyle and culture. But, it is necessary to remember that this sort of culture is the result of historical experience through which they have passed (Joshi, 1998). When the 'tribals' settled in the forests, the modern state did not exist there. It was only "by the end of the 19th century, steps were taken for survey and settlement of land revenue in the tribal areas directly governed by the British" (Trivedi, 1998). Prior to that the land where a tribal community had settled was held communally. A tribal farmer, with the permission of the ethnic chief, used to cultivate as much land as was sufficient for his family's maintenance.

But this relationship itself was problematic in the sense that the development model itself created problems for the tribals in the eastern belt. "Many problems concerning tribal development like displacement, poverty alleviation, health and disease, land alienation, indebtedness, criminalisation, etc., in fact, are the resultant effects of such a development model" (Kashyap, 1998). The biggest failure of this sort of consumerist model of development is that it has disintegrated the symbiotic relationship between man and nature, in general, and between tribals and forests, in particular. Moreover, it has also broken the self-generative and self-reliant system, hampered the community's creativity and made them dependent on market forces. The subjugated tribals could not enforce their development ideas against the larger forces. This is not to say that development has not taken place in tribal belt. Though there is a strong cooperative movement in the central belt, this has not touched even the fringe of the economic life of the people of the tribal region. Forest labour cooperative societies, groomed mainly by non-tribal Gandhian workers, soon after independence, have benefited some upper stratum tribals.

Though many big dams have came up in the tribal areas, irrigation benefits have gone to the non-tribals in the plains. Many tribals have lost land and the problem of their rehabilitation is alarming. A vast majority of the tribals depend on dry agriculture at subsistence level. As agriculture has not developed, the institutional set up and infrastructure for secondary and tertiary sectors are found absent here.

"Exceptions may be made in case of few tribal groups such as Dhodias and Chowdhrys of south Gujarat and Patelias of the Panchmahal district. But the vast majority of them still remains underdeveloped and lives a precarious economic existence (Lal, 1998). All 32 talukas of tribal areas are industrially backward talukas. Although there are concessions for establishing industrial units in backward areas, yet there are very few industrial units in this belt and these, also, have been established by non-tribal industrialists.

These are the three sub-cultures of Gujarat, each with a different ethos within the broader framework of the Gujarati culture. The Protestant ethic or the 'mahajan' culture of the central belt provides facilitation for individuals to develop on their own lines. Gujarati entrepreneurship has developed to its full potential in this belt. The semi-feudal culture, which has put more restrictions on the unfolding of capabilities of human beings, is now changing, at a time when development on the coastal belt of Saurashtra is becoming a reality. The third or the tribal belt is far behind. The non-tribal developers have provided whatever ceremonial development inputs are present in this belt. This has resulted in creating a dominant-submissive or patron-client relationship between the non-tribals and the tribals and the latter are far from asserting their cultural identity (Joshi, 2000).

Demography

Gujarat ranks tenth among the states of India in respect of population and twenty first in the case of population density. In terms of percentage, Gujarat accounts for 6.19 percent of the area of India. The population of the state, including estimated figures of the earthquake-affected areas, accounts for 4.93 percent of the India's population. The provisional figures for Census 2001 shows that the population of the state has increased by 7.08 million in ten years, even after excluding the areas where the census was postponed due to the earthquake. If we include the estimated population of the earthquake-affected areas, the absolute increase rose to 9.29 million from 7.22 million in 1991, which is the highest in all the decades since 1901.

Table 6.1
Decadal Growth Rate 1901-2001

Decades	Gujarat	India
1901-11	+ 7.79	+ 5.75
1911-21	+ 3.79	- 0.31
1921-31	+ 12.92	+ 11.00
1931-41	+ 19.25	+ 14.22
1941-51	+ 18.69	+ 13.31
1951-61	+ 26.88	+ 21.51
1961-71	+ 29.39	+ 24.80
1971-81	+ 27.67	+ 24.66
1981-91	+ 21.19	+ 23.85
1991-2001*	+ 22.66	+ 21.34

* Excluding badly affected earthquake areas, viz., entire Kachchh district; Maliya, Morbi and Wankaner talukas of Rajkot and Jodia taluka of Jamnagar district where Census 2001 was postponed.

The decadal growth rate of 1991-2001 has also increased in comparison to 1981-1991 from 21.19 to 22.66. In terms of percentage, it has increased by 432 percent since 1901, excluding Kachchh and others, while it is 456 percent including the estimated population of the earthquake-affected areas.

The district-wise population shows that Ahmedabad, which ranked 1st in 1991, has retained its position in the Census 2001. Similarly, Surat ranking 2nd, Vadodara 3rd, Rajkot 4th and Bhavnagar 6th have retained their same rank in 2001 also. Ahmedabad district has the highest contribution of 5.80 million to the population of the state. Smallest district, in terms of population, is the Dangs with 0.19 million persons. There are two more districts contributing less than one million population, viz., Porbandar and Narmada ranking 23rd and 24th. Banaskantha has gained the rank as 5th against 7th in 1991

Table 6.2

Ranking of Districts by Population Size in 1991 and 2001

Rank in 2001	District	Population, 2001	Percent to Total Population of the State, 2001	Population, 1991	Percent to Total Population of the State, 1991	Rank in 1991
1	Ahmedabad	5808378	11.48	4587491	11.1	1
2	Surat	4996391	9.87	3397900	8.23	2
3	Vadodara	3639775	7.19	3038127	7.35	3
4	Rajkot*	3157676	6.24	2514122	6.09	4
	(excluding earthquake-affected areas)	2571931	5.32	2514122	6.09	4
5	Banaskantha	2502843	4.95	1981513	4.8	7
6	Bhavnagar	2469264	4.88	2069953	5.01	6
7	Junagadh	2448427	4.84	2091182	5.06	5
8	Sabarkantha	2083416	4.12	1761086	4.26	9
9	Panchmahal	2024883	4.00	1682333	4.07	10
10	Kheda	2023354	4.00	1786794	4.33	8
11	Jamnagar**	1913685	3.78	1563558	3.78	13
	(excluding earthquake-affected areas)	1816029	3.75	1563558	3.78	13
12	Anand	1856712	3.67	1642615	3.98	11
13	Mahesana	1837696	3.63	1640251	3.97	12
14	Dohad	1635374	3.23	1274123	3.08	15
15	Kachchh ***	1526321	3.02	1262507	3.06	16
16	Surendranagar	1515147	2.99	1208872	2.93	17
17	Valsad	1410680	2.79	1087980	2.63	19
18	Amreli	1393295	2.75	1308867	3.17	14
19	Bharuch	1370104	2.71	1148252	2.78	18
20	Gandhinagar	1334731	2.64	1077406	2.61	21
21	Navsari	1229250	2.43	1085692	2.62	20

Contd...

Contd...

22	Patan	1181941	2.34	1036019	2.51	22
23	Porbandar	536854	1.06	469472	1.14	23
24	Narmada	514083	1.02	449376	1.09	24
25	The Dangs	186712	0.37	144091	0.35	25

* 2001 Census figures are presented including the estimated figures of Malia-miana, Morvi and Wankaner talukas where Census 2001 was postponed due to earthquake.

** 2001 Census figures are presented including the estimated figures of Jodia taluka where Census 2001 was postponed due to earthquake.

*** Census 2001 was not conducted due to earthquake; the estimated figures have been taken into account.

by replacing Junagadh from 5th to 7th. Other districts have also moved one rank above 1991. Amreli has gone down to the rank of 18th from 14th in 1991. District Kheda has also gone down from 8th to 10th rank. Rajkot still holds the same rank of Census 1991. However, some of these changes have taken place due to increase in the number of districts from 19 to 25.

According to the Census 1991, there were 19 districts, but six new districts were created during 1991-2001. In all, there are 25 districts according to the Census 2001. The newly created districts are shown below:

	New District	*Created from*
1.	Patan	Santalpur and Radhanpur talukas of Banas Kantha district, Sidhpur, Patan, Harij, Sami and Chanasma talukas of Mahesana district
2.	Porbandar	Porbandar, Ranavav and Kutiyan talukas of Junagadh district
3.	Anand	Anand, Petlad, Khambhat and Borsad talukas of Kheda district
4.	Dohad	Zalod, Limkheda, Dohad, Devgadbaria and Santrampur talukas of Panch Mahals district
5.	Narmada	Tilakwada taluka of Vadodara district and Nandod, Dediapada and Sagbara talukas of Bharuch district
6.	Navsari	Navsari, Gandevi, Chikhli and Bansda talukas of Valsad district

Table 6.3

Population Growth in Comparison to State Average

Highest Growth Rate	Higher than State Average	Lower than State Average	Lowest Growth Rate
1. Surat (47.04)	2. Valsad (29.66)	10. Jamnagar (22.40)	24. Amreli (6.45)
	3. The Dangs (29.58)	11. Panchmahal (20.36)	
	4. Rajkot (28.95)	12 Vadodara (19.80)	
	5. Dohad (28.35)	13. Bharuch (19.32)	
	6. Ahmedabad (26.61)	14. Bhavnagar (19.29)	
	7. Banaskantha (26.31)	15. Sabarkantha (18.30)	
	8. Surendranagar (25.34)	16. Junagadh (17.08)	
	9. Gandhinagar (23.38)	17. Narmada (14.40)	
		18. Porbandar (14.35)	
		19. Patan (14.08)	
		20. Kheda (13.24)	
		21. Navsari (13.22)	
		22. Anand (13.03)	
		23. Mehsana (12.04)	

The density of population of the state is 258 persons per sq km, calculated by including the estimated population of the earthquake-affected areas. The state ranks 21st in India in terms of population density. In the Census 1991, the state's density was 211 persons per sq km of area. Since the area of the state remains almost the same, change in the density from 1991 to 2001 reflects the effects of population growth. Percentage increase in density during 1991-2001 works out to about 22.27, which is very much nearer to the percentage decadal growth rate of 22.66 of population during the last decade. At the district level, the density is highest in Ahmedabad, which has population density of 718 persons per sq km; Surat follows with 653 persons per sq km. In the Ahmedabad district, 151 persons per sq km have been added, whereas Surat has added 209 persons per sq km during the decade.

The sex ratio of the state shows that it is generally decreasing except in 1931, 1951 and 1981 when it demonstrated an increase. The sex ratio in India has also the decreasing trend except 1981 and 2001 when it was increased. It can be seen that the sex ratio of Gujarat was less than India's sex ratio up to 1941. After 1941, Gujarat improved its sex ratio in comparison to India, but as per provisional results of Census 2001, the sex ratio of Gujarat has gone down by 15 females per 1,000 males in comparison to 1991, which is the greatest decrease since 1901. Such reduction in sex ratio in Gujarat is unfavourable for the future. Gujarat has only 919 females per 1,000 males while it comes to 921 when the estimated figures of earthquake-affected areas are included.

In the other districts of Gujarat, the Dangs and Amreli have the highest sex ratio at 986. Dohad follows with 985. The lowest sex ratio has been accounted in Surat district at 835. Ahmedabad, Anand and Surat are the districts, which have accounted less than the state sex ratio in both the 1991 and the 2001 censuses. The sex ratio of Surat district h has drally gone down from 901 to 835 during 1991-2001.

Table 6.4
District Literacy Rate, 2001

Districts below 50%		Below the State Average but more than 50%		Higher than the State Average	
1. The Dangs	48.99	8. Kheda	57.77	14. Ahmedabad	71.12
2. Surendranagar	48.72	9. Amreli	57.77	15.Navsari	68.74
3. Narmada	47.16	10. Junagadh	56.92	16.Rajkot	67.64
4. Patan	46.36	11. Jamnagar	56.90	17.Surat	66.71
5. Panchmahal	45.43	12. Bhavnagar	54.46	18.Bharuch	65.42
6. Banaskantha	34.54	13. Sabarkantha	52.85	19.Gandhinagar	64.85
7. Dohad	31.70			20.Mahesana	63.96
				21.Anand	62.53
				22.Vadodara	61.24
				23.Valsad	59.92
				24. Porbandar	58.83

There are eleven districts whose literacy rate is greater than the state average, while there are seven districts with less than even 50 percent literacy rate of females in 2001.

Natural Resources

Gujarat has a relatively poor and unevenly distributed natural resource base, an almost stagnant long-term growth in agriculture and wide regional disparities of growth. The state has lost heavily on its environment and ecology during the process of economic growth. It shows wide diversity of physiography, climate and hydrology. It can be described as arid, semi-arid and to an extent sub-humid in character. The state has been divided into seven agro-climatic zones as under:

- In the south, there are Southern Hills which is part of Saputara range (Dangs and Valsad districts) receiving more than 1800 mm of average annual rainfall.
- The rest of south Gujarat (Bharuch and Surat districts), receiving about 970 mm of average annual rainfall.
- Middle Gujarat (Kheda and Vadodara) with more than 900 mm of average annual rainfall.
- North Gujarat that is arid and semi-arid in character with an annual rainfall of 735 mm, (covering five districts, namely, Ahmedabad, Gandhinagar, Mehsana, Sabarkantha and Banaskantha).
- North-west arid zone (Kachchh district), that receives extremely low rainfall of about 340 mm annually.
- North Saurashtra (close to Kachchh) which is arid and semi-arid in character with 530 mm of annual rainfall (covering northern parts of Amreli, Bhavnagar, Rajkot, Jamnagar and Surendranagar districts).
- South Saurashtra or coastal Saurashtra that is dry and sub-humid in character.

The diversity has resulted in uneven distribution of land, water and vegetation in the state. Unfortunately, the state has mismanaged these resources (Hirway, 2000).

At present, the state is predominantly characterised by dry/semi-arid conditions with a large proportion of area facing frequent drought conditions. Of the total landmass, only 50 percent has been put under agricultural uses of which about 30 percent is irrigated. Since the major source of irrigation is ground water sources, covering 80 percent of the irrigated area, it poses serious problems of rainfall induced uncertainties and the depletion of the water table has reached a dangerous level in some parts of North Gujarat and coastal Saurashtra region. The land capitability is generally low in a large number of talukas in the state. The low productivity, coupled with frequent drought situation, had led to a further degradation of the land because of the poor vegetative cover resulting in increased soil erosion.

Agriculture

Agriculture in Gujarat is marked by erratic and uneven rainfall. The state receives only one rainfall, i.e., south-west monsoon, between the months of June/July and September/October. Precarious and uneven nature of rainfall often results in scarcity conditions, especially in Kachchh and parts of Saurashtra. The southern districts of the state generally receive high and assured rainfall, central districts medium and less assured rainfall, and rest of the state scanty and more irregular rainfall. The problem of water availability is manifested in its irrigation development. During 1991, agriculture engaged 56 percent of the total workforce, and 27 percent of the state domestic product originated from this sector. In the early Sixties, it was 64 and 48 percent respectively. It clearly shows that state is gradually reducing its dependence on agriculture for employment and income generation. It also shows that the state economy is witnessing structural transformation and it is more rapid compared to that of India. The cropping pattern of the state shows that there is a shift from traditional food crop to non-food crops like oilseeds, groundnut, etc. The land productivity in some selected crops has experienced significant deceleration after the 1980s (Mathur and Kashyap, 2000).

The district level analysis of levels and growth of agriculture output during 1961-63 to 1991-93 has brought out the changing nature of agriculture development in Gujarat in the post-green revolution phase, and particularly during the 1980s. These developments have led to the spread of new technological inputs on a wider scale. During the 1970s, the output in the state doubled compared to that recorded in the 1960s. Districts having greater input experienced faster growth of output. Thus, during 1970-71 to 1981-83, crop output recorded an unprecedented annual growth rate of 3.6 percent compared to 2.2 percent of the previous decade (Mathur and Kashyap, 2000).

Past trend shows that yield growth is the dominant source of output growth in the state and contribution of area to growth has declined in almost all the districts. The 1980s were marked by crop diversification towards non-traditional non-food crops. There has been a visible decline in the share of food crops and crop diversification away from coarse cereals towards oilseeds, which are perhaps more remunerative. There is an increase in area under crops other than food crops and traditional non-food crops of sugar cane, cotton and oilseeds. This is a positive development and would create opportunities for weaning away excess labour from agriculture.

Land productivity in these selected crops has experienced significant deceleration after the 1980s. Agriculture in the state is heading towards stagnation. Declining productivity levels of the selected crops perhaps indicate that increasingly productive and problem free lands are being allocated to 'other crops'. These crops perhaps also account for a major portion of purchased inputs (fertilisers, water, tractors, etc.). Male agriculture worker productivity up to the early 1970s registered a marked increase. Thereafter, labour productivity too has declined substantially. The fall in the productivity levels indicates that the state requires a rethinking on its resource use pattern.

Industry

Gujarat, the second most industrialised state in the country, has also emerged as the second most important investment destination, next only to Maharashtra. It is claimed that Gujarat has achieved this spectacular success because of its entrepreneurial endowment, progressive policies and political will of the government (irrespective of the political party in power), proactive and efficient bureaucracy, conducive industrial relations, relatively well-developed infrastructure, and its industrial structure. The state has responded well to the economic reforms sweeping the country. Consistent with the policies of the Government of India, it also undertook a serious exercise in economic reforms by setting up the State Finance Commission in 1992, which gave an 'Agenda for Reform' to the government. Its recommendations were accepted not only by the government, but also by all the political parties cutting across party lines. This kind of stability in policy formulation and execution has helped Gujarat generate confidence among investors. Several changes have taken place in the policy framework as well as industrial environment in Gujarat, especially after 1991 (Awasthi, 2000)

The industrial sector has performed consistently well with the growth rate of the manufacturing sector, continuously increasing from 3.04 percent in the 1960s, to 5.55 percent in the 1970s, 8.73 percent in the 1980s and 11.92 percent in the 1990s. Though Ahmedabad had developed as a major centre of the textile industry at the time of the independence, Gujarat ranked 8th in industrial development in 1960. Several factors led to this achievement. These included the establishment of industrial estates with all the required infrastructural facilities in several parts of the state by the GIDC (Gujarat Industrial Development Corporation). There was continuous availability of power to the industry, availability of water (from the major rivers) to the industry; availability of railway links with major industrial and trading centres, particularly in south Gujarat where the industries are concentrated. Four important corporations were set up, namely, GIIC (Gujarat Industrial Investment Corporation), GIDC, GSFC (Gujarat State Finance Corporation) and Indextb (Industrial Extension Bureau) to provide finance, power, facilities and all the required support to industries. There was also a generally highly positive and supportive attitude of the government to the new industries.

The industrial base of Gujarat became increasingly diversified gradually with petrochemicals and fertilisers, pharmaceuticals and drugs, dyestuff, as well as engineering and electronics industries developing in the state. The process of industrialisation in Gujarat has taken a new turn since the introduction of the economic reforms in 1991. After the Government of India announced the New Industrial Policy in 1991 with the objective of implementing the economic reforms in the industrial sector, the Government of Gujarat has also responded favourably and announced its own industrial policies. The State Industrial Policy, 1990-95 was already in operation when the New Industrial Policy, 1991 was declared by the central government (Hirway, 2000).

The Gujarat government declared the 'New Industrial and Incentive Policy 1995-2000' thereafter and 'Gujarat, 2000 AD and beyond' in 1994 for accelerated industrial development of the state. Though the policy declarations by the Government of Gujarat are essentially based on the general framework of the NIP, 1991, these are more aggressive in terms of promoting and facilitating new industrial investments. According to the Government of Gujarat, the new climate of economic liberalisation and globalisation has opened new opportunities to the states in India to attract industrial investments from India and abroad. The state's approach is to compete not only with other Indian states, but also with the newly emerging high growth regions of South-East and East Asian countries in the industrial sector.

As in the case of the central government, the main policy instruments of the state government are deregulation and liberalisation of the different markets, incentives and concessions to potential industrialists from India and abroad, and promotional and developmental work. The focus of the policy, however, has been relatively more on incentives and concessions, and on promotional and developmental works. There is also a clear emphasis on promoting larger units, which are described as 'premier units' (with investment between Rs 100 crore and Rs 500 crore) and 'prestigious units' (with investment of more than Rs 500 crore) in the policy statements.

The government has devised a generous package of concessions and incentives in turnover tax, sales tax on a whole range of goods such as raw materials, intermediate goods, packing materials, processing materials, consumable goods, by-products, scrap and waste materials, etc. In addition, there is transport subsidy and capital investment subsidy on a large number of products. These incentives are given at the taluka level to 128 talukas and eight regions of the total 184 talukas of the state, covering about 78 percent area of the state.

Secondly, certain industries such as electronics industry as well as the thrust industries, premier units, and prestigious units are eligible for the special incentives throughout the state except in the four banned areas. Tiny units set up and managed by the persons belonging to SCs/STs/OBCs or by women are eligible for the incentives throughout the state and the existing units undertaking expansion or diversification are also eligible for the special incentives as per rules. In addition, special incentives are provided to exporting units including the EOUs, employment-oriented small-scale units, units constructing project related infrastructure and units investing in social infrastructure construction and common and public purpose infrastructure. Special incentives are being given to NRIs that range from cash subsidies, tax concessions, out-of-turn allocation of sheds, power and other infrastructural facilities, to various types of escort services like providing facilities to their families and children. The Gujarat government has set up Single Point Contact, the NRI Cell in the Indextb, to assist NRIs right from the stage of concept to the stage of commissioning of industrial units.

Realising that subsidies and concessions are not adequate to attract industries in the state if the required infrastructure is not available, the Gujarat government has given a high priority to the promotion of infrastructure in the state. The state government has set up Gujarat Infrastructure Development Board (GIDB) in 1995 with the objective of attracting private sector investment in infrastructure such as roads, power plants, ports, jetties etc. GIDB has also set up guidelines for the involvement of the private sector, the banks and the financial institutions including the global financial institutions in funding infrastructural facilities in Gujarat and formulation and implementation of a long-term infrastructure policy in Gujarat.

In addition, the Gujarat government has also provided concessions to new industries in the acquisition of power, land, water and other infrastructure support, and assured these supplies within a limited time. The state government has also made special efforts to provide all the required information to prospective industrialists and has used the media extensively for this purpose. In short, the state government has been aggressive and determined to attract maximum industrial investments to the state (Hirway, 2000).

This approach has given rich dividends in terms of attracting industrial investments to the state, particularly in the large and medium industries. In fact, Gujarat has attracted the highest industrial investment in the large and medium sectors, more than Rs 1,70,000 crore, during 1991-1997 among all the states in India. This quantum jump implies more than ten times increase in the industrial investment per year, five-and-a-half time increase in the number of projects per year, and more than

60 percent increase in the average investment per unit, from Rs 24 crore to Rs 40 crore.

Employment and Labour Market

In the year 1991, there were about 16.6 million workers in the state (the workforce participation rate was about 40%), of whom 14.1 million (85%) were main workers and 2.5 million (15%) were marginal workers. Most of the male workers (about 99%) worked as main workers while only 53 percent of women workers worked as main workers. That is, about 47 percent of women workers in the state worked for less than six months in the year. The incidence of chronic unemployment (i.e., unemployment measured in terms of the usual status of the population) was fairly low, i.e., 0.62 percent and 0.30 percent for men and women respectively in rural Gujarat and 4.7 percent and 0.50 percent for men and women respectively in urban Gujarat. The current unemployment rates based on the daily status of the population in the state, however, were higher, i.e., 6 and 4.70 for men and women in rural Gujarat, and 5.70 and 7.8 for men and women in urban Gujarat, during 1993-94.

The overall employment scene in Gujarat is better than the same in India in some ways. Firstly, Gujarat has not experienced any decline in the level of employment in the recent decades. In fact, the workforce participation rate in Gujarat has shown a marginal increase between 1981 and 1991 while the same in India declined. And secondly, the rates of unemployment, including the daily status unemployment rates in Gujarat, are much lower for males and females both in rural and urban areas than the same in India. The dimensions of unemployment in the state, however, are far from insignificant. It has been estimated that the backlog of unemployment in the labour force will increase and reach 1.9 million to 2.2 million in 2001 (Hirway, 2000).

Water Resource

Overdrafting of ground water leading to water mining and salinity ingress has resulted in the deterioration of the quality of water available in the different regions of the state. The most important quality problems are pertaining to excessive salinity and excessive fluoride in water. About 14 percent of the villages in the state have ground water with excessive fluoride. Mehsana, followed by the Banaskantha, has the maximum villages facing this problem. Shortage of portable drinking water is one of the serious problems that the state is facing today. It has been estimated that about half of the villages face serious drinking water shortage during the summer months.

Salinity ingress is another serious environmental problem of the state. It has affected adversely the quality of water supply on the one hand and agricultural productivity of the land on the other. In 1960, the first salinity survey was conducted in Gujarat and reported this problem only in some villages along with coastal line in Saurashtra. However, by 1993, the saline area in the state has increased by more than eight times. This is primarily because of the destruction of mangroves on the seacoast and over drafting of ground water in the coastal and other regions of the state (Hirway, 2000). The Gujarat Ecology Commission has estimated that about 30 percent of the area will be affected by salinity problems in 2001. The most damaged area will be the region around the Gulf of Khambhat and the coastal Saurashtra (GEC, 1997).

Urbanisation

The state of Gujarat has experienced a rapid growth of population, much above that of the country since the beginning of the last century. This could be attributed, besides a lower death rate particularly of children, to a high rate of immigration. The latest census decade, however, reports a substantial decline in the population growth rate during the 1980s, bringing it down to below the national level for the first time. The pace of urbanisation in the state, on the other hand, has apparently been less than that in the country, except in a couple of decades. The urban population in the state during 1981-91, for example, has grown at 2.90 percent, which is less than that of the previous decade, i.e., 3.47 percent. Importantly, the corresponding rates for the country are higher, 3.09 and 3.83, respectively.

One may infer from this that the present rate of urbanisation in Gujarat is low and decelerating over time (Kundu, 2000). It must, however, be pointed out that the population in the rural areas of the state has grown at a rate much below than that of the country, going down further in recent decades. The annual exponential growth rate in the 1960s was 1.96, which has come down to 1.80 in the subsequent decades. As a consequence, the urban-rural growth differential for Gujarat during 1981-91 works out as much larger than that of the country and in fact most of the other (large) states. It was 1.46 in the state compared to 2.05 in the country during 1970s. The figure for the state has gone up to 1.51 in the 1980s, which is much above that of the country, viz., 1.29 percent. It would, therefore, be legitimate to argue that Gujarat has been one of the rapidly urbanising states in the country in recent years.

Gujarat has registered a reasonably high rate of inter-state (male) net immigration both in rural as well as urban areas during 1981-91. It is next only to Maharashtra. More importantly, Gujarat is the only state where the rate of net immigration from outside the state has gone up significantly during the 1980s, both in the rural as well as the urban areas. The only other state, which shows an increase in the net immigration rate, is Haryana but there the increment is negligible. It is, thus, evident that arrival of workers from outside the state is an important factor responsible for the pace of urbanisation in Gujarat. The distribution of population in different size-classes of urban centres in the state is similar to that of the country. About 66 percent of the total urban population is in class I cities having populations of one lakh or more. Another 24 percent live in class II and III towns in the size-class between 20,000 and 1,00,000.

Importantly, class I cities in Gujarat exhibit a higher growth rates than the smaller towns, as noted at the national level. A similar pattern emerges in the case of other developed states like Karnataka, Maharashtra, Punjab and Tamil Nadu. In most of the less developed states, however, the class I cities do not have an edge over other categories in terms of demographic growth. Furthermore, the class I cities in Gujarat have grown at a rate faster than those in the country during the 1970s. The gap between the two has, however, narrowed down in the 1980s. Also, the class VI towns in Gujarat have not grown at a faster rate than the class I cities, as is the case for several other states. This is because there are not many special purpose towns among them in Gujarat.

Another significant point is the deceleration of urban growth in Gujarat in all the size categories during the 1980s compared to the previous decade. This, however, is a national phenomenon since the decline is observed in all the states. Importantly, the ratio of the growth rate for class I cities to that of overall urban growth rate is higher in Gujarat than that in the country in 1981 as well as 1991. This highlights the primacy of these cities, not merely in terms of their share in urban population, but also a relatively higher growth rate. This is despite significant deceleration in the growth rate of these cities in Gujarat compared to smaller towns during the 1980s.

The pace of urbanisation varies across the districts in Gujarat but the disparity is not as high as in some of the backward states in the country like Orissa, Rajasthan and Bihar. The growth is fairly stable, ranging between 18 and 38 percent, except for three districts. Of these, Gandhinagar and Banaskantha register high growth due to special reasons like creation of state capital and low urban population in the base year. The growth rates, in general, are somewhat high in the developed districts like Surat, Rajkot and Vadodara with the sole exception of Ahmedabad.

Health Status

The health status in Gujarat shows considerable improvement and the state has been placed favourably on important indicators of health status in 1994. The state has made considerable progress in controlling mortality and reduction of infant mortality rate (IMR). The IMR has declined from 145 in 1970 to 62 in 1997, mainly due to decline in neo-natal mortality. The crude birth rate (CBR) that was 42.1 in 1971 has declined to 27 in 1997, and crude death rate (CDR) has reduced significantly from 18.1 to 8.3 during the same period. However, all these trends are different when we compare them in the rural-urban context. IMRs, CBRs and CDRs are much higher in rural areas than in urban Gujarat.

Table 6.5

CBR and CDR of Gujarat and India, 1971-1997

Year	Gujarat				India			
	Rural		Urban		Rural		Urban	
	CBR	CDR	CBR	CDR	CBR	CDR	CBR	CDR
1971	42.1	18.1	36.1	13.1	38.9	16.4	30.1	9.7
1981	36.1	12.4	29.8	10.7	35.6	13.7	27.0	7.8
1986	32.9	11.3	30.8	8.6	34.2	12.2	27.1	7.6
1990	30.2	9.6	28.3	7.2	31.7	10.5	24.7	6.8
1991*	28.2	8.8	25.9	7.9	30.9	10.6	24.3	7.1
1992*	29.5	9.5	24.6	8.3	30.9	10.9	23.1	7.0
1993*	29.1	8.9	25.8	6.8	30.4	10.6	23.7	5.8
1994*	28.5	9.6	24.5	6.9	30.5	10.1	23.1	6.7
1995*	27.9	8.3	24.0	6.2	30.0	9.8	22.7	6.5
1996*	26.9	8.3	23.0	6.3	29.3	9.7	21.6	6.5
1997*	27.0	8.3	22.6	6.2	28.9	9.6	21.5	6.5

* India excluding Jammu & Kashmir.

Source: SRS data, from Commissionerate of Health, Medical Services and Medical Education, cited by Mahadevia, 2000.

The CBRs and CDRs in Gujarat have reduced significantly during the last two decades, much more than at the all-India level. In 1971, the CBR in rural and urban Gujarat was 42.1 and 36.1 respectively, as against the all-India rates of 38.9 and 30.1. These have reduced to 27 and 22.6 respectively in Gujarat and to 28.9 and 21.5 respectively in India. The rural CBR, which was higher in Gujarat than in India in 1971, is lower than in India in 1997. Urban CBR continues to be higher in Gujarat than in India. Similarly, CDRs too have fallen significantly in Gujarat as compared to India. Both rural and urban CDRs were higher in Gujarat as compared to India in 1971 but are lower than that of India in 1997. The CDRs and CBRs have been higher in the rural areas as compared to the urban areas in Gujarat as well as in India. More importantly, the gap between the urban and rural rates has narrowed over time. Another important observation is that, since 1991, the CBR in urban Gujarat has remained higher than urban India. The same was the case with respect to CDR between 1991 and 1995, after which, the figures for urban Gujarat are lower than that for urban India.

In rural areas, the performance of Gujarat has been consistently better than India's. The IMR in Gujarat has declined more rapidly than in India during the last two decades, in both rural and urban areas. In 1971, rural and urban IMRs in Gujarat were higher than in India, while in 1994, the IMRs in Gujarat were significantly lower than in India. This improvement in IMR in Gujarat can be attributed to the significant decline of infant deaths in rural areas. The IMR has continued declining in rural areas of Gujarat, but in urban areas, there was some increase in 1994 as compared to 1993, after which, there is a decline once again.

Urban health status therefore requires deeper probing in Gujarat. As stated earlier the decline in the IMR is mainly attributed to the decline in neo-natal mortality due to the immunisation programme, and the extension of the health care system to take care of the complications of deliveries. Trained personnel are assisting more and more deliveries. The decline in neo-natal mortality (NNM) and, hence, the reduction in the IMR in Gujarat can be seen from the results of the National Family Health Survey (NFHS). In rural Gujarat, NNM rates have declined significantly from 59.2 in 1978-82 (10-14 years before) to 43.6 in 1988-92 (0-4 years before) period. In urban areas, the NNM has remained almost constant over the last decade and a half with a marginal increase during 1988-92. This is because the IMR during the same period in urban Gujarat has increased from 18.5 to 26.1 for 1,000 live births. Once again, urban Gujarat poses a special problem.

In Gujarat, it is observed that in the first year of life more male children died as compared to females. But more female children died in the age group of up to four years. All the fertility rates are lower in Gujarat in comparison to the rest of the country. Also, there has been decline in fertility rates during 1986-1993. Status of women's health is observed through female child mortality rates, fertility rates and maternal health. In spite of differing estimates of MMR of different sources, it appears that maternal health has improved over time, but not as much as desired. Also, on the whole, discrimination against the female child and women continue due to socio-economic conditions, which is reflected in higher death rates of female children as compared to male children.

Among the major states in India in 1994, Gujarat was placed in the middle on important indicators of health status. It ranked 16th with respect to CBR, and 14th with respect to CDR, out of 29 states and union territories. It is, in fact, surprising that the tribal-dominated Tripura and the non-urbanised state of Sikkim were doing better than Gujarat with respect to these two indicators of health. Even among the 15 large states, Gujarat was in the middle, seventh in CBR, sixth in CDR and IMR, and ninth in life expectancy at birth (LEB) in 1991 (Sundar, 1995).

The rate of prevalence of serious communicable diseases, in both rural and urban areas, is higher than the all-India average. However, in the case of chronic illness, its prevalence in Gujarat is much lower than national average. It is also interesting to note that in rural areas, the chronic illness prevalence rate is extremely low. Blindness, due to vitamin A deficiency, and goitre, due to iodine deficiency, are high in this state (Mahadevia, 2000). Prevalence of blindness is highest in Gujarat at the national level and its concentration is more in rural areas than in the cities. It is also reported that women are more affected than males. About one-fifth of the deaths are caused due to respiratory system diseases. Salinity is another major cause of deaths and it afflict persons aged 60 and above. Eleven districts of the state have an endemic prevalence of goitre due to iodine deficiency. All, apart from four of these districts, viz., Amreli, Mehsana, Kheda and Surendranagar, have a high proportion of tribal population.

While there is still a long way to go in improving the key health statistics, new dimensions of health status are emerging which need attention now. These are environmental health, occupational health, new contagious diseases such as AIDS, and diseases of prosperity. Also, much needs to be done with regard to women's health. Diseases of poverty continue to afflict a section of the population. Urbanisation has brought in a new set of health problems in the urban areas.

The problems of environmental pollution have become all pervasive in the developing countries, especially in the urban areas, because of high concentration of people, inadequate infrastructure for public hygiene, and uncontrolled and unregulated industrial activity. With continuous high rate of urbanisation, provision of basic services such as water supply, sanitation and solid waste collection do not keep pace with the rate of urban growth. As a result, water-borne infectious diseases are prevalent. The population, not having access to adequate water, does not maintain proper personal hygiene.

Skin diseases are common as a result. Risk to schistosomiasis, eye infections, and guinea worm diseases also increase due to lack of potable water supply. Air pollution, caused by vehicular traffic, thermal plants within the cities, industrial units and use of coal, is the other major environmental health problem in the developing countries. Studies show that in the Indian metropolises, air pollution levels far exceed the WHO standards. Air pollution damages human respiratory and cardio-respiratory systems. The elderly, children, smokers, and those with chronic respiratory and cardiovascular problems are more susceptible to damage because of air pollution.

The public expenditure for health was about 8 percent in the mid-1980s that came down to 6 percent in the mid-1990s. In Gujarat, in the mid-1980s, about 8 percent of the total budget was allocated to the health sector in the state. By mid-1990s, the proportion came down to about 6 percent. In the last few years, once again, there was an increase in this share, but not reaching the level that was in the mid-1980s. In terms of the proportion of NSDP, the expenditure on health sector was already very low in the 1980s (2.16% in 1986-87) and it has come down gradually since then. A disturbing aspect is that, as a percent of development expenditure, on the revenue as well as capital account, the allocation to health sector had declined for a decade (1987-96). In 1997-98, one can observe a slight increase in the proportion of the total budget as well as the NSDP spent on health.

In 1990-91, Gujarat incurred much lower per capita expenditure on health than the all-India average. However, if the expenditure of the union territories is excluded, the all-India average came to Rs 63.51, which is slightly higher than the Gujarat average of Rs 52.18. Gujarat ranked third among the 15 large states, with respect to per capita expenditure on nutrition. It ranked eighth in medical and public health and water supply and sanitation aspects, and ninth in family welfare. On the whole, Gujarat ranked sixth among the 15 large states. Tamil Nadu was at the top with per capita expenditure of Rs 77.18, followed by Kerala, with per capita expenditure of Rs 73.66. Gujarat incurred only 75 percent of the per capita expenditure incurred by Tamil Nadu. The state paid highest attention to medical and public health aspects followed by water supply and sanitation. In India, family welfare received higher per capita allocation than nutrition, while in Gujarat, nutrition received higher per capita allocation than family welfare, which is quite a rational and balanced situation.

According to Reddy and Selvaraju (1994), the expenditure on health in Gujarat was 10 percent of the total government expenditure on all activities in 1990-91, which was lower than that of all the state governments (12.6% of the total). Tamil Nadu, Kerala and Rajasthan had spent around 15 percent of their annual budget on health care in this year. The low importance of the health sector in Gujarat is also evident from the low share of health sector expenditure in NSDP. Only 1.63 percent of the NSDP was spent on health in 1990-91 in the state, whereas in India, 2.18 percent of the GDP was spent on health care. This figure was 3.17 percent for Kerala and 2.16 percent for all the states together (Reddy and Selvaraju, 1994). When ranked for the proportion of NSDP spent on health, Gujarat ranked fourth from the bottom out of 25 states and union territories in 1990-91. The high NSDP of Gujarat has not resulted in high government spending on health in the state, perhaps because of the lack of required political commitment.

As compared to India, Gujarat has a much higher availability of health facilities. That is because of urban Gujarat where the level of facilities is quite high. The number of hospitals and dispensaries per lakh population in Gujarat is more than three times than that in India. But, the difference between Gujarat and India is not large when sub-centres, beds per lakh population and doctors and nurses per lakh population are considered. With respect to primary health centres (PHCs), Gujarat's performance is poorer than India. This shows that with respect to high order health facilities, Gujarat's performance is better. High order health facilities are, however, generally located in the urban areas whereas the low order health facilities, such as the PHCs, sub-centres, etc., are located in the rural areas, where the state's relative performance is poor.

Urban-rural difference in high order health facilities is very high in Gujarat as compared to India. For example, in terms of hospitals, urban areas had 16 times higher facilities than rural areas in Gujarat. In India, this difference was only six times. However, with respect to beds per lakh population, the urban-rural difference was 11 in Gujarat as well as in India. Public health facilities in urban areas are under local bodies mainly the municipal corporations and municipalities, who incur expenditure on health care system from their own funds. For example, the Ahmedabad Municipal Corporation runs three general hospitals, 13 maternity hospitals, 25 dispensaries, five referral hospitals, one eye hospital, two TB clinics, four dental clinics and one contagious disease hospital. Similarly, the Employees State Insurance Scheme (ESIS) for industrial workers also runs three general hospitals and 49 dispensaries. But, given that the state is expected to rapidly urbanise and the municipal corporations may not be able to raise funds to meet health care demands of the increasing population, the state government will have to make budgetary allocation for the urban sector, which is low at the moment. With respect to PHCs, Gujarat was tenth among the 15 large states. Nevertheless, with respect to sub-centres, it was first.

While the health care facilities are at a medium level, their utilisation is low in Gujarat. A survey by the National Council for Applied Economic Research (NCAER), conducted in 1994, showed that the dependence of people on private facilities was higher than that on public facilities in rural as well as urban areas, and for both males and females. There is greater dependence on the private sector for hospitalisation, contrary to the all-India trend, despite hospitalisation involving higher expenditure than outpatient treatment. It is expected that the people would depend on public facilities for prolonged treatment of chronic illnesses and hospitalisation, which are expensive in private hospitals. However, for outpatient treatment, time is an important factor. Long waiting, non-availability of medical staff on time, and non-availability of quick treatment in government hospitals and dispensaries discourages the outpatients. In Gujarat, there are a large number of charitable trust hospitals providing hospitalisation at reasonable prices, which makes them popular compared to government hospitals for inpatient treatment.

The share of the private sector in treating patients outside the hospital was 65 percent in rural and 80 percent in the urban areas (Visaria and Gumber, 1994), which is closer to the NCAER trend for rural areas. In rural areas, even for non-hospitalised cases, poor households depended on the public facilities more than non-poor households. This was observed for cases of TB, malaria and dysentery. However, in urban areas, the dependence of the highest quintile of the expenditure classes on public outpatient treatment was the highest. This may be because of the acceptable level of public health facilities for the treatment of non-hospitalised illnesses. For inpatient care, the use of public hospitals is high. About 60 percent of the hospital treatment of illnesses in urban areas and about 55 percent of the same in rural areas depended on public facilities. The public sector hospitals are also well targeted towards the poor, more so in rural than in urban areas. Utilisation of non-governmental care for hospitalised cases increases with income in rural as well as the urban areas (Visaria and Gumber, 1994). Still, a significant proportion of the population has been using private health care facilities in the state.

Public expenditure on health care has also improved over time, and more so since the mid-1990s with the increase in overall awareness about health as an important development issue. However, Gujarat is far behind Kerala, which has a lower per capita income and higher incidence of poverty than Gujarat. Also, though the state has better performance in key health statistics, it comes in the middle order among the states in India. The overall improvement in the health statistics is because of significant improvement in rural areas, while urban areas remain a matter of concern and future policy interventions. Key health statistics have improved because of reduction in CBR and IMR (also reflecting in CDR), indicating reduced fertility and improvement in maternal and child health. There has also been progress in reducing post-neo-natal mortality (PNNM) and neo-natal mortality (NNM), which are noteworthy. This says a lot about the success of immunisation as well as nutrition programmes for mothers and infants in the state. In short, public health intervention towards improving maternal and child health and reducing fertility rates have been successful, especially where required, i.e., in rural areas.

There are, however, some paradoxes with regards to the health situation in the state. On the whole, the state did not fare well among the states in India with respect to the lower order health facilities such as PHCs and sub-centres, which are meant for rural areas. In spite of that, the rural health statistics have improved. On the other hand, in urban areas, where the state tops with regards to high order health facilities, the improvement in key health statistics has slowed down. The PRC and IIPS survey shows a reversal of trends in infant and child health in the urban areas in the mid-1990s. Nonetheless, urban areas have better performance in key health indicators than the rural areas. Much detailed investigation is required to understand whether slowing down of improvement in CBR, CDR and IMR in the urban areas is because of increasing exposure of urban residents to environmental pollution or lack of public health care system in the cities. As mentioned earlier, public health facilities are run in urban areas with the funds of the urban local bodies. Health department's budget is largely tied to providing rural facilities. The provision of urban public health facilities will therefore fluctuate greatly with the fortune of the urban local bodies, many of them, especially in the small and medium towns, are in dire financial conditions.

The health area that requires change in the mindset is women's health. Women's health has to be improved not only to ensure better health and survival of children and reduction of population growth rates, but also for women themselves and to improve the overall health status of the society. Till now, women's health has been viewed from the perspective of maternal health through immunisation and family planning programmes. Women constitute half the population. In Gujarat, as observed, health of the female child is neglected, which is reflected in the high mortality rate among the female child as compared to the male. In other words, socio-cultural change is required to approach women's health as their basic rights and improve their overall health. According to many researchers, improvement in female literacy will significantly reduce fertility and infant mortality rates.

The people and the progressive leadership of Gujarat have brought the state in the forefront of development in the country. The state has not only acquired and maintained its fourth rank in per capita NSDP but it has also taken a quantum jump in the post-independence period by attracting the highest industrial investment, particularly in large and medium industry, and experienced the highest growth in per capita NSDP during this period. In the process, the economy of Gujarat achieved a highly diversified economic structure. The process of this economic diversification, however, does not seem to be sustainable as the primary sector, and particularly agriculture, has lagged far behind distorting the agriculture-industry linkages. Along with agricultural near-stagnation, the environment has also experienced severe degradation, both of which have created constraints to the sustainability of economic growth in the state. The limited achievements of the state in the fields of employment and poverty, as well as in human development, are closely related to the macro development path. That is, these developments are not independent of each other, but are the consequences of the dynamics of development of the state.

7

The City of Ahmedabad

Ahmedabad (locally also known as *Amdabad*) is situated on the bank of river Sabarmati and is the largest city and the erstwhile capital of Gujarat. It nurtures in its fold, pages of history, a breath of harmony and a showcase of exquisite architecture. Named after the Sultan who founded it in 1411 and graced it with splendid monuments, it is associated with Mahatma Gandhi, the apostle of peace and non-violence, whose simple ashram on the banks of the river Sabarmati is now a site of national pilgrimage. Ahmedabad is renowned as a great textile and commercial centre and is also known as the "Manchester of India". It is also a land of gentle, dignified people, astute businessmen, gay and colourful peasants, and thriving industry. Ahmedabad is today the second largest prosperous city in western India and a place where tradition and modernity co-exist in harmony. On January 26, 2001, the city experienced devastating earthquake when about 750 people died and more than 100 buildings collapsed. In February 2002, the city faced large-scale communal problem that continued for more than three months and communally divided the city.

Ahmedabad has tropical monsoon climate characterised by hot and dry summer and semi-cold dry winter. Summer maximum reaches up to 44°C while the minimum temperature recorded in the city is 6.4°C in winter. Evidence of human settlement in the location of today's Ahmedabad dates back to a millennium. In the 11th century, there was a town called Ashaval founded by a Bhil ruler named Asha. Another settlement, known as Karnavati and founded by King Karnadev Solanki from Solanki dynasty, is believed to have been situated in the present location of Ahmedabad. Later on, it was famous as Ashapalli-Karnavati, during the reign of Siddharaja Jayasimhadeva (1094 to 1143 AD).

In the year 1411, Sultan Ahmed Shah (Ahmed Shah's forefather Zafarkhan revolted against the Delhi Sultan Mohammad-Bin-Tughlaq in 1392 AD and remained independent till the Mughal invasion.) built a citadel at the old site of the earlier Hindu town that was located on an open plain east of the river Sabarmati, near the area now known as 'Bhadra'. In 1456, a wall was constructed enclosing a group of villages to define the city limit and to protect it. Ahmedabad grew larger and wealthier for a century, but dynastic decay and anarchy brought decline, and the city was captured in 1572 by the Mughal emperor Akbar. Renewed eminence under the Mughals ceased with the death of Aurangzeb in 1707 and then it was occupied by the Marathas before finally handed over to the British in 1818.

The first textile mill in 1857 was a landmark in the growth history of Ahmedabad and was the turning point in the city's economic history, and was further facilitated by the railways in 1864. The city spread towards the north-east and south-east of the walled city after the spill over benefits from the textile industry was felt in a larger way. The industrial and residential growth however was confined to the eastern part of the river till the construction of the Ellis Bridge across the river in the late 19th century. The construction of six more bridges, namely, the Gandhi Bridge, the Sardar Bridge (1940), the Nehru Bridge (1959), the Subhash Bridge (1973), the Indira Bridge (1982) and the Shastri Bridge (1990) accelerated the developments in the western side of the river. These bridges are now extended to resolve the traffic problems.

Location of the temporary state capital following the bifurcation of the bilingual state of Bombay in the year 1960 and other related development also helped the growth of Ahmedabad. After the establishment of the permanent capital in Gandhinagar in 1970, Ahmedabad's importance did not suffer, because Gandhinagar could not become attractive as a residential or commercial city. Vatva, Naroda, Odhav, Rakhial and Asarva have been developed on the eastern part as industrial areas; and on the western part, Navrangpura, Ellisbridge, Naranpura, Memnagar, Paldi, Madalpur, Ambavadi, Vastrapur, Ghatlodia, Thaltej, Bodakdev, Vejalpur etc. have developed as residential areas. Commercial activities remain concentrated within the walled city area although there is a gradual shift towards Ashram Road on the western bank of the river Sabarmati. After a series of communal violence and redevelopment of some areas like the C.G. Road in the western part of the city, rapid growth of commercial activities has been seen.

Ahmedabad has a locational advantage as it lies along the growing Mumbai-Mehsana corridor. Also, recent industrial success in the region has favoured high potential urban growth. As a result, the city is on the way to becoming a mega city. It is one of the largest urban centres in the country and now is also the second largest city in western India, after Mumbai. Ahmedabad has already become a metropolis with more than three million population. Roads from the city lead to Mumbai, Central India, the Kathiawar peninsula and the Rajasthan border. It is a major junction on the Western Railway, with lines running to Mumbai, Delhi and the Kathiawar peninsula. Ahmedabad was historically an important trading town and then it was transformed into one of the major industrial centres in the country mainly due to the entrepreneurial abilities of its business communities. The multiplier effects of the textile industry have been evident in the rapid growth of the commercial sector, chemical and dyes industries and light engineering industries, all of which are dependent on this sector. Though the era of textile industry in the city is declining and many mills have been closed down, still some mills are producing quality clothes like denim jeans, synthetic saris, etc.

The magnetic effect of the employment potential of the premier city of Gujarat is fairly strong due to its well-developed industrial base, educational facilities, trade and commercial activity. Ahmedabad functions as the financial capital in Gujarat. Successful industrial policies have led the state of Gujarat as one of the most industrialised states in the country. Industrial growth and urbanisation have created the Western Indian Golden Corridor, which spread linearly from Mehsana to Mumbai (Mahsena-Ahmedabad-Baroda-Bharuch-Ankleshwer-Surat-Vapi-Mumbai). Stock market in the city is growing and large capital investments are taking place. Due to abnormal increase in land price and housing rent in Mumbai, corporate offices are shifting to Ahmedabad (AUDA, 1997).

Ahmedabad is also an important educational centre with nationally and internationally renowned institutions such as Physical Research Laboratory (PRL), Indian Space Research Organisation (ISRO), Indian Institute of Management (IIM), National Institute of Design (NID), Centre for Environmental Planning and Technology (CEPT), etc. Many new educational institutions are coming either within the city or in nearby areas.

City Administration

City administration in Ahmedabad commenced with the establishment of a statutory committee in 1830, initially for the repair and preservation of the city wall, which was in a dilapidated condition at that time. Later on, the committee started carrying out other important works such as water supply, streetlighting etc. In 1858, this committee was replaced by a municipal committee with well-defined constitutional

power, under the Municipal Act XXVI of 1850. In the year
1873, the Bombay District Municipal Act VI of 1873 replaced
the Municipal Act XXVI of 1850, and Ahmedabad
Municipality was reconstituted. In 1884-85, when Lord Rippon
conferred local self-government on municipalities, the
municipality of partly elected and partly nominated members
came into being. With the application of the provision of the
Bombay Provincial Municipal Corporation Act, 1949, the
municipality was transformed into a corporation from 1st July,
1950. The number of members was increased and the area
within the municipal jurisdiction, which was 5.72 sq km in
1850, was extended to 190.86 sq km in 1986. It may be extended
further on the western side, as many small municipalities are
not in a position to provide and manage essential services.

The Municipal Corporation is now composed of four
different bodies:
1. the General Board of Elected Members, including Mayor;
2. the Statutory Committee with the Standing Committee,
   the Transport Committee and the School Board;
3. the Special Committee; and
4. the Executive Body.

The Corporation has vested with the power to impose
various specific types of taxes on the citizens in order to enable
it to undertake different kinds of civic activities as imposed on
it by the virtue of the BPMC Act of 1949, in the public interest.

During the early years of 1990s, new constitutional
amendments such as 73rd and 74th, have provided substantial
powers to both rural and urban local governments in India.
Urban local governments now not only decide the fate of a city
but also of a larger region. Policies of local government will
determine the attractiveness of a city for foreign as well as
domestic private investment, which can bring rapid economic
changes not only in the city, where investments have direct
implications but also in the surrounding region according to the
city's intensity of interaction with the region. To create the

required environment to accommodate changes due to liberalisation in a city is a complicated job, which will also determine the successful nature of the changes. The Ahmedabad Municipal Corporation (AMC) today has challenging path ahead in identifying the proper methods to achieve the development objectives and should also be careful enough in establishing a vision for the city. A new initiative has been undertaken with the help of the World Bank in the name of City Development Strategy (CDS) for the future growth of the city.

Demography

Ahmedabad is one of the largest cities in western India. As usual phenomenon in many other Indian cities, urban area of Ahmedabad and area under the local authority do not match each other. It is only because of the continuous expansion of 'urban' activities whereas the jurisdiction of an urban local body gets expanded after certain period. Urban activity area of Ahmedabad goes far beyond the AMC limit. On the other hand, the Planning and Development Authority of Ahmedabad, which prepares the 'Development Plan' for Ahmedabad, occupies larger area than the urban sprawl of the city, engulfing hundreds of villages and many small towns in the surrounding region being cautious of the future expansion of it. But, any study on Ahmedabad should incorporate the actual urban area of the city at the present-day context. In census documents, the same area has been defined as Ahmedabad Urban Complex with areas under AMC and the areas of immediate urban expansion, which fall outside the Corporation's jurisdiction. There are 190.84 sq km of land area under AMC, but total urbanised area (both in east and west) outside the AMC's boundary is 67.79 sq km and the total area is 258.63 sq km.

Ahmedabad is the seventh largest city in India. According to Census 1991, the city (AMC) has more than 2.9 million of

Figure 7.1
Ahmedabad, Growth of Population

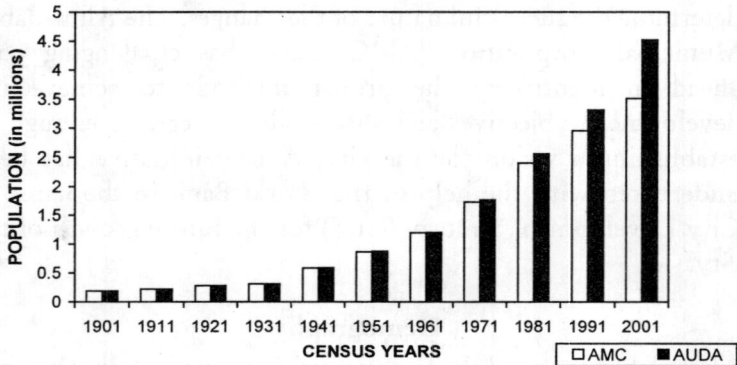

population. During that time population of total urban agglomeration area was more than 3.3 million. Decadal growth rate in the AMC area during the time period from 1981 to 1991 was 22.99 percent and the same in the total urban agglomeration area was 29.51 percent. There is spatial variation and differentiation of distribution of population density in the city. Different wards under AMC exhibit differential pattern of

Table 7.1
Demography: Ahmedabad City

Parameter	AMC Area (1991)	AMC Area (2001)
Population (in million)	2.9	3.5
Total area (sq km)	190.84	190.84
Density (persons/sq km)	15,402	18,420
Growth (%)	22.99	20.69
Number of households	552,164	N.A.
Average household size	5.9	N.A.
Sex ratio (F/1000M)	889	885
Literacy rate (%)	68.58	73.38

Source: Statistical Outline of Ahmedabad City, 1998-99

Figure 7.2

Ahmedabad Urban Agglomeration Distribution of Population, 1991

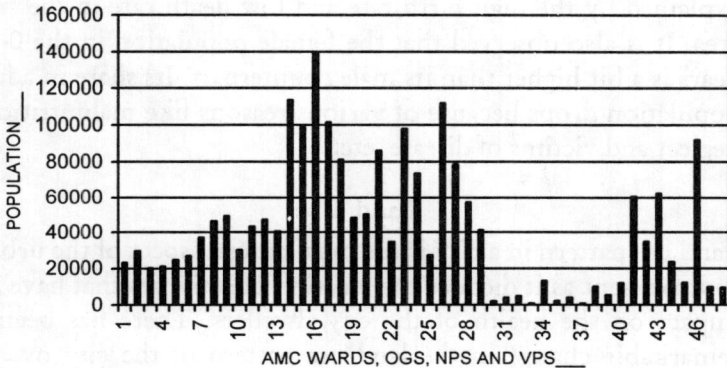

density. The AMC wards falling under the walled city area show the highest level of density in the city. The average density pattern in the eastern part of the city is higher than that of the western part. The peripheral areas in the city exhibits comparatively lower density level, but the rate of growth of annual density figure is very high.

Literacy and Sex Ratio

As stated earlier, although Ahmedabad is famous for a number of prestigious educational institutes of national and international reputation, primary education is lagging behind, as only 68.58 percent of population are literate (according to Census 1991). The male literacy is about 75 percent as compared to 62 percent for females. In an urban area, literacy is expected to be much higher than the state or the national average. In Ahmedabad agglomeration, the rate is higher by one percent. Sex ratio, which is an important demographic indicator, shows a gradual improvement from 766 in 1951 to 889 in 1991. The ward-wise information shows that it is quite low in the wards of Bapunagar, Rajpur, Danilimada and Isanpur. These wards are also having low levels of literacy.

The age-sex composition of the city population shows that the base of the population is very high. The heavy base can be explained by the high birth rate and low death rate in the city area. It is also observed that the female population in the 0-14 years is a bit higher than its male counterpart. Its share in adult population drops because of various reasons like malnutrition, neglect and victims of disease, etc.

Land Use

Land use pattern in a city is the most crucial aspect of the urban environment as it dictates the location of activities that have an impact on the health of the city dwellers. There has been a remarkable change in the land use pattern of the city over a period of time. In the first decade after independence, during 1950-1961, the residential land use had increased considerably. The same trend is continuing from 1961 onwards. In 1986, a large area on the eastern part of the city had been incorporated within city limit and the urban area doubled from a modest 92.15 sq km to 190.84 sq km. Land under commercial use has increased from 1.2 percent in 1950 to more than 3 percent in 1991. During the same period, industrial land uses reduced slightly. Roads and streets cover only 14.3 percent of the total developed area, which is far below the desirable standard. Public amenities like parks, gardens and other open space, which generally act as the breathing spaces, are also insufficient as compared to prescribed standard. Area under parks and gardens has reduced from 13.4 percent to 11.6 percent between 1950 and 1981.

Economy

Ahmedabad is a major industrial centre with many textile, chemical and pharmaceutical industries. It has three industrial estates within the municipal limits. Economy of Ahmedabad is gradually changing from secondary base to tertiary base. Now, Ahmedabad has more than five hundred thousand tertiary workers which accounts for about 60 percent of the total main workers in the city. On the other hand, there are three hundred thousand workers in the secondary sector, which is 38 percent of the total (Census, 1991). It implies the decreasing secondary sector activity or faster rate of growth in tertiary sector based activity.

There is a clear decline in the textile sector, which saw closing down of many of the textile mills during the last decade. The fall of textile industry also affected other ancillary industries in the city. There is a sectoral shift in industrial growth in Gujarat, after liberalisation, and this shift also exhibits an unequal spatial pattern of distribution. There is rapid growth of chemical and petrochemical industries in South Gujarat districts, such as Bharuch, Surat and Valsad. The South Gujarat districts of Bharuch and Surat, and Jamnagar from Saurashtra, account for 58 percent of the investment envisaged in the state in the year 1995-96. On the other hand, there is a significant decline in the share of industries in and around Ahmedabad (Kundu, 1999b). On the other hand, there is a rapid growth in the tertiary sector that includes business and commerce, transport and communication, construction activities and other services.

In the post-liberalisation era, corporate business and other related activities are booming in the city. Due to rapid growth of the tertiary sector, the growth of employment in Ahmedabad Urban Agglomeration (AUA) area is much higher than in other parts of urban Gujarat. As a consequence, the work participation ratio for males in AUA has gone up from 49.6 percent in 1981 to 55.7 percent in 1991 (for urban Gujarat, from 49.8% to 50.8 only). Furthermore, the unemployment rates in AUA are also declining sharply during the early nineties, although they show still higher figures (Kundu, 1999b).

Infrastructure

Planning, development and maintenance of infrastructure facilities in the city have been exercised by the AMC and by the Ahmedabad Urban Development Authority (AUDA). Electrification, sewerage network, drinking water facilities and transport installations are considered as the most important infrastructure requirements by the authorities. All parts of the city are now accessible (spatially) for electricity, which is provided by a private enterprise called Ahmedabad Electricity Company (AEC). But still the city does not have complete electrification, as many low-income families cannot afford to have a connection and many enjoy it by unauthorised connections. AMC area has 13,08,453 total connections and the total AUA area has 13,76,870 connections (Census, 1991). Ahmedabad has long history of installing and managing sewerage network. AMC has covered most of its areas by sewerage network except some areas in the eastern part that was incorporated within municipal limit in 1986. AUDA also has started constructing it in the areas under its jurisdiction. Drinking water in the AMC area has been provided by AMC in hourly basis in a day. Generally, flow continues in a day for two hours with varying intensities and at different time. To fulfil the requirements, people of Ahmedabad generally depend upon ground water. Almost all the middle and higher income households have electric motors for ground water draft. The industrial consumers depend significantly on the private bore wells to meet their requirements. This is especially alarming, as the water table is already low and is dropping rapidly.

Ahmedabad has all sorts of transport installations, except water transport. Total road length in the city is 1384.5 km. Out of it 1103.3 km is paved and 998.3 km comes under jurisdiction of AMC (Census, 1991). Hierarchy of roads vary from national highways to the local roads. The National Highway 8 links Ahmedabad to Delhi and Mumbai and an express highway is under construction to link it with Baroda. There are other state highways to connect it with other urban areas in Gujarat and the surrounding states. During the early years of 1990s, a massive road upgradation operation was done in the city by the city authority. Presently, upgradation (four laning) of the state roads is being done by the state government of Gujarat. The city has a congested and overused regional bus terminus in the Gita Mandir area of the old part of the city. The only means of public transportation in the city is city bus service, which has been provided by Ahmedabad Municipal Transport Service (AMTS), an AMC operated service. Private auto rickshaws provide semi-public passenger service in the city. Regional freight traffic by roads has been served by many trucks 'addas' in the periphery of the city and goods inside the city are being transported by various modes from handcarts and camel carts to mini-trucks and three-wheelers. Increasing private vehicles in the city is becoming a major problem with the incompatible nature of it with road space and with growing environmental pollution. Ahmedabad's connectivity with Delhi and other places in North India has been recently improved by replacing the old metre gauge rail line by a broad gauge track. There was already a broad gauge connection with the eastern and southern part of the country.

In Ahmedabad, roads cover approximately 8 percent of the AMC area. The total length of all the roads is 1,217 km, of which 1,050 km are surfaced. Till recently, most roads consisted of no more than an asphalt strip in the centre, dirt on both side, rudimentary streetlighting and a haphazard maze of utility lines underneath. With rapid increase in traffic volumes in the last decade, the road network of Ahmedabad has come under severe strain. Due to a lack of well-designed streets, traffic in the city is disorganised and slow, pedestrians are unsafe and noise and air pollutions are high. The annual expenditure on road maintenance in Ahmedabad was as low as Rs. 10 million per year till 1994.

From November 1994 onwards, the AMC has increased its financial and management capacity by diligently enforcing the rule of law, as well as by rejuvenating the revenue recovery systems. Following this, the AMC embarked upon a major programme of road improvement. For this, the AMC has initiated public-private partnerships aimed at improving the streets of Ahmedabad to make them efficient and safe. Under this project, streets are to be designed and constructed to ensure smooth flow of traffic while ensuring the safety of pedestrians, reducing pollution and beautifying the cityscape. Aimed at upgrading the quality of streets in Ahmedabad and channelling private finance to be recovered through advertisement rights, C.G. Road, the prime commercial street in Ahmedabad, was redeveloped in partnership with Arvind Mills Ltd., a private industrial company.

Solid Waste Disposal

The Ahmedabad Municipal Corporation manages to collect about 85 percent of the solid waste generated in the city. The average generation in the city is about 1,430 tonnes per day while collection is 1,215 tonnes per day. The total number of vehicles deployed for the purpose, including trucks, lorries, tippers, dumpers, compactors, etc., comes to 116. The total manpower employed for the solid waste removal and street cleaning is 7,531. The system of solid waste management in Ahmedabad is most efficiently managed with low manpower deployed per tonne of waste collected and not too large a fleet of specialised vehicles. In some areas non-governmental agencies are also collecting solid waste from the residential areas.

Attempts have been made to involve NGOs in Ahmedabad for solid waste management as well. The Corporation has the responsibility of collecting garbage only from streets, bins and dumpers. AMC, in collaboration of NGOs like SEWA, organised training programmes for informal garbage collectors and tried to ensure their access to industrial/commercial establishments and housing societies. They were also given bags for separating reusable items from composting material and their appropriate disposal. The AMC tried to strengthen this decentralised model of garbage collection since October 2000, starting with the commercial areas. It is proposed to extend this, step by step, to cover industrial as well as residential areas. Unfortunately, the system is functioning only in a limited way, covering less than 4 percent of the households as the NGOs have failed in ensuring greater acceptability of these rag-pickers and adequate earnings to them.

The AMC had been 'selling' municipal solid waste (MSW) about 10 percent of the total collection, to a private company, Excel Industries, since the 1980s. The revenue that the AMC earned was so low that it did not cover even the cost of transportation. A new arrangement has been worked out now, and it has contracted out the responsibility of managing 40 percent of the MSW to the same industry. The arrangement has come into effect from January 2000, which involves conversion of 500 metric tonnes of garbage every day into manure by the company and the rest to be taken to a landfill site. It has been argued that this would result in substantial cost saving for the AMC and, at the same time, make it possible for the company to conduct its business profitably (Kundu, 2002).

The Excel Industry is expected to pay a royalty payment of only 2.5 percent of the total ex-plant realisation of receipts, excluding levy, cess, etc., which is a very small amount. This is unlikely to cover the cost of delivery of the MSW to the Excel receipt point, as was the case before. The only change in the arrangement is that AMC now is under the obligation of providing 500 metric tonnes of garbage every day, failing which it would invite a penalty equivalent to the cost of collection of deficit amount from the city. The economics of the arrangement and net saving to the corporation, as a consequence, is yet to be established. There are, however, apprehensions that the AMC may fail in its commitment of providing the required volume of garbage, leading to penal payment to the company. It is also not very clear why the corporation has accepted such unfavourable conditionality in case of its failure to meet the delivery obligations when it stands to gain almost nothing through its compliance. Most importantly, AMC has not been able to pass on any part of its responsibility such as collection of garbage, sorting out debris, industrial and toxic wastes or transportation of MSW to the receipt point (Kundu, 2002).

SWM is one service where the AMC is very hopeful that its subcontracting arrangements will succeed. The major problem here is segregation and door-to-door collection of waste through participation of common people and groups or the NGOs and transportation of waste to the receipt point. Some high and middle-income housing societies have shown willingness to bear the financial burden and also engage informal rag pickers for improving the system of separation, collection and disposal of waste in municipal bins.

Slums and Chawls

Rapid industrialisation and urbanisation have also worked as a catalytic factor in the mushrooming of low-income localities in Ahmedabad. There are two types of low-income settlements in the city, which differ from one another in terms of their origin and growth. First, out of the two, is the 'slums', which can be found in any other city with similar nature of occupants and with identical physical conditions. The second type of these settlements in Ahmedabad is known as 'chawls'. Initially, chawls were built to house the textile workers the early decades of the 20th century. These chawls do have some basic infrastructure such as water supply and community latrines. Now, they are occupied by the workers of the closed textile mills in the city and due to their old age, low-income occupants and the initial design, they are in dilapidated condition. Today, their physical status and their occupants' economic status are more alike slums. According to the Census 1991, within the limit of AMC, there were 91,188 families with 474 thousand persons living in the slums. Population in chawls in the city transcended the upper limit of that in the slums and around 1,33,000 families with 696 thousand persons lived in them. Therefore, a total of 2,25,000 families with more than 1,170 thousand population are distributed over 2,432 low-income localities that accounts for nearly 41 percent of the total population in the city.

The living environment in these low-income settlements today is a serious concern to the local authority and the people in the city. It is estimated that around five hundred thousand of the slum dwellers have no toilet facilities and they defecate in the open. The community toilets are constructed in many slums by the city authority, which do not fulfil the full requirements in those areas and are poorly maintained. Few households have individual facilities. There are many such settlements, which are connected to the sewer network in the city, but still most of them are yet to be linked. In the slums established prior to the year 1976, there is water supply either by public stand posts or by individual connections from the AMC. There is a serious problem of water in the remaining areas. Lack of storm water drains and the provision for household liquid waste management, along with ill-managed solid waste in these localities, have created 'hell' in them.

Contamination of drinking water with resultant occurrence of water-borne diseases, continuous presence of odour and anarchic sights are the main characteristics of these settlements. Narrow lanes inside the settlements are the lines of communication, which are normally unpaved and also work as dirty drains. The legal status of these settlements is a critical subject in urban development planning. Although the origin and growth of these settlements are illegal, the residents in many of them have been allowed to settle down permanently during late 1970s. Legalisation of these localities, which are illegally established in the land belonging to AMC, is followed by various settlement upgradation programmes taken by the authority. But, there are also many slums and chawls, on private land and under the Bombay Municipal Act, where the city authority is not responsible for street sweeping and solid waste collection (CEPT, 1997). Nowadays, many non-government organisations are also engaged in developmental activities in the slums and the chawls in the city.

Slum Networking

'Slum networking' is a development strategy which attempts to tackle the infrastructural and environmental problems of slums in such a manner that the city as a whole benefits. Slum networking is the integrated upgradation of the city slums, not as isolated islands but as an urban network. The spatial spread of slums over a city, contiguity between slum settlements, and a close correlation between the slum locations and the natural drainage paths of a city, gives an opportunity to strengthen the city level infrastructure through networks. Within slums, unconventional concepts such as topography management, earth regradation and constructive landscaping are introduced. The service infrastructure is simplified and modified so that individual services (instead of shared facilities) can be offered to slum families at lower costs. At the same time, the maintenance burden is reduced and can be shifted from the local government to the individual householders.

The strategy prescribed requires sensitive and intense participation of the public in the development process, through self-help. NGOs can play an active role in motivating the communities, mobilising resources from slum dwellers and converging them with the various programmes and resources of the local government and the business community of the city. The mechanisms evolved for community interaction can be gainfully extended to health, education and income generation programmes. This leads to holistic development, which changes the functional, physical, socio-economic and environmental qualities of a city, at a fraction of the cost of the conventional approaches.

In Ahmedabad, the AMC is the nodal basic service provider of the slum dwellers since few decades of its existence. Until date, it has yet to make a large-scale impact on the quality of the life of the people living in slums. It has in turn raised the issues like health and sanitation of the city and needs attention for its improvement in terms of upgrading physical environment, provision of health services, improving the level of education and income generating opportunities with participation of the slum dwellers.

Slum networking represents a new vision for the urban poor living in the slums. Slums were looked as fabric and beauty of the city. Upgradation will include improving infrastructure provision of the city connecting the slums apart from providing all other services within slums. The project has been named as Pandit Deen Dayal Upadhyay Antyodaya Yojana – Slum Networking Project. At present, this project is on going in nine different slum pockets of the city in which two NGOs, namely, SEWA and SAATH, are working together. Mostly, they are involved in community-based activities, such as educational programmes, health programmes, and other income-generating activities.

Green Partnership

In 1996, the AMC prepared an urban forestry programme as partnership programme for environmental improvement of the city. A proposal was prepared by the Municipal Commissioner and submitted before the Standing Committee of the Corporation that was subsequently passed without any debate on 20th June 1996. To finalise the programme details, a workshop was organised on April 13, 1996 with the support of RUDO/USAID which was attended by a large number of NGOs and local institutions. The workshop evolved a detailed proposal to give AMC-owned vacant plots in partnership with local NGOs and community organisations without any ownership right of the land for planting trees, flowering trees, fruit trees, nurseries and medicinal plants. It was also decided that initially plots can be given only for five years which can be extended to another five years if the Corporation finds it necessary and work done satisfactorily. Three years of registration was decided as the minimum requirement for any NGOs or other organisations to participate in this activity (Raval, 2000).

The basic objective of the project was to contribute in greening the city through development of urban forest and other greening-related activities in AMC-owned vacant plots designated for this or other purposes. It was also intended to facilitate and encourage participation of low-income residents through public-private partnership and to increase the income generation possibilities for low-income groups. AMC prepared a list of 44 vacant plots that can be brought under the Ahmedabad Green Partnership (AGP) programme and requested to apply for each of the plots. AMC promised to provide free water connection and 'no objection' for getting electric connection. It also promised to assist NGOs in getting loan facilities if required. However, the AMC reserved its right to terminate the agreement without paying any compensation by giving an advance notice of 15 days. The Director of Parks and Gardens entertained applications, revised the proposals and then prepared the agreements signed by the Municipal Commissioner and the implementing NGOs. The Director of Parks and Gardens was entrusted with the sole responsibility of coordination with the NGOs whereas the General Manager in this department was to report to the Municipal Commissioner. A financial allocation of Rs 25.4 lakh was made for the first year. For the next four years, the Corporation approved Rs 21.4 lakh as grants during 1996-97. In the first year a total of 18 plots were allotted to 13 NGOs.

Raval (2000) studied some of the NGOs participating in this programme and observed several problems in the implementation of this scheme. It is found that in some cases local political leaders have opposed AGP and forced some NGOs to surrender the plot as they were using these plots for various purposes. There were several coordination problems between the AMC and NGOs and also within the AMC administration that resulted in delay of handing over the plot and release of funds. It is reported that only 50 percent of the promised fund was released during 1987-88 and since then no fund was released to any NGOs. In many cases NGOs have complained about the topography, soil condition, water availability and criteria for safeguarding the plots as some of the encroached plots were given under the AGP.

Along with the AGP a separate strategy of roadside tree plantation was also undertaken with active support from the corporate and industrial houses. The Rotary Club of Ahmedabad (North) has played an important role in bringing corporate houses as partner of this project. Under this scheme corporate and business houses adopted certain road for tree plantation by bearing the cost of plantation and of tree guards. AMC prepared a list of about 15 plants and given it to the sponsoring agency for selection of road and plants. A detailed cost estimate was made for digging, weeding, watering, etc., and finally decided to charge Rs 1,000 for each plant which also include cost of guard and maintenance. AMC permitted the sponsoring agency to put its name on the tree guard. As a result of this initiative about 8.1 km of road length was brought under plantation programme by planting about 7,150 plants. It can be extended to 1,217 km of road length within the Municipal Corporation area.

Municipal Finance

AMC was formed in 1950 under the Bombay Provincial Municipal Corporation Act. The main infrastructure services as provided under the Act include a protected water supply, sewerage and storm water drainage, the construction and maintenance of roads, street-lighting, disease prevention and monitoring, solid and liquid water disposal, public transport, and parks and gardens. The city has 43 wards and the city's Mayor is elected for a term of two-and-a-half years.

In the midst of the overall prosperity of the city, a large poor population has suffered from deprivation of basic services and amenities. The proportion of the total population in slums and low-income housing was 41 percent in 2000. The bulk of the residents in slum areas had a shared water supply and more than a quarter of them had no toilet facilities.

In the mid-1990s the AMC began instituting significant fiscal and management reforms, including improving tax collection, computerising the accounting system, strengthening AMC's workforce and financial management, and developing a comprehensive capital improvement program. These reforms laid the necessary groundwork for AMC to issue the first municipal bond issued in India without a state guarantee and enabled AMC to partner with the business community, NGOs and other organisations to undertake new development initiatives. The bonds represented the first step towards a fully market-based system of local government finance.

Before 1993, AMC was a loss-making urban local body with accumulated cash losses of Rs 350 million (US $9.2 million). During a deteriorating financial situation in 1994 the AMC launched a major effort to strengthen its capacity to develop commercially viable projects. As a result, it was able to turnaround its financial position and achieve a closing cash surplus of Rs 2,142 million (US $50 million) in March 1999.

The main credit for the financial turnaround of the Corporation and other development initiatives and administrative reforms goes to the dynamic leadership of a Municipal Commissioner, Mr. Keshav Varma, who remained at the helm from 1994 to 1997. The reforms first initiated under

Varma's leadership included restructuring the Corporation and upgrading its workforce, and improving revenue collection, accounting and financial management systems.

Octroi (a tax on goods coming into the city) has traditionally been AMC's major source of revenue, accounting for about 70 to 75 percent of total revenue. Knowing that the tax was not being collected effectively, the AMC increased octroi collection by updating the valuation manual for tax assessment based on current market prices. Octroi collection was further improved through deploying police personnel for controlling touts and catching defaulters, linking all checkposts with a wireless network to facilitate 24-hour communication, forming 13 vigilance squads to conduct spot checks of vehicles, and installing weighing machines at the check posts. A system of backtracking of the goods (taxing items that previously went untaxed) was also introduced. Strict action was taken against corrupt and negligent employees. Because of these measures, annual octroi collection increased by 60 percent.

Similarly, in 1994, the AMC introduced a series of measures to improve property tax collection, which accounts for about 30 percent of AMC's tax revenues. The tax assessment system is based on annual ratable value (British system of assessing property tax), which can be subjective and inequitable. A computer database was created to identify defaulters, while attention was focused on recovering major outstanding tax amounts. These measures included issue of notices and warrants, disconnection of water supply and sewerage, publishing of the defaulters' names, attachment of property, and restructuring and strengthening of the property tax department. These steps helped to increase annual property tax collection by 55 percent. AMC has recently introduced an area-based system for assessment of property tax, which will further improve the tax collection.

Beginning in the mid-1990s, the AMC also introduced a number of management reforms such as computerising the accounts and upgrading the workforce. AMC had been using a single-entry cash-based accounting system until 1996-97. In April 1996, it introduced a computerised double-entry accounting system, purchased new computers, developed a new accounting system and recruited chartered accountants to introduce the new system. AMC's electronic data processing department worked closely with the city's finance department to build in-house capacity. In the first year, both single and double entry systems were operated on a parallel basis. A local chartered accounting firm was appointed to assist AMC in preparing its first balance sheet in 1996. The new system is now operational.

Traditionally, promotions in the AMC were based on seniority and not merit. There was hardly any recruitment of new talent from outside the organisation. Performance was not rewarded and the administration lacked new ideas and a professional culture. The Corporation then decided to change its resulting negative image. It began by upgrading its workforce by recruiting a group of professional middle level managers. AMC also revised its recruitment rules to enable it to make such direct recruitment. In 1997, about 40 chartered accountants and business management graduates were recruited. The Corporation placed them in key administrative and operational positions. These new officers are improving AMC service delivery, while introducing a new work ethic.

In 1996, the AMC prepared a five-year capital investment plan for investing Rs 5,973 million (US $150 million) for water supply, sewerage, roads, bridges and solid waste management projects and allocated Rs. 4,393 million ($US 110 million) for the water supply and sewerage component. It proposed to meet 30 percent of the total investment requirement from internal sources of financing while mobilising the remaining amount through municipal bonds and loans from financial institutions. The project was structured within an urban financial framework that was predicated on receipt of significant transfers from general revenues such as octroi and property taxes.

The availability of the cash, however, permitted the AMC to rapidly respond to an impending water crisis. The Corporation was able to expend bond proceeds to successfully implement an emergency bulk water supply scheme known as the 'Raska Project' in a record five months. AMC claims that this availability of cash enabled it to obtain highly competitive tenders from the private contractors, which came in at 10 to 15 percent below the estimated cost. AMC estimates that this more than offset the loss of interest on the debt.

In addition to the water project, the healthy state of municipal finances enabled the AMC to go into partnership with the business community, NGOs and other organisations to undertake new initiatives. For example, AMC partnered with a prominent textile company to redevelop an important commercial artery called C.G. Road. The textile company funded the estimated project cost of Rs 35 million and all additional costs were borne by the AMC. The company expects to recover its contribution from advertising and parking revenues. Following recovery of the capital investment, these revenues will go to AMC. AMC also set up a 'green partnership' whereby private companies share the cost of upgrading and maintaining parks, gardens and roadside plantation in exchange for advertising rights.

Finally, in the Slum Networking Project, the Corporation partnered with a prominent textile company, an NGO and the slum community to improve basic infrastructure and provide water and toilets to households. The textile company set up a Trust and executed the project while the NGO mobilised the community and AMC acted as facilitator for a pilot community called Sanjay Nagar. The project was completed within the stipulated time and without any cost overruns.

With the success of the first municipal bond issue, the AMC has gone ahead with another bond issue of the same amount, i.e., Rs 1,000 million. However, the second bond launched in March 2002 is tax exempt. AMC is again the first municipal corporation in India to issue tax-free municipal bonds. This bond will be used to complete its original water and sewerage infrastructure scheme.

Municipal Bond

In the midst of the overall prosperity of the city, a large proportion of the poor population has suffered from deprivation of basic services and amenities. In 2000, 41 percent of the population lived in slums and low-income housing, with the bulk of the slum residents sharing the water supply, and many living without toilet facilities. Prior to 1993, the AMC had accumulated a cash loss of over US $9 million and their financial situation was deteriorating. In 1994, the Corporation launched a major effort to strengthen its capacity to develop commercially viable projects. As a result, the AMC was able to turnaround its financial position and achieve a closing cash surplus of US $50 million in 1999.

The main credit for the financial turnaround and other development initiatives and administrative reforms goes to the dynamic leadership of a Municipal Commissioner who remained at the helm from 1994 to 1997. One of the initial reforms addressed octroi. Octroi (an entry tax on goods) has traditionally been the AMC's major source of revenue, accounting for about 70 to 75 percent of total revenue. To increase octroi revenues, the valuation manual for tax assessment was updated based on current market prices. Octroi collection was further improved through a number of means including the deployment of police personnel for controlling touts and catching defaulters and installation of weighing machines at spot checks. Annual octroi collection increased by 60 percent.

Similarly, in 1994, the AMC introduced a series of measures to improve property tax collection, which accounts for about

30 percent of tax revenues. A computer database was created to identify defaulters, while attention was focused on recovering major outstanding tax amounts. Annual property tax collection increased by 55 percent.

In the mid-1990s, as stated earlier, the AMC also introduced a number of management reforms such as computerisation of accounts and upgrading of the workforce. In April 1996, the Corporation introduced a computerised double-entry accounting system, purchased new computers and recruited chartered accountants to introduce the new system. In 1997, about 40 chartered accountants and business management graduates were recruited. Placed in key administrative and operational positions, these new officers are improving Ahmedabad's service delivery while introducing a new work ethic.

In 1996, the AMC prepared a five-year capital investment plan worth US $150 million for water supply, sewerage, roads, bridges and solid waste management projects. It proposed to meet 30 percent of the total investment requirement from internal accruals, while mobilising the remaining amount through municipal bonds and loans from financial institutions.

Ahmedabad became the first city in India to request and receives a credit rating for a municipal bond issue. The US Agency for International Development's Financial Institutions Reform and Expansion (FIRE) Project played a multifaceted role in assisting Ahmedabad in developing the bond issue. The city was ultimately assigned an 'AA' rating. In 1998, the AMC publicly issued secured redeemable bonds aggregating to a total of 1 Rs billion. City bonds, as they are popularly known, had a face value Rs 1,000 (US $25) each (for cash at par). AMC sold 25 percent of the bonds to the Indian public and the remaining 75 percent to institutional investors.

Because of the fiscal and management reforms, Ahmedabad built an extensive water project, developed mutual partnerships to improve traffic congestion and improved conditions in slums. Ahmedabad demonstrated that municipal bonds could work in India for raising finances for infrastructure projects. However, before actual issuance of bonds, local governments need to institute efficient project management systems and procedures to reduce time delays and cost overruns. The most critical factor for obtaining market finance is a healthy municipal revenue base.

The Rs 1,000-million municipal bond issue of the Ahmedabad Municipal Corporation was a landmark in that it was the first such instrument issued in India without a state guarantee and represented the first step towards market-based system of local government finance. Significant fiscal and management reforms, including improved tax collection, computerisation of the accounting system, an upgradation in the AMC's workforce and financial management and development of comprehensive capital improvement programme, laid the necessary groundwork for AMC's access to domestic capital markets. National and state-level legislations and policies, such as the passage of the 74th Constitutional Amendment Act and the introduction of various economic reforms, provided ample opportunities to the AMC to access the capital market (Vaidya and Johnson, 2001).

Prior to the inception of reforms in 1994, the AMC did not have a long-term capital investment plan. There existed a physical development plan, which was not based on any financial analysis or projections. Investment decisions were generally made on a year-to-year basis. In 1996, the AMC took the decision to prepare a five-year capital investment or corporate plan. The USAID supported studio on urban environment mapping and environmental risk assessment provided critical impetus for this plan. Based on an analysis of the existing situation, preliminary cost estimates were made for capital investments in water supply, sewerage, roads and bridges, and other services. The preliminary cost of various projects worked out around Rs 11,000 million.

The AMC's intention was to finance the corporate plan through internal accruals, loans from financial institutions, and debt from capital markets. AMC appointed IL&FS as the investment banker for the debt portion of the financing. AMC also invited the FIRE project to provide technical assistance in financial analysis. IL&FS and the FIRE team carried out preliminary revenue and expenditure forecasts. Various options were analysed in terms of alternative revenue assumptions, expenditure forecasts and borrowing. Utilising an iterative process and the most optimistic financial performance levels and lending terms, it was determined that the AMC could afford an investment of Rs 5,500 to Rs 6,000 million. Based on this analysis, AMC reviewed different project priorities and worked out a capital investment plan of Rs 5,974 million for the period from 1996-97 to 2000-01.

8

Health Facilities in Ahmedabad

Ahmedabad is the largest city in the state and provides an extensive network of medical services in the form of hospitals, dispensaries and maternity homes. Ahmedabad Municipal Corporation (AMC) is providing basic amenities according to the provisions of Bombay Municipal Corporation Act, 1949. Along with the obligatory functions like water supply, solid waste management, it provides a large number of voluntary services like undergraduate and postgraduate medical education, hospital services having speciality and superspeciality in various subjects, wide network of health services, maternity home facilities, etc. The Corporation manages three general hospitals, one ophthalmic hospital, one TB hospital, five referral hospitals and 22 allopathic dispensaries. It also provides 18 maternity homes, three ayurvedic dispensaries, two unani dispensaries and four dental clinics. Recently, the Corporation has also taken many measures to provide special health care services for low-income areas in the city. AMC has decided to improve the primary health care and family welfare services the financial assistance of the World Bank.

However, apart from the AMC, the state government is also providing health services through the civil hospital, which has 1,470 beds and treats about half-a-million patients through the outpatient department. The municipal general hospitals put together have the capacity of 1,754 for indoor treatment. The municipal health service with its limitation is offering medical care through its health department. The three general hospitals and other specialised services offer through eye hospitals, infectious disease hospitals, etc., are covering the entire city and the people living in the nearby areas. Nevertheless, the Corporation has not been able to improve the services and infrastructure because of financial limitations. The health infrastructure, which has been created by the AMC over a period, is not getting adequate funds to offer services required in the present context.

Expenditure on Health

The time series data of the AMC health budget show increase in budget allocation each successive year. The budget has increased from Rs 5.4 million in 1987-88 to Rs 53.8 million in 1998-99. The break-up of the health budget across different heads shows that maternity homes have been allocated around 20 percent, of the budget till 1993-94, after which it has gone down each successive year. Other important heads as far as the budget is concerned come out to be health department, dispensaries, national malaria prevention, and mosquito repellent. Another head that has gained importance is road cleaning, which received around 5 percent to 7 percent of the budget till 1994-95, but after which it has started receiving nearly 60 percent to 70 percent of the budget allocated for health. Other heads under the health budget consist of public health, disinfectants, TB, smallpox, family planning, births and deaths registration, food inspection, infectious hospitals, etc.

Average Births and Deaths

The monthly average births in the city of Ahmedabad range between a minimum of 6,520 in 1993 and a maximum of 6,992 in 1990. The average daily births have been in the range of a

Table 8.1
Expenditure on Health

	1987-88	1988-89	1989-90	1990-91	1991-92	1992-93	1993-94	1994-95	1995-96	1996-97	1997-98	1998-99	17/2/2000
Health Department	8497	9548	10769	10900	12676	16973	19389	20279	17799	34637	29539	30165	32910
Public Health Laboratory	347	476	460	469	646	697	789	854	359	609	666	881	1131
Disinfectants	145	139	131	190	177	219	250	265	198	202	239	298	345
Mosquito Repellent	4435	4904	5565	5072	5725	8780	9678	10450	9773	10759	14137	16294	15811
National Malaria Prevention	4525	5125	6722	6626	6919	10131	11549	12535	13432	9939	11639	10311	12200
TB	271	303	353	363	360	530	603	649	481	533	544	649	520
Smallpox	775	902	1048	1083	1129	1584	1826	1966	1669	1830	2460	3393	1450
EPI Scheme	1676	1839	2211	2188	2339	4278	4914	5366	3431	3726	4365	4760	4910
Family Planning	53	67	74	26	98	225	264	284	110	157	124	131	135
Mortuary	1032	942	883	907	863	1438	1553	2027	2099	1625	1275	1713	1887
Births and Deaths Registration	2277	4755	3730	2888	2757	4478	5261	5122	3564	4677	5669	7168	6956
Food Inspection	2227	2338	2716	2993	2970	4574	5177	5672	6014	5386	6479	8432	10244
Road Cleaning	3174	3678	4757	6298	5174	6868	7750	162176	201797	233243	275483	380748	346022
Special Expenditure	1507	2268	2360	4103	2392	16115	15045	18618	0	0	0	0	0

Contd...

Contd...

Baal Vikas Yojana	2522	2650	0	0	0	0	0	0	0	0	0	0	0
Grants to Ayurvedic Institutes	51	50	0	0	0	0	0	0	0	0	0	0	0
Slums	0	0	0	0	0	0	0	0	0	0	17383	22604	23878
Dispensaries and Referrals	7102	8707	10632	10097	10049	14990	17510	18645	14195	15977	14894	18999	16081
Maternity Homes	10947	13016	14650	14698	15524	24394	27456	35658	20914	21996	21331	24981	25731
TB Clinics	1298	1693	1561	1862	1780	3060	3428	3669	2573	3033	3416	3553	3948
Infectious Hospitals	903	1510	1319	1198	1580	2215	2836	2529	2416	2656	2204	2959	3390
	53764	64910	69941	71961	73158	121549	135278	306764	300824	350985	411847	538039	507549

Source: Health Department, AMC. Average Births and Deaths

Figure 8.1
Monthly Average Births and Deaths

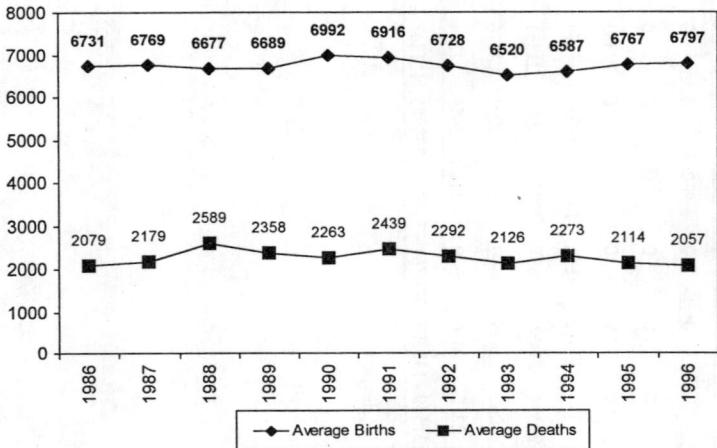

minimum of 214 in 1993 and a maximum of 230 in 1990. The monthly average deaths fall in the range of a minimum of 1,990 in 1997 and a maximum of 2,589 in 1988. The daily average deaths fall in the range of a minimum of 65 deaths in 1997 and a maximum of 85 in the year 1988. Birth and death rates in the past ten years have remained unchanged with some minor variation in some years.

Infant and Maternal Mortality Rates

The infant mortality rate (IMR) has gone down from 45.74 deaths per 1,000 live births in 1986 to 27.63 in 1997. However, it increased to 31.32 in 1998. The IMR has been in the range of a minimum of 27.63 deaths per 1,000 live births in 1997 and a maximum of 56.83 in 1988. The infant death in absolute terms has also decreased from 3,695 in 1986 to 2,297 in 1997. A steady decline has been observed in the infant deaths with the exception of the years 1988 and 1998 when the number exceeded that of previous year and was 4,554 in 1988 – the

Figure 8.2
IMR and MMR

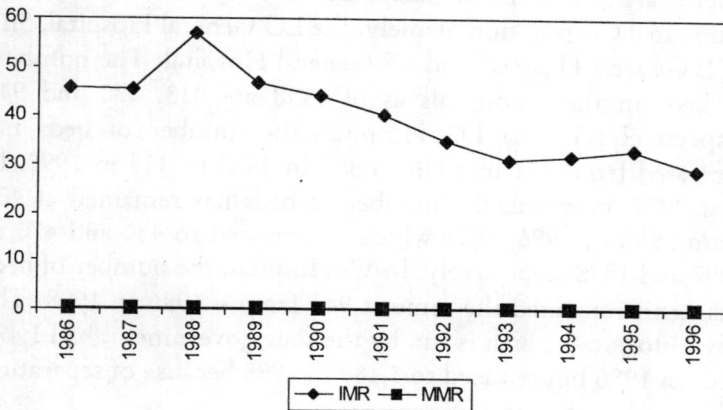

highest ever in the twelve years examined. The number of stillbirths has declined from 1,430 in 1986, and to 665 in 1997. The number of stillbirths falls in the range of a minimum 640 in 1994 and a maximum of 1,579 in 1989.

The number of maternal deaths has also decreased from 30 in the year 1986 to 12 in the year 1998. A general decline has been observed after 1986 with the exception of the years 1991 and 1992. The maternal mortality rate (MMR) has gone down from a maximum of 0.37 in 1986 to 0.15 in 1998.

The city has created a wide network of immunisation centres under the Universal Immunisation Programme (UIP) with the help of the state government and NGOs. The coverage, which was under 50 percent, has substantially increased and it has now reached almost 100 percent in the case of infants. As against only 31 immunisation centres that existed in the city till the year 1986-87, the number has increased to more than 100. It has helped to reduce the IMR. But, the incidence of vaccine preventable diseases has increased tremendously.

Municipal Hospitals

There are three main hospitals run by the Ahmedabad Municipal Corporation, namely, the LG General Hospital, Smt SCL General Hospital and VS General Hospital. The numbers of beds in these hospitals as of 1998 are 413, 470 and 945 respectively. In the LG Hospital, the number of beds has increased from 391 in 1986 to 395 in 1990 to 413 in 1998. In Smt. SCL Hospital, the number of beds has remained at 406 from 1986 to 1996, after which it increased to 430 and 470 in 1997 and 1998 respectively. In VS Hospital, the number of beds has again remained the same at 945 from -- 1986 to 1998. The Civil Hospital, which is run by the state government, had 1,470 beds in 1986 but reduced to 1,189 in 1998 because of separation of some department.

Registered Nursing Homes

The number of private nursing homes has increased steadily from 219 in 1986-87 to 976 in 1998-99. One of the reasons is the static public health facility and quality of services. The numbers of beds in the nursing homes have been categorised as maternity and others.

The numbers of beds for maternity homes have increased from 1,160 in 1986-87 to 2,423 in 1998-99. The number of beds for others has again shown an increase each year since 1986-87. The total number of beds has increased from 2,251 in 1986-87 to 8,330 in 1998-99.

Treatment at Municipal Medical Institutions (General Medical Institutions)

The total number of municipal medical institutions has declined from 36 in 1986 to 29 in 1998. A rise in the number of medical institutions has been observed in 1989 to 37 which remained till 1992. Thereafter, it started declining since 1993 when it was 34 and finally in 1998 it declined to 29.

Table 8.2

Beds in Municipal Hospitals

Name of Hospital	1986	1987	1988	1989	1990	1991	1992	1993	1994	1995	1996	1997	1998
LG Hospital	391	391	391	391	395	403	403	403	403	403	403	413	413
Smt. SCL Hospital	406	406	406	406	406	406	406	406	406	406	406	430	470
VS Hospital	945	945	945	945	945	945	945	945	945	945	945	945	945
Civil Hospital	1470	1209	1209	1209	1209	1209	1209	1209	1209	1209	1209	1189	1189

Source: Statistical Outline of Ahmedabad City, 1998-99.

Table 8.3
Registered Private Nursing Homes

No. of Nursing Homes		Number of Beds		
		Maternity	Others	Total
1986-87	219	1,160	1,091	2,251
1987-88	234	1,238	1,239	2,477
1988-89	268	1,368	1,346	2,714
1989-90	285	1,438	1,406	2,834
1990-91	337	1,570	1,593	3,163
1991-92	408	1,736	1,967	3,703
1992-93	447	1,759	2,230	3,989
1993-94	510	1,854	2,688	4,542
1994-95	574	1,927	3,110	5,037
1995-96	681	2,115	3,804	5,919
1996-97	786	2,212	4,523	6,735
1997-98	853	2,323	4,928	7,305
1998-99	976	2,423	5,907	8,330

Source: Statistical Outline of Ahmedabad City, 1998-99.

Although the total number of beds in medical institutions have remained more or less the same, i.e., 1,886 in 1986, and 1,887 in 1996, it increased to 1,921 and 1,953 in the next two years respectively. There has been fluctuation in the number of beds between a maximum of 1,934 in 1992 and a minimum of 1,887, 1993 onwards. The total number of outdoor cases treated declined for two years after 1986 at the rate of 20.84 percent and 2.23 percent respectively; after which there was an increase of 12.4 percent in 1989. There has been a decline in the number of outdoor cases treated ever since with the exception of 1996 when it has increased by 7.57 percent, after which it increased noticeably reaching 19.25 percent increase in 1997-98. The maximum number of outdoor cases treated has been 22,45,249 in the year 1989 and the minimum 14,59,104 in the year 1995.

Table 8.4
Treatment at Municipal Medical Institutions
(General Medical Institutions*)

Year	Total No. of Units	Total No. of Beds	Cases Treated			
			Outdoor	Percent Change	Indoor	Percent Change
1986	36	1886	2,429,525		100,696	
1987	36	1904	2,010,575	-20.84	98,966	-1.75
1988	36	1904	1,966,730	-2.23	117,561	15.82
1989	37	1923	2,245,249	12.40	109,974	-6.90
1990	37	1926	1,924,981	-16.64	104,485	-5.25
1991	37	1934	1,811,042	-6.29	101,481	-2.96
1992	37	1934	1,738,310	-4.18	96,485	-5.18
1993	34	1887	1,544,967	-12.51	87,484	-10.29
1994	34	1887	1,532,636	-0.80	85,100	-2.80
1995	34	1887	1,459,104	-5.04	83,684	-1.69
1996	30	1887	1,578,577	7.57	93,755	10.74
1997	30	1921	1,718,076	8.12	100,953	7.13
1998	29	1953	2,127,705	19.25	103,285	2.26

* Includes three general hospitals, five referral hospitals, all dispensaries and Kashiben General Hospital, Vatwa.

Source: Statistical Outline of Ahmedabad City, 1998-99.

A general decline has been observed in the indoor cases treated with the exception of the years 1988 and 1996 when these have increased by 15.82 percent and 10.74 percent of the previous year. The maximum rate of decline has been observed in the year 1993 at 10.29 percent of the previous year. The maximum number of indoor cases treated has been 1,17,561 in the year 1988 and the minimum number has been 83,684 in the year 1995. Both the indoor and outdoor cases are declining over a period of ten years and it again a serious concern for the health planners and city managers.

Treatment at Municipal Medical Institutions
(Specialised Medical Institutions)

The number of specialised municipal medical institutions indicates a similar trend as that of the general municipal medical institutions. The number of such institutions has remained the same at 25 from 1986 to 1992. The specialised municipal medical institutions have reduced to 20 in 1993, 19 in 1996 and 1997 and reached the lowest of 14 at 1998. The total number of beds in the specialised medical institutions has remained 702 from 1986 to 1992; after which as with the decrease in the actual number of the medical institutions themselves, the number of beds has reduced to 491 in 1993, 457 in 1996 and 1997 and reached 376 in 1998.

Table 8.5
Treatment at Municipal Medical Institutions
(Specialised Medical Institutions*)

Year	Total No. of Units	Total No. of Beds	Cases Treated			
			Outdoor	Percent Change	Indoor	Percent Change
1986	25	702	350,574		19,430	
1987	25	702	323,070	-8.51	17,959	-8.19
1988	25	702	357,294	9.58	18,696	3.94
1989	25	702	348,656	-2.48	16,180	-15.55
1990	25	702	363,680	4.13	15,798	-2.42
1991	25	702	314,745	-15.55	15,778	-0.13
1992	25	702	319,417	1.46	14,582	-8.20
1993	20	491	310,255	-2.95	16,211	10.05
1994	20	491	315,966	1.81	15,874	-2.12
1995	20	491	328,730	3.88	19,843	20.00
1996	19	457	357,387	8.02	22,047	10.00
1997	19	457	360,960	0.99	22,574	2.33
1998	14	376	247,878	-45.62	11,811	-91.13

* Includes three specialised hospitals, all maternity homes and dental clinics.
Source: Statistical Outline of Ahmedabad City, 1998-99.

There has been a rise and fall in successive years in the number of both the outdoor and the indoor cases treated, showing no definite trend until 1993. Since 1994, there has been a steady rise in the number of outdoor cases treated. The maximum number of outdoor cases treated has been 3,63,680 in 1990 and the minimum being 3,10,255 in 1993. The indoor cases treated have shown a sudden increase in 1995 and 1996 of 20 percent and 10 percent respectively over the previous year. The maximum number of indoor cases treated has been 19,843 in 1995 and the minimum being 14,582 in 1992.

Treatment at Municipal Dispensaries and Referral Hospitals

The number of municipal dispensaries has remained 28 since 1986 to 1992, after which it has declined to 25, and finally to 20 in 1998. The number of referral hospitals has remained the same at five since 1986 until 1998. The number of beds at the referral hospitals, however, has decreased from 162 in 1992 to 115 in 1993 and remained the same till 1998.

In municipal dispensaries, both the new and old cases treated are reducing during the years between 1986 and 1997 with some variations in some years. However, in 1998, both the new and old cases treated show a major increase with new being 3,09,907 and old being 3,92,026. The total cases range between a maximum of 8,43,972 in 1988 and a minimum of 3,62,081 in 1996. There are two cases where the Corporation has handed over the dispensary to a charity trust. The Corporation is now ready to hand over more dispensaries to charity trusts and other organisations, just for reducing their own burden of providing services.

The Paldi Child Welfare Centre was handed over to the Divyajyot Ayurvedic Research Foundation in 1996. The centre was closed for several years, when a proposal from the Foundation was received for running it. The Foundation pays

Table 8.6
Treatment at Municipal Dispensaries and Referral Hospitals

Year	No. of Dispensaries	No. of Beds	Cases Treated			
			Outdoor			Indoor
			New	Old	Total	
1986	28		262365	449,717	712,082	
	5*	162	114030	379,866	493,896	4,993
1987	28		267223	424,656	691,879	
	5*	162	84222	239,428	323,650	3,998
1988	28		339502	504,470	843,972	
	5*	162	105088	287,684	392,772	3,967
1989	28		329127	506,037	835,164	
	5*	162	97765	241,949	339,714	2,902
1990	28		301,308	425,575	726,883	
	5*	162	66,380	121,435	187,815	2,987
1991	28		251,360	335,280	586,640	
	5*	162	31,665	148,799	180,464	2,343
1992	28		274,245	314,893	589,138	
	5*	162	76,744	129,714	206,458	2,250
1993	25		211,823	279,986	491,809	
	5*	115	31,590	87,638	119,228	2,693
1994	25		222,159	277,119	499,278	
	5*	115	65,338	125,073	190,411	2,345
1995	25		154,709	218,790	373,499	
	5*	115	37,134	130,925	168,059	3,922
1996	21		155,748	206,333	362,081	
	5*	115	39,546	130,541	170,087	4,894
1997	21		149,153	240,474	389,627	
	5*	115	42,958	142,208	185,166	6,719
1998	20		309,907	392,026	701,933	
	5*	115	35,067	122,542	157,609	4,944

* referral hospital
Source: Statistical Outline of Ahmedabad City, 1998-99.

Rs 101 as token fee per year. It has to submit a report to the Municipal Commissioner every six months giving all the details concerning running of the centre, the number of cases, type of diseases, etc. The kinds of services offered are treatment of kidney problems, cancer and heart diseases along with other general health problems.

Likewise, the Tapiben Hiralal Babalal Mehta Dispensary and Maternity Home was handed over to the Polio Foundation in June 4, 1992. The dispensary was given for five months after which the agreement was renewed. The cost of running the dispensary was turning out to be greater than the benefit to the citizens. A proposal was received from the trust for running the dispensary, which was accepted by the Corporation. The Foundation pays a token fee of Rs 101 per year to the Corporation. The services provided include treatment, operation, callipers and a physiotherapy centre for polio patients. They also have a marriage bureau for polio-affected people.

Referral Hospitals

The number of beds in the referral hospitals has remained 162 from 1986 to 1992. In 1993, the number of beds has declined to 115 and has remained the same until 1998. The new cases treated at the referral hospitals range between a maximum of 1,14,030 in 1986 and a minimum of 31,590 in 1993. The number of old cases treated at the referral hospitals range between a maximum of 3,79,866 in 1986 and a minimum of 87,638 in 1993. Similarly, the indoor cases treated at the referral hospitals range between a maximum of 6,719 in 1997 and a minimum of 2,250 in 1992. The trend shows a general decrease in the number of indoor cases treated since 1986 until 1994. A sudden increase in the number of indoor cases treated by the referral hospitals has been observed from 1995 onwards.

Treatment at VS General Hospital

The VS Hospital, which is run by the Ahmedabad Municipal Corporation (AMC), caters not only to the population residing within the boundary of the Corporation but much beyond. Although, due to lack of data availability, it is difficult to assess the actual number of cases treated from within and outside the municipal boundary. The number of beds in the VS General Hospital has remained the same at 945 since 1986. Since 1986, the number of new outdoor cases has increased for two years, the increase has been more in the year 1988, at 11.85 percent over the previous year; after which, there has been a decline in the number of new outdoor cases. Maximum decline of 19.85 percent over the previous year has been observed in the year

Table 8.7
Treatment at VS General Hospital

Year	No. of Beds	Cases Treated						Indoor
		Outdoor						
		New	Percent Change	Old	Percent Change	Total	Percent Change	
1986	945	176,566		301,733		478,299		50,698
1987	945	186,665	5.41	307,885	2.00	494,550	3.29	49,127
1988	945	211,747	11.85	363,928	15.40	575,675	14.09	59,426
1989	945	198,388	-6.73	366,251	0.63	564,639	-1.95	56,580
1990	945	186,284	-6.50	294,049	-24.55	480,333	-17.55	51,900
1991	945	155,436	-19.85	282,876	-3.95	438,312	-9.59	50,639
1992	945	145,911	-6.53	260,100	-8.76	406,011	-7.96	46,644
1993	945	132,675	-9.98	236,859	-9.81	369,534	-9.87	42,524
1994	945	123,339	-7.57	215,409	-9.96	338,748	-9.09	41,192
1995	945	124,999	1.33	272,358	20.91	397,357	14.75	39,204
1996	945	120,238	-3.96	290,558	6.26	410,796	3.27	42,768
1997	945	149,946	19.81	300,230	3.22	450,176	8.75	44,520
1998	945	161,730	7.26	356,456	15.77	518,186	13.12	45,525

Source: Statistical Outline of Ahmedabad City, 1998-99.

1991, after which there has been a further decline of 6.53 percent, 9.98 percent and 7.57 percent in three consecutive years. However, after 1996, the number of cases has increased for the two successive years of 1997 and 1998.

The old outdoor cases have increased for three consecutive years since 1986. The maximum increase as in the new outdoor cases has been observed in 1988 of 15.4 percent over the previous year. There is a very slight increase in 1989, after which the number of cases treated has shown a sudden decline of 24.55 percent in 1990. The number of cases has steadily declined since 1990 until 1994. A sudden increase in the number of old outdoor cases has been observed in 1995; there has again been an increase of 6.26 percent in 1996 and the increase continued till 1998. The total number of cases treated has been the maximum in 1988 at 5,75,675 and the lowest in 1994 at 3,38,748. Indoor cases have shown a decline from 1986 to 1987; after which following a similar trend as the outdoor cases there has been a sudden increase of 17.33 percent over the previous year in 1988. Since 1988, there has been a decline in the number of cases till 1987, and has been the maximum in 1993 of 9.69 percent over the previous year. There has been an increase in 1996 of 8.33 percent.

Treatment at LG General Hospital

The number of beds in LG General Hospital was 391 in 1986 until 1989; it increased to 395 in 1990, to 403 from 1991 to 1996, to 413 in 1997 and remained the same in 1998. The number of new cases treated has shown a rise for two years after 1986 at the rate of 8.53 percent and 15.82 percent respectively. After 1988, there has been a general decline in the number of new cases treated until 1994. The year 1996 has shown a sudden increase of 16.65 percent over the previous year. The new cases treated at the LG General Hospital range between a low of 73,806 in 1994 to a high of 1, 05,502 in 1998. The number of old outdoor cases fluctuated greatly, with one year showing a decrease by approximately 50,000 patients, the following year showing an increase by approximately 50,000 patients, and this trend continued till 1991 starting from 1986. After 1990, the number has shown a steady decline for five consecutive years and has shown a sudden increase of 18.19 percent over the previous year in 1996 and continued to increase fractionally for the next two years. The number of old outdoor cases ranged between a minimum of 1,31,327 in 1995 and a maximum of 2,09,257 in 1986. The number of indoor cases is fluctuating over a period of ten years.

Table 8.8
Treatment at LG General Hospital

Year	No. of Beds	Cases Treated							
		Outdoor						Indoor	Percent change
		New	Percent Change	Old	Percent Change	Total	Percent Change		
1986	391	75,600		209,257		284,857		22,071	
1987	391	82,654	8.53	156,399	-33.80	239,053	-19.16	22,061	-0.05
1988	391	98,193	15.82	198,502	21.21	296,695	19.43	26,783	17.63
1989	391	89,574	-9.62	159,700	-24.30	249,274	-19.02	24,835	-7.84
1990	395	86,353	-3.73	199,421	19.92	285,774	12.77	25,876	4.02
1991	403	91,677	5.81	194,952	-2.29	286,629	0.30	25,722	-0.60
1992	403	90,565	-1.23	170,995	-14.01	261,560	-9.58	24,881	-3.38
1993	403	82,636	-9.60	144,667	-18.20	227,303	-15.07	21,527	-15.58
1994	403	73,806	-11.96	131,722	-9.83	205,528	-10.59	21,485	-0.20
1995	403	74,701	1.20	131,327	-0.30	206,028	0.24	20,954	-2.53
1996	403	89,628	16.65	160,533	18.19	250,161	17.64	23,637	11.35
1997	413	95,579	6.23	162,533	1.23	258,112	3.08	25,049	5.64
1998	413	1,05,502	9.41	173,128	6.12	278,630	7.36	25,743	2.70

Source: Statistical Outline of Ahmedabad City, 1998-99.

Treatment at Smt. SCL General Hospital

The number of beds at Smt. SCL General Hospital has remained 406 since 1986 until 1996. It increased to 430 in 1997 and further to 470 in 1998. The treatments of new outdoor cases have shown an increase for three consecutive years starting 1986, after which there has been a decline for three consecutive years. In terms of percent change, the largest decline of 12.13 percent, over the previous year has been observed in 1989, and the largest increase of 19.66 percent over the previous year has been observed in 1996. The number of cases has ranged between a minimum of 67,485 in 1990 and a maximum of 1,09,122 in 1998. The old outdoor cases have shown a small decline for five years starting 1986, after which there has been great fluctuation in the number of cases treated with an increase of 28.08 percent over the previous year in 1991, then a decrease of 29.06 percent in 1992 and again followed by a decrease of 25.17 percent in 1993. The indoor cases treated have shown an increase in number for two years starting 1986, when the number increased from 22,934 in 1986 to 27,385 in 1988, and 1989 onwards there has been a decline till 1995, after which there has been a sudden increase by 12.92 percent over the previous year.

Treatment at Civil Hospital (Government)

The Civil Hospital, which is run by the state government, is the largest hospital in the entire state. It caters not only to the residents of Ahmedabad city but also to the population of the entire state. The numbers of both indoor and outdoor cases treated at this hospital far exceed the other hospitals. However, the number of beds has reduced from 1,470 in 1986-87 to 1,209 in 1987-88. This decrease in the number of beds has been due to the separation of ophthalmology, nephrology and paraplegia sections from Civil Hospital. Since 1987-88, the number of beds has remained the same till 1996-97. After that it decreased further to 1,189 and remained the same till 1997-98. The outdoor cases treated have ranged between a minimum of 4,09,868 in 1986-87 and a maximum of 5,69,410 in 1994-95. Overall, there has not been much fluctuation in the number of

Table 8.9

Treatment at Smt. SCL General Hospital

Year	No. of Beds	Cases Treated							
		Outdoor						Indoor	Percent Change
		New	Percent Change	Old	Percent Change	Total	Percent Change		
1986	406	76,603		183,788		260,391		22,934	
1987	406	79,386	3.51	182,057	-0.95	261,443	0.40	23,780	3.56
1988	406	84,362	5.90	173,254	-5.08	257,616	-1.49	27,385	13.16
1989	406	75,236	-12.13	166,613	-3.99	241,849	-6.52	25,037	-9.38
1990	406	67,485	-11.49	164,693	-1.17	232,178	-4.17	23,160	-8.10
1991	406	75,897	11.08	229,003	28.08	304,900	23.85	22,394	-3.42
1992	406	78,620	3.46	177,436	-29.06	256,056	-19.08	22,394	0.00
1993	406	76,371	-2.94	237,121	25.17	313,492	18.32	20,449	-9.51
1994	406	68,266	-11.87	210,639	-12.57	278,905	-12.40	19,860	-2.97
1995	406	71,148	4.05	216,663	2.78	287,811	3.09	19,295	-2.93
1996	406	88,558	19.66	265,425	18.37	353,983	18.69	22,158	12.92
1997	430	97,813	9.46	298,298	11.02	396,111	10.64	24,354	9.02
1998	470	109,122	10.36	320,349	6.88	429,471	7.77	26,736	8.91

Source: Statistical Outline of Ahmedabad City, 1998-99.

outdoor cases treated. The trend has been of a small increase each year. Nevertheless, there has been a decrease in the number in the years 1995-96 and 1996-97.

The number of indoor cases treated has remained more or less the same since 1986-87 until 1996-97. The absolute numbers of cases have ranged between a minimum of 49,671 in 1989-90 and a maximum of 65,579 in 1995-96. The numbers of deliveries each year have ranged between a maximum of 5,835 in 1997-98 and a minimum of 4,802 in 1986-87. The number of major operations has ranged between a minimum of 10,171 in 1989-90 and a maximum of 15,237 in 1998-99. The number of minor operations has ranged between a minimum of 10,071 in 1998-99 and a maximum of 19,119 in 1987-88. The numbers of deaths each year have ranged between a minimum of 3,400 in 1989-90 and a maximum of 4,425 in 1995-96. The average number of deaths each year between 1986 and 1999 comes out to be 4,149.

Table 8.10
Treatment at Civil Hospital (Government)

Year	No. of Beds	Cases Treated		No. of Deliveries	No. of Major Operations		No. of Deaths
		Outdoor	Indoor		Major	Minor	
1986-87	1470	409868	55810	4802	11255	14324	3818
1987-88*	1209	459870	58578	5309	10942	19119	3730
1988-89	1209	450740	59158	5227	11026	17169	4430
1989-90	1209	468728	49671	5023	10171	12667	3400
1990-91	1209	457327	62672	5096	11650	12261	3982
1991-92	1209	458740	64095	5044	12427	14716	4392
1992-93	1209	487070	62203	5346	11486	14876	4263
1993-94	1209	507998	56270	5145	12796	13937	3969
1994-95	1209	569410	63586	5325	11781	13304	4133
1995-96	1209	555495	65579	5578	13712	11380	4425
1996-97	1209	487613	62339	5278	14124	10727	4355
1997-98	1189	524256	61470	5835	14742	10827	4304
1998-99	1189	521629	62528	5390	15237	10071	4736

* Number of beds reduced due to separation of ophthalmology, nephrology and paraplegia sections from Civil Hospital.

Source: Statistical Outline of Ahmedabad City, 1998-99.

Treatment at Municipal Maternity Homes

The total number of maternity homes has decreased from 18 in 1986 to 13 in 1993, to 12 in 1996 and to 8 in 1998. The number of beds has decreased along with the decrease in the number of maternity homes, from 460 in 1986 to 249 in 1993, to 215 in 1996 and finally to 134 in 1998. The new outdoor cases treated range between a low of 32,853 in 1987 to a maximum of 58,582 in 1996. The number fluctuated between 1986 and 1990, after 1990 it decreased in 1991, after which it has shown a steady increase. It started decreasing again after 1996 and became 57,417 in 1997 and a very low 22,605 in 1998.

Table 8.11
Treatment at Municipal Maternity Homes

Year	No. of Maternity Homes	No. of Beds	Cases Treated			
			Outdoor			Indoor
			New	Old	Total	
1986	18	460	46,051	105,756	151,807	13,399
1987	18	460	32,853	73,161	106,014	10,139
1988	18	460	40,445	92,449	132,894	10,097
1989	18	460	39,581	99,116	138,697	8,505
1990	18	460	48,549	121,008	169,557	8,922
1991	18	460	42,178	77,274	119,452	8,079
1992	18	460	43,880	77,192	121,072	7,838
1993	13	249	47,182	75,875	123,057	8,761
1994	13	249	48,451	65,908	114,359	8,497
1995	13	249	56,964	72,687	129,651	13,131
1996	12	215	58,582	74,932	133,514	15,065
1997	12	215	57,417	76,345	133,762	15,993
1998	08	134	22,605	36,002	58,607	5,332

Source: Statistical Outline of Ahmedabad City, 1998-99.

Following the same trend as the new outdoor cases, old outdoor cases too slumped after 1986, and then kept on increasing till 1990, when it reached the maximum at 1,21,008. After 1990, the number has suddenly plunged and has remained more or less the same until 1996. It increased marginally in 1997 but fell again in 1998. Apart from this, there are three cases of handing over of maternity homes to private trusts for running, one of the cases of Tapiben Hiralal Babalal Mehta Dispensary and Maternity Home has been discussed earlier, and the other two are as follows:

- Chhipa Jamal Municipal Maternity Home: It was given to the Chhipa Welfare Organisation in June 4, 1998. It primarily provides services for poor and middle class patients. The facilities provided are x-ray, sonography, pathology and minor operations. This Home provided great help during the GE epidemic of January 2000.
- Seth Bhikabhai Trikamlal Municipal Maternity Home: It was given to the Karuna Trust in November 3, 1997. It provides facilities for polio operations, eye operations, homeopathic centre, child health centre, oxygen centre, ambulance and wheel chair. There is also a proposal for giving C.C. Gandhi Maternity Home (Relief Road) to Samjubhai Charitable Trust.

Treatment at Specialised Medical Institutions

The Ahmedabad Municipal Corporation (AMC) also runs one TB hospital. The number of beds in this hospital has remained 32 since 1986 until 1996. The number of new outdoor cases ranges between a minimum of 6,521 in 1986 and a maximum of 9,318 in 1989. The highest numbers of cases were witnessed in the years 1987 to 1991, after which the number of cases has declined. The old outdoor cases too show an upward trend in the years 1986 to 1989, after which the average number of cases each year has declined to the range of 9,697 in 1991 and 11,779 in 1994. Again, in 1996, the number has shown a sudden increase. Overall, the old outdoor cases range between a minimum of 9,697 in 1991 and a maximum of 20,023 in 1988. The number of beds in Nagri eye hospital, which offers specialised eye care service, has remained 100 since 1986 until 1998. The number of beds at infectious diseases hospital has remained 110 since 1986 until 1998. There are also four dental clinics run by the AMC. This number has remained the same till 1997 and then reduced to three in 1998.

Figure 8.3
Yearwise GE Cases

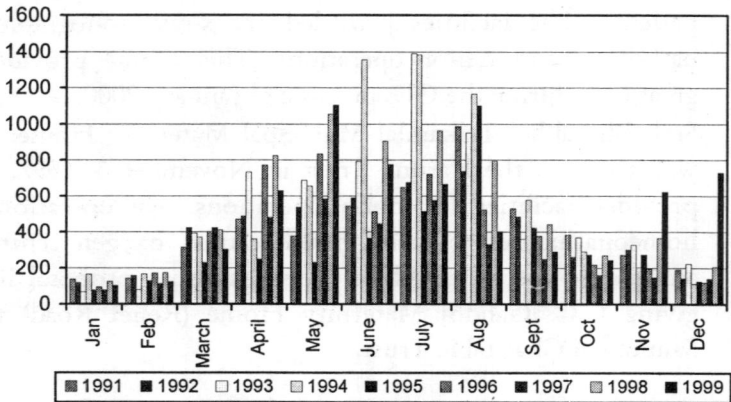

Source: Health Department, AMC.

Year-wise GE Cases and Deaths

The maximum numbers of GE cases are observed in the months of May, June, July and August, with the peak being in June and July and continue up to October. The greatest numbers of GE cases in the ten years under observation are observed in the year 1993 with 1,389 cases in July and in the year 1994 with 1,355 cases in June and 1,383 cases in July. The incidence of GE cases was also high in January 2000 with 1,205 cases. The number of GE cases ranges between a maximum of 6,811 cases in 1994 to a minimum of 3,729 cases in 1997. The number of deaths caused by GE ranges between a maximum of 58 in 1991 and a minimum of nine in 1997, which amount to 1.16 percent and 0.24 percent respectively of the total number of cases.

Year-wise Viral Hepatitis Cases and Deaths

The highest incidence of viral hepatitis cases is noticed in the months of November and December 1993, with the number of cases being as high as 1,069 and 1,020 respectively. The number of cases is also observed to be high in June 1999 with 483 cases being recorded.

The number of viral hepatitis cases in the years under observation ranges between a maximum of 2,591 in the year 1993 and a minimum of 512 in 1998. Although, the actual number of cases of viral hepatitis is observed to be lower than that of GE cases, the percentage of deaths is much more. The percentage of deaths vary between a maximum of 5.15 in 1991 to a minimum of 0.39 in 1999. In absolute numbers, the maximum number of deaths (80) has been observed in 1993, which is 3.09 percent of the total cases, and a minimum of five deaths in 1999, which is also the year with the minimum percentage of deaths.

Year-wise Typhoid Cases and Deaths
The typhoid cases are observed to be the highest (323) in June 1994, the minimum number of cases (4) is observed in January 1999. In general, a higher incidence of cases is noticed from April to July each year. The number of typhoid cases each year

Figure 8.4
Year-wise Typhoid Cases and Deaths

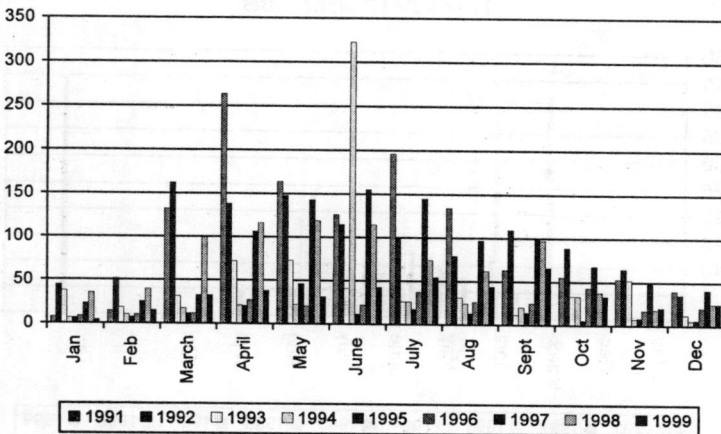

ranges between a minimum of 164 in 1995 and a maximum of 1,247 in 1991. The number of deaths caused by typhoid ranges between no deaths in the years 1996 and 1999 to eight deaths that comes to 0.64 percent of the total number of cases in 1991.

Year-wise Cholera Cases and Deaths

The maximum number of cholera cases (45) in a month has been recorded in December 1999. A high incidence of cholera has also been observed in March and April 1996. The number of cholera cases each year varies between a minimum of 20 in 1995 to a maximum of 100 in 1996.

In the years under observation, only one death has been recorded due to cholera in the year 1994.

New Initiative

A new programme under *Jeevan Daan* (Gift of Life) or Child Survival Programme was introduced in Ahmedabad. These four-year *Jeevan Daan* programmes are implemented in the urban slums within the Jamalpur, Raipur, Baharampura, Danilimda

Figure 8.5
Year-wise Cholera Cases

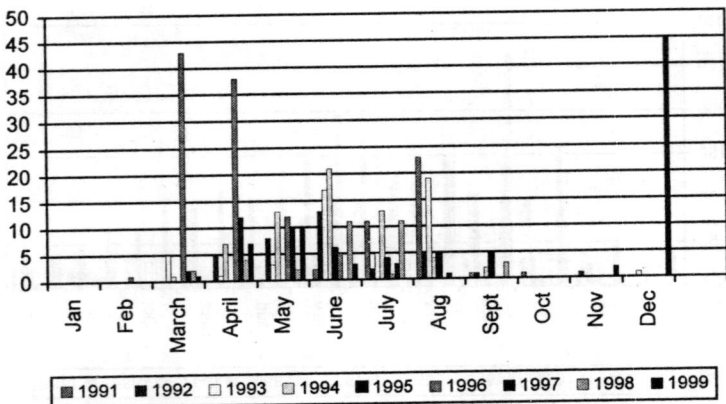

Source: Health Department, AMC.

and Dariyapur municipal wards. The programme is funded by the U.S. Agency for International Development (USAID) Bureau of Humanitarian Response, Office of Private and Voluntary Cooperation, and is benefiting some 45,000 children. The programme builds on USAID's experience in managing public health education, child survival and family planning programmes, and applies lessons learned from previous USAID-funded child survival programmes in the South Pacific. Counterpart's Senior Public Health Specialist, Darshana Vyas, who has over 12 years of experience in the design, implementation and evaluation of health programmes in India, manages the programme.

Counterpart's local NGO partner, Sanchetana, provides public health education and other social services in the targeted slums. The state government of Gujarat and the Ministry of Health, as well as the Ahmedabad Municipal Corporation (AMC), have played a vital role in the child survival programme's design. The programme is focused on four interventions, viz., pneumonia case management, diarrhea case management, nutrition, and immunisation, which address the major causes of child mortality and morbidity in the urban slums.

The programme's main strategy is to promote healthy behaviours in mothers and other caretakers in the home, through health education initiatives, which improve their access to information and services. Counterpart is working with local NGOs to assist them in training and community mobilisation, and to help them develop public health education strategies. Counterpart and its partner NGOs will train community health workers and local AMC staff to communicate messages to mothers, who will also be exposed to the same messages via mass media and other channels. In addition, the programme will provide training for AMC health staff in the case management of pneumonia and diarrhea, increasing access to higher quality services.

9

Educational Facilities in Ahmedabad

The Ahmedabad Municipal Corporation (AMC) is providing primary education through different types of schools within its jurisdiction. The Primary School Board is responsible for the management of these schools. Its activities are divided into five zones: zone 1 consists of Kankaria area, zone 2 consists of Jamalpur area, zone 3 consists of Ellisbridge area, zone 4 consists of schools of other mediums like Urdu and Hindi, and the last zone 5 consists of the east zone which was transferred from Jilla Panchyat to the Corporation when it was merged with the municipal limit.

The primary schools run on 80 percent grants and the Corporation provides 20 percent of the expenditure. The Corporation provides uniforms to some children, free textbooks to all and scholarships are given to students belonging to SCs/STs/OBCs. In each of the 43 wards of the city there is at least one primary school. Each year, the best teacher award also known as the Mayor's Award is given to a teacher from the primary school who is recognised for his/her efforts towards education, or starting some innovative activity for students or the results of the students make evident the quality of education provided by that teacher.

Figure 9.1
Organisational Set-up

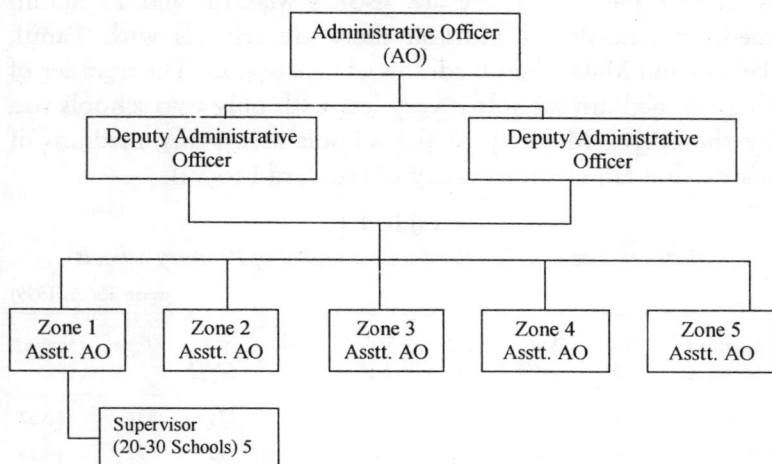

In addition, the Primary Education Department has ten part-time doctors working for them. These doctors visit schools, examine the student's eye, nose, ear, skin, teeth, etc., and if a student is affected by some ailment, they fill a yellow card for the student. They administer medicines and an affected student is supervised regularly. A supervisor is the person who is directly responsible for schools falling under his bid. One bid consists of around 20-30 schools. The supervisors make daily visits to the schools falling under their bid, supervise proper functioning, and report to the Assistant Administrative Officers.

Medium-wise and Standard-wise Number of Primary Schools

It is evident from Table 9.1 that the largest number of schools are Gujarati medium schools, which amount to nearly 60.67 percent of the total number of primary schools. Next in number follow the Urdu medium schools, which amount to nearly 16.23 percent. Then follow the Hindi medium schools with 12.7 percent. There are also 28 Marathi and 19 Sindhi medium schools. In addition there are schools with Tamil, Telugu and Malayalam mediums of instruction. The number of English medium schools is very less with only two schools run by the AMC. Majority of the schools across any medium of instruction fall in the category of standard I to VII.

Table 9.1

Medium-wise and Standard-wise Number of Primary Schools

(as on 30/09/1999)

Medium/ Standard	Std. I-II	Std. I-III	Std. I-IV	Std. I-V	Std. I-VI	Std. I-VII	Total	Percent
Gujarati	8	88	68	6	3	171	344	60.67
Urdu	5	26	21	2	0	38	92	16.23
Hindi	5	23	1	0	1	42	72	12.70
Marathi	0	7	4	0	1	16	28	4.94
Sindhi	0	0	4	2	0	13	19	3.35
Tamil	0	0	0	0	0	7	7	1.23
Telugu	0	0	0	0	0	2	2	0.35
Malayalam	0	0	0	0	0	1	1	0.18
English	0	0	0	0	0	2	2	0.35
Total	18	144	98	10	5	292	567	100.00

Source: Annual Report, 1998-99, District Primary Education Department.

The AMC is mainly responsible to provide primary education services through pre-primary and primary schools. It was running about 187 pre-primary schools in 1998-99. However, the available statistics shows a clear declining trend, from 240 in 1994-95 to 205 in 1996-97, to 189 in 1997-98 and to 187 in 1998-99. The number of students attending these classes also declined from 11,486 to only 7,642 during the period of 1989-90 to 1998-99. The number of primary schools, on the other hand, remained constant during 1991-99 (about 487). This is also true for numbers of students and teachers with some

Figure 9.2

Education: Percentage of Revenue Expenditure

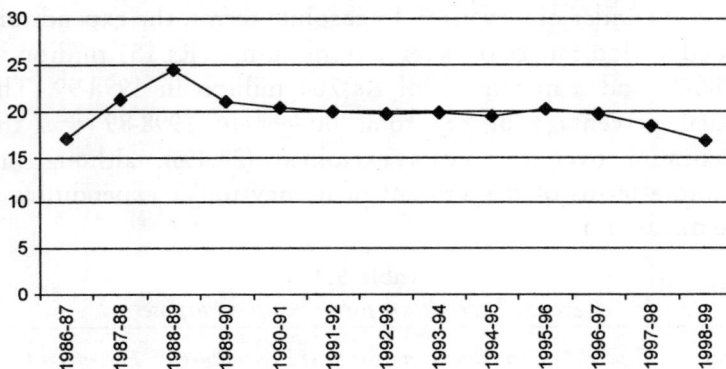

Table 9.2

Expenditure for Education Purposes

Year	No. of Schools	Average Expenditure in Rs		Average Number of Students per School		No. of Primary School	
		Per School	Per Student	Municipal	Private	Municipal	Private
1961-62	247	32126	65	298	196	412	196
1971-72	371	95916	222	433	258	371	348
1981-82	496	163099	373	437	357	496	374
1991-92	555	585604	1260	465	399	555	587
1994-95	570	796009	1752	454	427	570	707
1995-96	564	952918	2118	450	450	564	720
1996-97	565	1047113	2473	423	498	565	720
1997-98	567	1083421	2644	410	525	567	624
1998-99	567	1316755	3301	399	529	567	650

marginal variations. However, the number of private primary schools increased rapidly from 376 in 1985-86 to 720 in 1996-97.

It fell sharply to 624 in 1997-98 but again rose to 650 in 1998-99. The general trend of expenditure on education has been in the range of 19 percent to 21 percent of the total expenditure, in the 13 years under observation. In absolute terms, the expenditure on education ranges between a minimum of Rs 151 million in 1986-87 and a maximum of Rs 704 million in 1998-99. The actual percentage of the total budget in 1998-89 was the maximum over the years examined (24.4%), although in absolute terms of the amount of money under expenditure is the maximum.

Table 9.3

Revenue Expenditure for Education Purposes

Year	Expenditure on Education (Rs. in million)	Revenue Expenditure (Rs. in million)	Percentage to Total
1986-87	151	889	17
1987-88	221	1034	21.3
1988-89	304	1243	24.4
1989-90	298	1420	21.0
1990-91	326	1604	20.3
1991-92	348	1749	19.9
1992-93	395	1998	19.7
1993-94	445	2249	19.8
1994-95	483	2477	19.5
1995-96	577	2849	20.3
1996-97	634	3219	19.7
1997-98	665	3614	18.4
1998-99	704	4189	16.8

Source: Statistical Outline of Ahmedabad City, 1998-99.

Primary Educational Institutions

The number of primary educational institutions has increased over the years. Of the primary schools run by the AMC majority are in owned premises. The number of schools in both the owned and rented premises has increased steadily since

Figure 9.3

Number of Municipal and Private Primary Schools

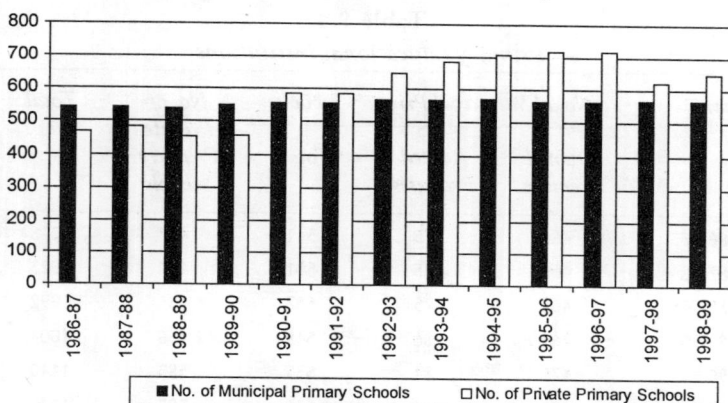

No. of Municipal Primary Schools   □ No. of Private Primary Schools

1990-91. There were about 541 schools run by the AMC in 1986-88, the number declined to 537 in 1988-89, after which there has been a steady increase each year till 1994-95. A marginal decline is observed in the year 1995-96 to 564 but it increased over the next few years till 1998-99.

At times the municipal primary schools receive donations from NGOs and other groups like the Lions Club, the Rotary club, etc. who give small funds for up gradation of facilities like installation of water coolers, renovation work, etc.

The private primary schools that were lesser in number than the municipal primary schools in 1986 to 1990, exceeded in number since 1990-91 and ever since their number has remained higher. The number of private primary schools declined to 455 in the 1988-89 from 482 in 1987-88. After which there has been a constant increase in the number of private primary schools each year, and the number rose to 720 in 1996-97. It fell to 624 in 1997-98 but went up to 650 in 1998-99. As far as the total number of primary schools is concerned including the municipal and private schools, with the exception of 1988-89 when there were 992 schools, there has been an increase each year with the maximum number being 1,285 schools in 1996-97.

Table 9.4
Primary Educational Institutions

Year	No. of Municipal Primary Schools			No. of Private Primary Schools	Total
	Owned Premises	Rented Premises	Total		
1986-87	466	75	541	467	1008
1987-88	466	75	541	482	1023
1988-89	462	75	537	455	992
1989-90	462	86	548	456	1004
1990-91	471	84	555	585	1140
1991-92	471	84	555	585	1140
1992-93	486	80	566	648	1214
1993-94	488	80	568	687	1255
1994-95	490	80	570	707	1277
1995-96	484	80	564	720	1284
1996-97	485	80	565	720	1285
1997-98	487	80	567	624	1191
1998-99	487	80	567	650	1217

Source: Statistical Outline of Ahmedabad City, 1998-99.

Student-Teacher Ratio for Municipal Primary Schools

Barring the year 1986-87, when the student-teacher ratio was 36.6 students per teacher, the student-teacher ratio is observed to be in the range of 39.7 in 1989-90 and 43.4 students per teacher in 1999-99. As of 1998-99, there are about 2,26,153 students.

In the 13 years under examination, the range of students has been between 2,10,317 students in 1986-87 and 2,73,590 students in 1990-91. The number of teachers has been in the range of 5,212 in 1998-99 and 6,889 in 1987-88. Since 1992-93, there has been a decline in the absolute number of teachers each

Figure 9.4
Student-Teacher Ratio

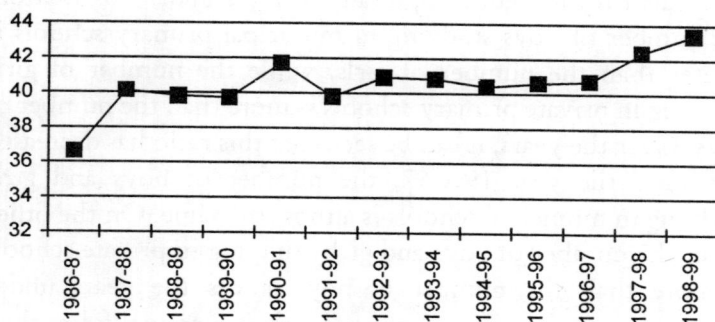

year, finally reaching 5,212 in 1998-99. There has also been a decline in the absolute number of students each year, since 1992-92 to 1998-99 reaching 2,26,153.

Table 9.5
Student-Teacher Ratio for Municipal Primary Schools

Year	Teachers	Students	No. of Students per Teacher
1986-87	5740	210317	36.6
1987-88	6889	253742	40.1
1988-89	6508	261081	39.8
1989-90	6557	260123	39.7
1990-91	6558	273590	41.7
1991-92	6489	257942	39.8
1992-93	6677	273269	40.9
1993-94	6519	266010	40.8
1994-95	6409	258966	40.4
1995-96	6245	253788	40.6
1996-97	5880	239273	40.7
1997-98	5481	232348	42.4
1998-99	5212	226153	43.4

Source: Statistical Outline of Ahmedabad City, 1998-99.

Municipal and Private Primary Schools and Students

As evident from Figure 9.5, in all the years under observation, the number of boys studying in municipal primary schools is greater than the number of girls, while the number of girls studying in private primary schools is more than the number of boys. Over the years, it can be seen that this ratio has decreased and since the year 1996-97, the number of boys and girls studying in municipal schools is almost the same. On the other hand, the number of boys and girls studying in private schools is more than the number of boys across the years under observation; in fact, the number of girls is marginally less than the number of boys only in 1990-91.

Table 9.6
Municipal Primary Schools and Students

Year	No. of Primary Schools	Number of Students			Average No. of Students per School
		Boys	Girls	Total	
1986-87	541	134628	119114	253,742	469
1987-88	541	145547	115534	261,081	483
1988-89	537	135720	123302	259,022	482
1989-90	548	135073	125050	260123	475
1990-91	555	141282	132308	273590	493
1991-92	555	131317	126152	257469	465
1992-93	566	139317	133952	273269	483
1993-94	568	134616	131394	266010	468
1994-95	570	130252	128714	258966	454
1995-96	564	127728	126060	253788	450
1996-97	565	120167	119106	239273	423
1997-98	567	116612	115736	232348	410
1998-99	567	112847	112847	226153	399

Source: Statistical Outline of Ahmedabad City, 1998-99.

Figure 9.5

Ratio of Boys and Girls in Primary Schools: Municipal and Private

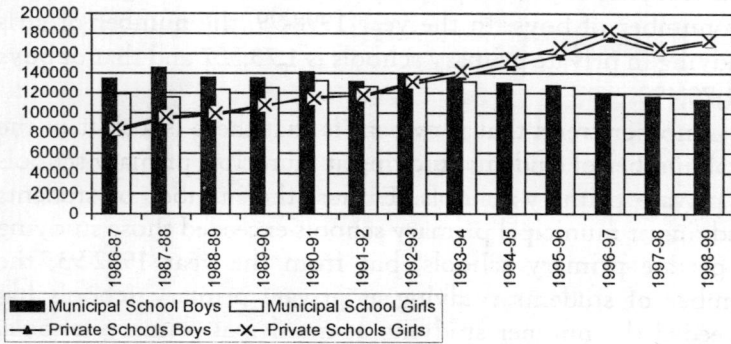

Municipal School Boys ☐ Municipal School Girls
▲ Private Schools Boys ✕ Private Schools Girls

Table 9.7

Private Primary Schools and Students

Year	No. of Primary Schools	Number of Students			Average No. of Students per School
		Boys	*Girls*	*Total*	
1986-87	461	81731	84052	165783	360
1987-88	482	94238	95720	189958	394
1988-89	455	97819	99396	197215	433
1989-90	494	106,210	107,692	213,902	433
1990-91	535	117,025	114,630	231,655	433
1991-92	587	116,205	117,926	234,131	399
1992-93	648	129,320	131,264	260,584	402
1993-94	687	137,705	142,766	280,471	408
1994-95	707	147,369	154,609	301,978	427
1995-96	720	157,680	166,039	323,719	450
1996-97	720	175,680	183,080	358,760	498
1997-98	624	162,372	165,245	327,617	525
1998-99	650	170,490	173,507	343,997	529

Source: School Board Ahmedabad Municipal Corporation.

Over the years, a steady increase has been observed in the number of students, both boys and girls, studying in private primary schools. Starting from the year 1991-92, the number of girls studying in private primary schools has starting exceeding the number of boys. In the year 1998-99, the number of girls studying in private primary schools is 1,73,507 and that of boys is 1,70,490.

Another trend that is evident is that there is a shift in the total number of students studying at municipal primary schools to private primary schools. Earlier, the number of students studying at municipal primary schools exceeded those studying at private primary schools, but from the year 1992-93, the number of students studying at private primary schools has exceeded the number studying at municipal primary schools. With each year, this gap has increased. At the same time, the absolute number of students studying at private primary schools is increasing with rapid speed while those studying at municipal schools are observed to be on the decline ever since 1992-93.

Secondary Educational Institutions

Since 1991-92, when there were about 210 institutions, secondary education institutions declined in the year 1992-92 to

Table 9.8
Secondary Educational Institutions and Pupils

Year	No. of Institutions	Pupils	Teaching Staff	Non-teaching Staff
1991-92	210	70247	2446	805
1992-93	166	43493	1416	830
1993-94	172	44172	1431	834
1994-95	175	47261	1510	874
1995-96	175	50713	1692	874
1996-97	219	56893	1723	870
1997-98	219	56258	1704	870
1998-99	228	58030	1751	910

Source: Statistical Outline of Ahmedabad City, 1998-99.

Figure 9.6

No. of Secondary Educational Institutions

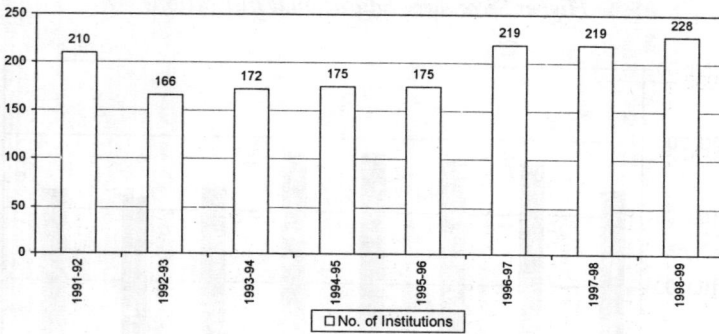

166 institutions, after which, the number increased again to around 175 and remained the same for a couple of years. In the year 1996-97, the number increased to 219 and again to 228 in 1998-99. The number of pupils studying at the secondary schools has also decreased considerably since 1991-92.

Figure 9.7

Number of Students and Teachers in Secondary Educational Institutions

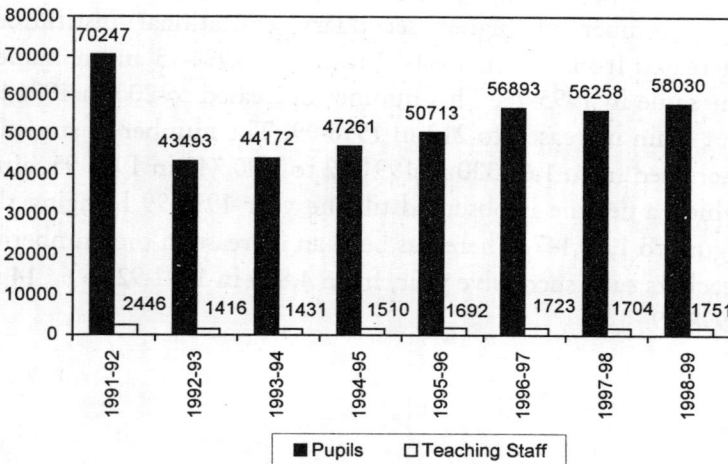

Figure 9.8
*Number of Pupils and Teaching Staff in
Higher Secondary Educational Institutions*

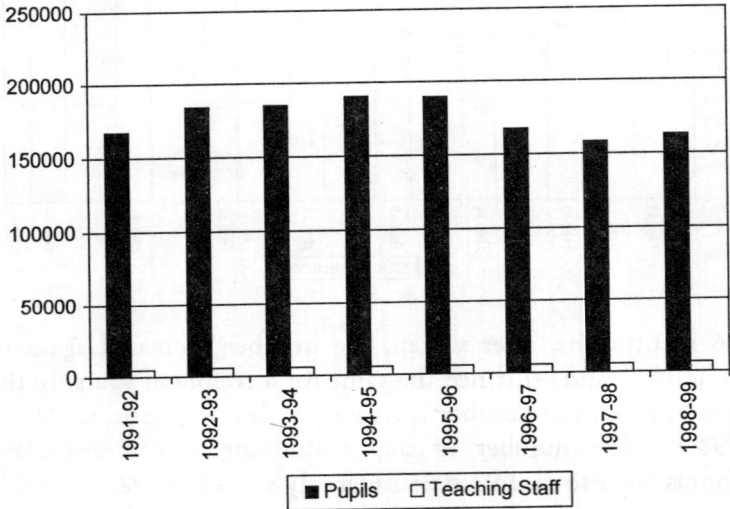

Higher Secondary Educational Institutions

The number of higher secondary educational institutions increased from 212 in 1991-92 to 232 in 1994-95 and remained the same in 1995-96. This number decreased to 205 in 1996-97 but again increased to 212 in 1998-99. The number of students increased from 1,67,330 in 1991-92 to 1,90,748 in 1994-95, after which a decline is observed till the year 1998-99 bringing the figure to 1,63,147. There has been an increase in the number of teachers each successive year, from 4,803 in 1991-92 to 6,214 in 1998-99.

Table 9.9
Higher Secondary Educational Institutions

Year	No. of Institutions	Pupils	Teaching Staff	Non-teaching Staff
1991-92	212	167330	4803	1821
1992-93	228	184232	5318	1832
1993-94	230	184865	5325	1836
1994-95	232	190748	5520	1935
1995-96	232	189374	5523	1935
1996-97	205	167815	5609	1933
1997-98	205	158425	5672	1930
1998-99	212	163147	6214	1950

Source: Statistical Outline of Ahmedabad City, 1998-99.

10

Household Profile of the Study Area

Religion

The household survey reveals that Hinduism is the most dominant religion at the sampled localities. At all the localities, Hindu dominance by number of households is more than 90 percent and out of the total households surveyed, 98 percent practise Hinduism. At three localities, viz., Lakhudi slum, Lakhudi non-slum, and Omnagar slum all the households surveyed are Hindu. At Machhipir and Omnagar non-slums, Hindu households account for 98 percent of the total. On the other hand, non-Hindus account for 2 percent of the total. Compared to the Hindus, Muslims and Christians are negligible in the sampled households. Muslim households account for less than 2 percent of the total surveyed households. Out of them 75 percent are there at the slum of Machhipir and rest belong to the Machhipir non-slum (both the localities are situated in the Maninagar area of south-eastern Ahmedabad). At the slum of Machhipir, Muslim households account for 6 percent and in the nearby non-slum areas for 2 percent of the total households. Only 0.7 percent of the total sampled households are Christians and they live at Machhipir slum and Omnagar non-slum, in equal proportion. At both these localities, 2 percent of the total households are Christian.

Table 10.1

Religion

	Religion				Percentage			
	Hindu	Muslim	Chris-tian	Total	Hindu	Muslim	Chris-tian	Total
Lakhudi slum	50	0	0	50	100.0	0.0	0.0	100.0
Lakhudi non-slum	50	0	0	50	100.0	0.0	0.0	100.0
Macchipir slum	46	3	1	50	92.0	6.0	2.0	100.0
Macchipir non-slum	49	1	0	50	98.0	2.0	0.0	100.0
Omnagar slum	50	0	0	50	100.0	0.0	0.0	100.0
Omnagar non-slum	49	0	1	50	98.0	0.0	2.0	100.0
Total	294	4	2	300	98.0	1.3	0.7	100.0

Caste Pattern

Four different categories are chosen for examining the distribution pattern of castes in the surveyed localities. They are general, scheduled caste (SCs), scheduled tribes (STs) and other backward castes (OBCs). The survey reveals that out of the selected types, households with general castes people have the largest share, which is 46.3 percent of the total households. Second are the SC households with 29 percent of the total. The OBC category comes next with a percentage share of 22 while the STs occupy the lowest and a miniscule portion of the total at only 2.7 percent. The highest number of households in general castes are found at the non-slum locality of Lakhudi, which accounts for 84 percent of the total households surveyed there. In general, the non-slum areas have a higher percentage of general caste persons than their slum counterparts. In Machhipir, the non-slum area has 70 percent general category while the slum area has 22 percent. The Omnagar non-slum area has 66 percent in the general category while the slum area has about 10 percent. SC households are the highest at the slum of Omnagar with a 10 percent share of the total of the all households at all the localities. It is 60 percent of the total households at Omnagar slum. The share of the total SCs found at Lakhudi and Machhipir slums are 9.33 percent and 7.33 percent respectively, where they account for 50 and 44 percent respectively of the total households. Likewise, the ST households are found only in the locality of Machhipir slum, where they are 16 percent of the total households. The OBC households are the highest at Omnagar slum and non-slum. They account for 23 percent of the total OBC households at the all localities and 30 percent of the total households at that locality. The presence of OBC households is the lowest at Lakhudi non-slum, which comprises only 10.6 percent of the total OBC households at all the localities and accounts for only 14 percent of the locality's households. Rest of the localities, slum and non-slum, both have more or less similar figures ranging from 16 to 24 percent share of OBC households at each of them.

There is a clear-cut distinction between the distribution of general and SC category in the localities. In all the non-slum localities, there is dominance of the general castes while the slums are dominated by the SCs. The OBC households are more or less equally distributed at all the localities without having any distinction between slums and non-slums.

Table 10.2
Caste

	Caste					Percentage				
	General	SC	ST	OBC	Total	General	SC	ST	OBC	Total
Lakhudi slum	13	25	0	12	50	26.0	50.0	0.0	24.0	100
Lakhudi non-slum	42	1	0	7	50	84.0	2.0	0.0	14.0	100
Machhipir slum	11	22	8	9	50	22.0	44.0	16.0	18.0	100
Machhipir non-slum	35	7	0	8	50	70.0	14.0	0.0	16.0	100
Omnagar slum	5	30	0	15	50	10.0	60.0	0.0	30.0	100
Omnagar non-slum	33	2	0	15	50	66.0	4.0	0.0	30.0	100
Total	139	87	8	66	300	46.3	29.0	2.7	22.0	100

House Types

Four major housing types are observed at the sampled localities: informal (temporary huts), flats in apartment blocks, row houses and bungalows. The informal houses are temporary structures mostly built by the economically weaker sections of the society. They are cheaply built by using low-cost materials. In Aḥmedabad, most of them are made up of brick walls with asbestos or polythene roofs and situated in congested conditions sometimes in inappropriate public land and sometimes in private land. The informal houses are predominant with a share of 50 percent of the total households surveyed. Row houses are those houses where residential building units stand in a row, with common sidewalls. There are also large numbers of row houses, which account for more than 32 percent of the total. Flats are groups of residential units in a multistoried building block, where all the houses generally have a common entrance. The survey has shown that 13 percent of the samples are from flats and rest 4 percent from bungalows. Here bungalow means an independent unit of residence, with efficiently maintained private outdoor space.

Informal houses are the major features of the slums. They are observed for all the households surveyed at Omnagar slum. At Lakhudi, they are 96 percent and at Machhipir, they are 94 percent of the total. There are also few informal houses at the non-slum localities and they account for nearly 4 percent of the total informal houses. Most of the row houses are present at Omnagar non-slum with 49 percent of the total row houses, while they account for 96 percent of the total houses surveyed at Omnagar non-slum. At Lakhudi non-slum, it is 64 percent while at Machhipir it is 30 percent of the total row houses. Flats are largely present at Machhipir non-slum. They account for 62 percent of the total surveyed houses in that locality and account for 80 percent of the total flats surveyed. Bungalows are found mostly at the Lakhudi non-slum area, with 66 percent of the total bungalows surveyed; but they share only 16 percent of the houses surveyed in that locality. In rest of the localities, they are negligible with less than 10 percent of the total houses at each of them. In the Omnagar locality, both slum and non-slum, there is an absence of bungalows.

Built environment largely affects the living environment, which is a major factor in overall development of a community. The differences in the utilisation of built facilities make the differences in quality of life as well as determine the potentialities of growth in a community. Here, the picture shows that major shares of built facilities in terms of quality of residential houses are below average. The upgradation of the built environment is therefore necessary.

Table 10.3
Types of Houses

	House Type					Percentage				
	Informal	Flats	Row houses	Bungalows	Total	Informal	Flats	Row houses	Bungalows	Total
Lakhudi slum	48	0	1	1	50	96.0	0.0	2.0	2.0	100
Lakhudi non-slum	3	7	32	8	50	6.0	14.0	64.0	16.0	100
Machhipir slum	47	1	2	0	50	94.0	2.0	4.0	0.0	100
Machhipir non-slum	1	31	15	3	50	2.0	62.0	30.0	6.0	100
Omnagar slum	50	0	0	0	50	100.0	0.0	0.0	0.0	100
Omnagar non-slum	2	0	48	0	50	4.0	0.0	96.0	0.0	100
Total	151	39	98	12	300	50.3	13.0	32.7	4.0	100

Household Size

Four different categories are selected to examine the household size pattern. They are 'one to three', 'four to six', 'seven to nine' and 'ten or more than that'. The category of the 'four to six' has the highest share out of the all the categories, which accounts for 68 percent of the total in all the localities. The lowest share is exhibited by the category of ten or more than that, with a share of only 1 percent of the total. The other two groups 'one to three' and 'seven to nine' have equal shares of households, with 15 percent of share in them. The 'four to six' category, with the highest share, has more or less equal distribution of households at all the localities. This category remains at the top with more than 60 percent of the households at each of them. Machhipir non-slum exhibits the highest share with 78 percent of the total in the locality. In the category of 'one to three' persons per household, there is clear-cut distinction between the slums and non-slums. All the non-slums have more number of households in this category than the slums. In this category, the household share at the non-slum areas is on the higher side with 16, 18 and 33 percent households at Lakhudi, Machhipir and Omnagar non-slum localities respectively; on the other hand, the figures in the slums are lower, i.e., 14, 8 and 4 percent households, respectively. This reveals that non-slum localities have greater number of households with a smaller household size. Contrary to that, the categories of higher household size, such as 'seven to nine' and 'ten or more than that', reveal a reverse picture with slum localities having greater number of households in these categories than the non-slums. In both these categories, Omnagar slum shows the highest household number.

The overall picture that the survey reveals is that in all the localities the size of the households is becoming lesser than it used to be previously. However, it has still not come down to the desired lowest category but is still one level above it. Another observation that can be drawn from the survey is that while the highest category is that of 'four to six', the rest of the households of the slums and non-slums lie in categories either above or below it. The non-slums, in particular, lie mostly on the lowest category of 'one to three' with very few in the 'seven to nine' and none above it. The slums, on the other hand, show the opposite picture. Of the remaining, very few are in the lowest category, while the majority of the rest are in the 'seven to nine' category. A few are also in the 'above ten' category. In case of the slums, this distinction can be explained by the fact that in the slum households most of the household members who are of working capacity are earning members of the family. This indicates the size of larger households. Also, among the economically weaker sections, the concept of family planning measures is not as effective as in the non-slum households. This also depicts the difference in lifestyles of people.

Table 10.4
Household Size

	One to three	Four to six	Seven to nine	Ten or more than ten	Total	One to three	Four to six	Seven to nine	Ten or more than that	Total
Lakhudi slum	7	31	11	1	50	14.0	62.0	22.0	2.0	100
Lakhudi non-slum	8	34	8	0	50	16.0	68.0	16.0	0.0	100
Machhipir slum	4	37	9	0	50	8.0	74.0	18.0	0.0	100
Machhipir non-slum	9	39	2	0	50	18.0	78.0	4.0	0.0	100
Omnagar slum	2	32	14	2	50	4.0	64.0	28.0	4.0	100
Omnagar non-slum	15	32	3	0	50	30.0	64.0	6.0	0.0	100
Total	45	205	47	3	300	15.0	68.3	15.7	1.0	100

Tenure Status

The survey on ownership clearly shows that the self-owned households dominate the scene. The share of self-owned houses is 86.6 percent of the total. On the other hand, rented houses are 13 percent of the total in all the localities. Other tenure status comprises of negligible 0.33 percent share. The Lakhudi slum and Machhipir non-slum show the highest shares of 96 percent self-owned houses by each. The least figure is from Omnagar non-slum, where self-owned houses account for 72 percent of the total houses surveyed in that locality. Rest of the localities have self-owned houses ranging from 80 to 92 percent in them. On the other hand, the share of rented houses to the total surveyed houses at each of the locality is on the higher side at Omnagar non-slum, Omnagar slum and at Machhipir slum, which ranges from 16 to 28 percent. The share of rented houses is the highest in Omnagar non-slum, which is 35 percent of that of all the localities and comprises 28 percent of the total houses surveyed in that locality. At Lakhudi slum, Lakhudi non-slum and Machhipir non-slum, the share of rented houses to the total at each is negligible. Other status of tenure is found at Lakhudi non-slum, which is only 1 percent of the all types of tenures.

More households in self-owned houses denote permanent nature of the dwellers in terms of their occupation and livelihood. Even in slums, people are living in their own houses. Although the proportion of self-owned houses is more in the non-slums than in the slums of all the localities, the difference between the two is too miniscule to come to any wide conclusion.

Table 10.5
Status of Tenure

	Own	Rented	Others	Total	Own	Rented	Others	Total
Lakhudi slum	48	2	0	50	96.0	4.0	0.0	100.0
Lakhudi non-slum	46	3	1	50	92.0	6.0	2.0	100.0
Macchipir slum	42	8	0	50	84.0	16.0	0.0	100.0
Macchipir non-slum	48	2	0	50	96.0	4.0	0.0	100.0
Omnagar slum	40	10	0	50	80.0	20.0	0.0	100.0
Omnagar non-slum	36	14	0	50	72.0	28.0	0.0	100.0
Total	260	39	1	300	86.7	13.0	0.3	100.0

Number of Rooms

The survey shows that various categories of number of rooms in the surveyed houses of the localities can be formed, as the range of number of rooms is very wide. Finally, four different categories are chosen. They are one, two, three to five, and more than five. The study has shown that most of the houses in the locality fall in the category of 'two', which accounts for 34 percent of the total houses surveyed in all the localities. The next category 'three to five', accounts for 33.7 percent of the total, which is followed by the category of 'one' with 25.7 percent of the total households. The last category is that of 'more than five' with only 6.7 percent of the total households.

The results can be related to both the differences that exist between the slums and non-slums as well as the size of the households in these localities. The number of rooms in a household is obviously a function of the size of the household. Apart from this, the considerations include the costs involved and the economic condition of the household. The result is that the households in the slums have more persons per room and live in slightly cramped conditions while the non-slum households have fewer persons per room and live in more spacious conditions. Rooms in slums are multifunctional and for practical uses for this reason while in the non-slums rooms they are generally unifunctional and are used for recreational purposes as well.

Thus, it is the category of 'two' which is the highest in all the localities. But, here, the slums are higher than that of non-slums. This can be explained by the fact that while the overall picture show 'two' as the highest category, in the case of non-slums, the highest category is that of 'three to five'. Only Lakhudi non-slum has households with more than five rooms that are 6 percent of the total in Lakhudi non-slum. In the case of slums, most of the houses are equally distributed between the categories of 'one' and 'two' with an even distribution of 23 percent of all slum households. Very few households have greater number of rooms in slums. The exception is Omnagar slum with 26 percent in the 'three to five' category and 10 percent in the 'more than five' category. This can be explained by the fact that the Omnagar slum has 4 percent of the families with household size more than ten (i.e., 15 households; only Lakhudi slum has one household of this great size). This is also a fact that Omnagar slum has 80 percent of houses in the self-owned category that is higher than that of Omnagar non-slum with 72 percent in the self-owned category. The large size of these households necessitates greater number of rooms and self-owned houses make it easier to add rooms by constructing them.

The distribution of the number of rooms at localities shows that the average number of rooms per household is 2.72. In the slums it is two rooms per household while in the non-slums it is three to five rooms per household. In slums there are 77 households having only one room and the largest number of such households is from Machhipir slum. In non-slum area, about eight households are living in one room accommodation with separate kitchen. Only in three households there are more than nine rooms and they all belong to the Lakhudi non-slum. From field observation, it is found that in the slums people use whatever little open space available le near (. use for various activities including cooking. But, the size of the room varies and the total covered area may give a better picture rather than simply looking at the number of rooms.

Table 10.6
Number of Rooms

	One	Two	Three to five	More than five	Total	One	Two	Three to five	More than five	Total
Lakhudi slum	12	36	2	0	50	24	72	4	0	100
Lakhudi non-slum	2	1	32	15	50	4	64	30	6	100
Machhipir slum	37	12	1	0	50	74	24	2	0	100
Machhipir non-slum	2	2	46	0	50	4	98	0	0	100
Omnagar slum	20	23	7	0	50	40	46	14	0	100
Omnagar non-slum	4	28	13	5	50	8	56	26	10	100
Total	77	102	101	20	300	25.7	34	33.7	6.7	100

The average unit size of all the localities together is 584.15 sq ft per household. But it is only 119 sq ft in Machhipir, 166 in Lakhudi and 182 in Omnagar slum. In the non-slum areas, it is 1,801 sq ft in Lakhudi, 797 in Machhipir and 442 in Omnagar. What is clearly emerging is that while there is some similarity between the slums, in the case of the non-slums, it is directly related to the socio-economic condition of that particular neighbourhood.

Water Facility

Availability of water in the households exhibits a more or less satisfactory picture. At all the non-slum localities, except Machhipir non-slum, all the households have water connections at their houses. Machhipir non-slum is just short of it. All the slums have at-home connections covering more than 80 percent of the households. The households with the at-home connections accounts for 92 percent of the total in all the localities. The households in all the localities, which depend upon near-to-house connections are 7 percent of the total. At the slum of Machhipir, nearly 20 percent of the households have to use such facilities. There are only three households in Lakhudi slum, which responded talking about their problem of collecting water from a far-off location.

Table 10.7
Water Facility

	At-home	Near-to-house	Far-off	Total	At-home	Near-to-house	Far-off	Total
Lakhudi slum	40	7	3	50	80.0	14.0	6.0	100
Lakhudi non-slum	50	0	0	50	100.0	0.0	0.0	100
Machhipir slum	40	10	0	50	80.0	20.0	0.0	100
Machhipir non-slum	49	1	0	50	98.0	2.0	0.0	100
Omnagar slum	47	3	0	50	94.0	6.0	0.0	100
Omnagar non-slum	50	0	0	50	100.0	0.0	0.0	100
Total	276	21	3	300	92.0	7.0	1.0	100

The existing scenario depicts that a little more effort will definitely help in achieving the availability of a water connection in every household. Adequacy of water in a sufficient amount in the localities depends not only on a tap connection, but also on various other factors such as availability of water at the source, efficiency of the distribution system, etc.

Toilet Facility

To understand the present scenario of toilet facilities in the surveyed localities, three criteria were selected. Firstly, it has been emphasised to check whether toilet is available in each house or not. The presence of toilet inside a house has lot of advantages. From the economic and hygienic points of view, it is favourable as the family itself normally takes care of it and efficiency in service is definitely higher than other provisions invented till date. Secondly, there was a check for the presence and use of the community toilets (near-to-home facilities), the use of what are common for several households in a locality. They have certain disadvantages as the public authorities normally responsible for their maintenance and in terms of service too, they are inefficient. It is also seen that sometimes they become unacceptable to people socially. Toilet facility that is far-off indicates that there is no such physical installation as toilet and people defecate either in open grounds near the settlement or use drains and low-lying areas to do so.

The survey has shown that all the households at the non-slum localities of Lakhudi and Machhipir have individual toilets. Omnagar non-slum has household coverage of 96 percent with an individual toilet. On the other hand, the same scenario in the slum household is disappointing. The highest number of households with individual facility is there at Omnagar slum, covering 58 percent of the total surveyed households. Rest of the slums, Lakhudi and Machhipir comprise only 2.7 and 2.1 percent of the households with individual toilets. They cover only 10 percent households at Lakhudi slum and 8 percent of the same at Machhipir slum. The near-to-home facilities are the highest at slum of Machhipir, which accounts for 51 percent of the total of these facilities in all the localities and nearly 48 percent of the households use them in that slum. Lakhudi and Omnagar slums have near about equal share of households with the near-to-home facilities, both accounting more or less than 20 percent of the total in all the localities. In Omnagar non-slum, nearly 4 percent of the households use these facilities, which also accounts for 4 percent of that in all the localities.

Households using far-off facilities are found only in the slums. Out of this category, 52 percent are found in Lakhudi slum, 32 percent in Machhipir slum and 14 percent in Omnagar. At Lakhudi slum 70 percent of the total households face such conditions, at Machhipir it is 44 percent and at Omnagar it is 20 percent.

Table 10.8
Toilet Facility

	At-home	Near-to-house	Far-off	Total	At-home	Near-to-house	Far-off	Total
Lakhudi slum	5	10	35	50	10	20	70	100
Lakhudi non-slum	50	0	0	50	100	0	0	100
Machhipir slum	4	24	22	50	8	48	44	100
Machhipir non-slum	50	0	0	50	100	0	0	100
Omnagar slum	29	11	10	50	58	22	20	100
Omnagar non-slum	48	2	0	50	96	4	0	100
Total	186	47	67	300	62	15.7	22.3	100

It has been seen that Lakhudi and Machhipir non-slums do not have any trouble with the existence of the toilet facilities as all the households have them at their home. Omnagar slum has yet to cover up 4 percent of the households with the at-home facilities. All the slums suffer from the inadequacy in provision of toilets. Conditions are somewhat better in Omnagar slum, but still it is not satisfactory.

Electric Connection

The survey also enquired about the presence and absence of the legal electric connection in the localities. All the households at the non-slum localities are connected to electricity. On the other hand, inadequacy of the connection is prominent at all the slums. The share of connected households is as low as 44 percent of the total households at Machhipir slum. The connections in the Omnagar slum have coverage of 70 percent and the same at the Lakhudi slum is 60 percent.

The distribution of electric connections is probably affected by the pattern of lifestyle and income at the localities. It also may happen due to the free use of electricity illegally by many of the slum households.

Table 10.9
Electric Connection

	Con-nected	Not connected	Total	Connected	Not connected	Total
Lakhudi slum	30	20	50	60.0	40.0	100.0
Lakhudi non-slum	50	0	50	100.0	0.0	100.0
Machhipir slum	22	28	50	44.0	56.0	100.0
Machhipir non-slum	50	0	50	100.0	0.0	100.0
Omnagar slum	35	15	50	70.0	30.0	100.0
Omnagar non-slum	50	0	50	100.0	0.0	100.0
Total	237	63	300	79.0	21.0	100.0

Bathroom Facility

Regarding the availability of a bathroom in a household, here too, the non-slums are better off than the slums. Out of the total available 'at home' facilities, non-slums' share is as high as 71 percent with more or less equal percentage share exhibiting by each of the localities. In Lakhudi and Machhipir non-slums, all households have a bathroom at their home. In Omnagar non-slum, it is 96 percent. In the slums, the figures are disappointing. Omnagar slum has highest, i.e., 62 percent coverage of households by a bathroom. In Machhipir and Lakhudi slums, 'at home' facilities are very less, i.e., 34 and 20 percent respectively. This is unfortunate because most of the slum households have water connection and the presence of bathrooms and toilets within the house will improve hygienic and health conditions remarkably.

Condition in Lakhudi slum is the worst and to par with the other non-slum localities only in terms of availability of an individual bathroom facility per household, conditions at all the slums have to be improved dramatically.

Table 10.10
Bathroom Facility

	At home	Not available	Total	At home	Not available	Total
Lakhudi slum	10	40	50	20.0	80.0	100.0
Lakhudi non-slum	50	0	50	100.0	0.0	100.0
Machhipir slum	17	33	50	34.0	66.0	100.0
Machhipir non-slum	50	0	50	100.0	0.0	100.0
Omnagar slum	31	19	50	62.0	38.0	100.0
Omnagar non-slum	48	2	50	96.0	4.0	100.0
Total	206	94	300	68.7	31.3	100.0

Sewerage Connection

All the households in the non-slum localities have sewerage connection. Interestingly, the slum of Omnagar also has shown 100 percent accessibility to sewerage connections by its surveyed households. Connections in other two slums, viz., Lakhudi and Machhipir, have already reached 96 and 86 percent respectively. Therefore, connections have to be improved in these two localities to acquire full coverage.

Table 10.11
Sewerage Connection

	At home	Not available	Total	At home	Not available	Total
Lakhudi slum	48	2	50	96	4	100
Lakhudi non-slum	50	0	50	100	0	100
Machhipir slum	43	7	50	86	14	100
Machhipir non-slum	50	0	50	100	0	100
Omnagar slum	50	0	50	100	0	100
Omnagar non-slum	50	0	50	100	0	100
Total	291	9	300	97	3	100

Approach Road

All the households in the non-slum localities and Omnagar slum have proper access to a motorable approach road. However, in the slums of Lakhudi and Machhipir, only 96 percent of the households agree to the availability of an easy access road directly linked to their houses. While 4 percent in Machhipir and 2 percent in Lakhudi slums told about a 'near' access road and 1 percent of the samples from Lakhudi say about 'far-off' access to any road.

Table 10.12
Accessibility of Approach Road

	Con-nected	Near-to-house	Far-off	Total	Con-nected	Near-to-house	Far-off	Total
Lakhudi slum	48	1	1	50	96.0	2.0	2.0	100
Lakhudi non-slum	50	0	0	50	100.0	0.0	0.0	100
Machhipir slum	48	2	0	50	96.0	4.0	0.0	100
Machhipir non-slum	50	0	0	50	100.0	0.0	0.0	100
Omnagar slum	50	0	0	50	100.0	0.0	0.0	100
Omnagar non-slum	50	0	0	50	100.0	0.0	0.0	100
Total	296	3	1	300	98.7	1.0	0.3	100

Although most of the slum dwellers told about the near access to an approach road, but reconnaissance concludes that the conditions of the inner lanes in the slums are not in a desirable condition. Most of them are unpaved, the surface quality bad and they also perform the works of surface drains for sullage. The provision of toilets will help reduce the latter while the condition of surface roads can only be helped with regular maintenance.

Use of Fuels

There are mainly four different types of fuel use in the surveyed households in all the six localities. They are firewood, kerosene, cowdung and LPG. Amongst all the fuels, the use of LPG is the highest, where 47 percent of the total households use this fuel. Kerosene rests in the second place with 32 percent of the households using it. There are 19 percent households still using firewood as a fuel. The households using cowdung are negligible in comparison to those of other fuels. They comprise only 0.7 percent of the total households. The use of LPG is also the highest in the households at the non-slum localities. They account for 98 percent at the both Lakhudi and Machhipir non-slum areas, while it is somewhat less at Omnagar non-slum area, i.e., 73 percent. The figures at all the slums are in sharply contrasting positions to those of the non-slums. The highest figure appears at Lakhudi slum, which is 21 percent of the total households using different fuels. Lakhudi slum's figure accounts for 10 percent of the LPG use in all the localities. The figure exhibited by both the other slums are less than 20 percent. The households using kerosene are the highest at Lakhudi slum, which accounts for 30 percent of the households using kerosene and 43 percent of the households in that locality. Except Omnagar non-slum, where 26 percent households use kerosene, negligible share of households at all other non-slum localities use kerosene. The use of firewood is found only at the slums. About 30 to 35 percent of the households in all the slums use firewood. Lakhudi slum has the highest number of households, i.e., 38 percent of the total firewood using households and it is lowest at the Machhipir slum. Cowdung as a fuel is used in the localities of Lakhudi and Omnagar slums, but its use negligible in comparison to other types of fuels.

The use of LPG is a good sign, but is restricted mainly to the non-slum localities. It is obvious that its use correlates positively with living standard. In the slum localities, the use of kerosene and firewood is extensive. The use of kerosene is most probably due to the fair-price shops, which are selling it at a subsidised price. On the other hand, the use of firewood is undesirable in a state like Gujarat, where most of the area is under semi-arid conditions.

Table 10.13

Fuel Use (Multiple Responses)

	Fire-wood	Kero-sene	Cow-dung	LPG	Total	Fire-wood	Kero-sene	Cow-dung	LPG	Total
Lakhudi slum	30	39	1	19	89	33.7	43.8	1.1	21.3	100
Lakhudi non-slum	0	1	0	50	51	0	2	0	98	100
Machhipir slum	21	37	0	11	69	30.4	53.6	0	15.9	100
Machhipir non-slum	0	1	0	50	51	0	2	0	98	100
Omnagar slum	26	33	2	13	74	35.1	44.6	2.7	17.6	100
Omnagar non-slum	0	17	0	47	64	0.0	26.6	0.0	73.4	100
Total	77	128	3	190	398	19.3	32.2	0.8	47.7	100

Educational Status

Education has been accepted as one of the important indicators of socio-economic development. It is also a decisive power in order to promote welfare of the family. Table 10.14 shows that about 23 percent of the total sample population are illiterate and 25 percent are just literate. On the other hand, 31 percent of the total population are having education above 12th standard and only 4 percent are having professional qualification. Settlement-wise analysis shows that illiterates are from slums while professionals and higher educated people are mainly from the non-slum localities. Slum-wise population

Table 10.14
Educational Status

		Lakbudi slum	Lakbudi non-slum	Macchipir slum	Macchipir non-slum	Omnagar slum	Omnagar non-slum	Total
Illiterate	% Row	27.60	0.59	19.29	9.20	28.19	6.23	100
		93	2	65	31	95	21	337
	% Column	39.91	0.83	26.53	14.49	36.26	10.71	24.24
Up to 5th standard	% Row	22.54	11.56	25.14	6.36	22.25	12.14	100
		78	40	87	22	77	42	346
	% Column	33.48	16.67	35.51	10.28	29.39	21.43	24.89
6 to 10th standard	% Row	14.87	16.91	14.87	10.50	20.12	22.74	100
		51	58	51	36	69	78	343
	% Column	21.89	24.17	20.82	16.82	26.34	39.80	24.68
11 to 12th standard	% Row	8.14	25.58	6.98	15.12	11.63	32.56	100
		7	22	6	13	10	28	86
	% Column	3	9.17	2.45	6.07	3.82	14.29	6.19
Above 12th standard	% Row	0.89	38.84	2.23	45.98	3.57	8.48	100
		2	87	5	103	8	19	224
		0.86	36.25	2.04	48.13	3.05	9.69	16.12
Pro-fessional	% Row	3.70	57.41	1.85	16.67	5.56	14.81	100
		2	31	1	9	3	8	54
	% Column	0.86	12.92	0.41	4.21	1.15	4.08	3.88
Total		233	240	245	214	262	196	1390

distribution shows that in Lakhudi about 30 percent are illiterates, 23 percent are educated up to primary level, and 15 percent are in the category of 6th to 10th standard. In Omnagar, the situation is more or less same as in Lakhudi but Machhipir is slightly different.

Occupational Pattern

The occupation largely decides the economic status of the households and directly related to many aspects of family life. Table 10.15 clearly shows that among the employed population a large number belong to the category of self-employed (44.85%). The self-employed are engaged in different types of income generating activities like vegetable vendors, hawkers, small traders etc. in slums while it is builders, contractors, showroom owners, etc. in non-slum settlements. However, in terms of total number, it is very clear that more people are working as self-employed in slums compared to non-slum areas. Daily wage labourers mainly stay in slums as only eight households from non-slums reported to be daily wage labourers. In Lakhudi slum, self-employment is the most important occupation, but, in Machhipir and Omnagar slums, a large number of people are working as daily wage labourers. About 17 percent of the total employed persons are in regular jobs and the number is more in private job category as only about 6 percent are in public jobs. Unemployment is also very high but more prevalent in non-slum settlements of Machhipir and Omnagar in compare to nearby slum settlements.

A problem faced during the primary survey was in identifying the unemployed, as it is normally defined as a person not doing any useful work to earn his/her livelihood. While talking to the respondents it was observed that some of the family members are identified as unemployed because they are not earning enough or doing something on a regular basis. In such a situation, their opinion was recorded, which may not be an acceptable definition of unemployment. It is also observed that about 37 persons below 15 years are also included in the list of unemployed when they are not yet in the working age group. It simply shows that the concept of occupation has different meanings and formal interview method is not very appropriate to capture it in totality. Case study methods will certainly take care of such situations to a great extent.

Table 10.15
Occupational Pattern

		Lakhudi slum	Lakhudi non-slum	Machhipir slum	Machhipir non-slum	Omnagar slum	Omnagar non-slum	Total
Self-employment	% Row	25.69	16.06	18.81	10.09	19.27	10.09	100
		56	35	41	22	42	22	218
	% Column	36.84	30.42	20.52	10.89	21.73	12.28	20.94
Daily wage labour	% Row	21.11	0	35.56	4.44	34.44	4.44	100
		19	0	32	4	31	4	90
	% Column	12.50	0	16.02	1.98	16.04	2.23	8.65
Private job	% Row	12.93	19.83	16.38	15.52	9.48	25.86	100
		15	23	19	18	11	30	116
	% Column	9.87	19.99	9.51	8.91	5.69	16.75	11.14
Public jobs	% Row	4.84	37.10	9.68	24.19	9.68	14.52	100
		3	23	6	15	6	9	62
	% Column	1.97	19.99	3	7.42	3.10	5.03	5.96
Unemployed	% Row	7.25	3.96	18.24	29.23	18.46	22.86	100
		33	18	83	133	84	104	455
	% Column	21.71	15.64	41.54	65.81	43.46	58.07	43.71
Total		152	115	200	202	193	179	1041

Household Income

The average monthly income of all the households together is Rs 7,930. The slum and non-slum average is Rs 3,510 and Rs

12,349 respectively. Among the slum settlements, there was a marked difference observed in income as Omnagar reported Rs 4,240 as average monthly income while it was only Rs 3,384 and Rs 2,906 in Lakhudi and Machhipir slums. A similar situation also prevailed in the non-slum settlements. Lakhudi non-slum has reported Rs 22,368 as average monthly income against Rs 9,752 in Machhipir and only Rs 4,928 in Omnagar. In Omnagar, the income difference between slum and non-slum is not very high as in other two settlements.

Table 10.16
Household Income

Income Group	Lakhudi slum	%	Lakhudi non-slum	%	Omnagar slum	%	Omnagar non-slum	%	Machhipir slum	%	Machhipir non-slum	%
0-2500	22	44	2	4	10	20	13	26	25	50	1	2
2501-5000	20	40	3	6	30	60	24	48	23	46	15	30
5001-7500	6	12	1	2	6	12	6	12	2	4	7	14
7501-10000	2	4	6	12	3	6	4	8	0	0	12	24
10001-20000	0	0	20	40	1	2	3	6	0	0	13	26
20001-40000	0	0	11	22	0	0	0	0	0	0	1	2
40001-75000	0	0	5	10	0	0	0	0	0	0	1	2
>75000	0	0	2	4	0	0	0	0	0	0	0	0
Total	50	100	50	100	50	100	50	100	50	100	50	100

* Average income is Rs 7,930, in slum Rs 3,510 and Rs 12,349 in non-slum settlements.

We have also analysed the pattern of household income in different income groups that gives more detailed information. Table 10.16 shows that about 24.33 percent of the total households are earning only up to Rs 2,500 per month and they are mainly living in slums except in 16 cases. In Machhipir and Lakhudi slums about 44 percent of the sample households

belong to this category. The largest numbers of sample
households belong to the income category of Rs 2,501 to Rs
5,000 (38.33%). Rest are distributed in other three income
categories. But, only two households are in the income category
of above Rs 75,000 and both are from Lakhudi non-slum
settlements.

Household Expenditure

Household expenditure also gives clear indication of economic
status of the sample households both in slums and nearby
non-slum areas. Table 10.17 gives details of the expenditure and
the average expenditure is Rs 3,776 only. The settlement-wise
analysis clearly shows differences between slum and non-slum
areas. In Lakhudi, non-slum people are spending more than
other areas and it is lowest in Machhipir slum. In slums people
are spending more than half of their total expenditure for food
and it is about 75 percent of the total in Machhipir and
Omnagar. In Lakhudi, non-slum people are spending about 20

Table 10.17
Household Expenditure

Localities	Av. cost per HH on food	Av. cost per HH on clothes	Av. cost per HH on medi-cines	Av. cost per HH on educa-tion	Av. cost per HH on trans-port	Av. cost per HH on enter-tain-ment	Av. cost per HH on other heads	Total av. cost/ month per HH
Lakhudi slum	1496	33	35.57	7.08	187	300	507.10	2566
Lakhudi non-slum	3574	102	85.18	132.8	1544	849.20	1818	8106
Machhipir slum	1522	31	17.35	15.67	187	94	151.5	2018
Machhipir non-slum	3050	42	42.59	78.5	606	287	62	4168
Omnagar slum	1984	35	14.29	19.65	120	177	289	2639
Omnagar non-slum	2040	23	17.21	31.33	189	126	132	2558
Total	13666	266	212.19	285.03	2833	1833.2	2959.6	3676

percent on transportation and related activities. In all other areas, people are spending very small amount for medical, education and clothing purposes. In Omnagar, there is hardly any difference between the expenditure pattern of slum and non-slum areas.

Other Assets

Distribution of assets reflects the lifestyle of people living in an area. Here few assets are identified, which are normally used in a developing country such as ours with typical climatic conditions and behavioural preferences of the people. The assets, which are identified to check their presence or absence in the surveyed households, are bicycle, electric fan, black and white television, coloured television, refrigerator, motorbike, car, air conditioner and others. Amongst all these assets bicycle is the most evenly distributed asset in all the localities and its share in all the assets and localities is the highest with more than 84 percent. Locality-wise distribution shows that except Machhipir non-slum at rest of the localities more than 75 percent of the households have bicycles. The figure is the highest at Omnagar non-slum, where 96 percent of the households have one or more bicycles. In terms of the distribution of electric fans, slum and non-slum localities have shown large differences. The share of households with electric fans in the slum localities rests below 15 percent and except three in Omnagar non-slums all non-slum households are having at least one fan.

Assets such as black and white television again show the uneven distribution in all the localities but it is found to be more among slum households. But maximum numbers of black and white TV are seen in Omnagar non-slum. In slums, their percentage shares vary from 13 to 18 percent of the total assets. The distribution of the coloured television that is more expensive is skewed towards the non-slums. About 91 percent of the total households with coloured television are from non-slums. Lakhudi non-slum has the largest share with 44 percent of the total televisions, which also accounts for 7 percent of the total assets at that locality. The non-slum of Omnagar has a comparatively a low share of 11 percent of the total.

Table 10.18
Distribution of Assets

Settlement	Cycle	Fan	B/W TV	Colour TV	Re-frig-era-tor	Motor bike	Car	AC	Others
Lakhudi slum	38	32	19	2	0	0	0	0	8
%	15.08	13.39	15.15	2.15	0	0	0	0	27.59
Lakhudi non-slum	42	50	12	41	44	41	20	4	14
%	16.67	20.92	9.89	44.08	47.31	42.71	86.96	36.36	48.28
Machhipir slum	45	22	16	1	0	0	0	0	1
%	17.86	9.20	13.11	1.07	0	0	0	0	3.45
Machhipir non-slum	34	50	16	34	44	36	2	3	4
%	13.49	20.92	13.11	36.56	47.31	37.5	8.7	27.27	13.79
Omnagar slum	45	38	22	4	0	0	0	0	0
%	17.86	15.89	18.03	4.30	0	0	0	0	0
Omnagar non-slum	48	47	37	11	5	19	1	4	2
%	19.04	19.67	30.33	11.82	5.38	19.79	4.35	36.36	6.9
Total	252	239	122	93	109	96	23	11	29

Refrigerators are noticed only at the non-slum localities. The Lakhudi non-slum households are having maximum number (88%) while it is lowest in Omnagar non-slum (10%). In the similar fashion, motorbikes, which include motorcycles, scooters and mopeds, are also present only at the non-slum localities. A total of 82 percent households at Lakhudi non-slum are having it. Omnagar non-slum exhibits the lowest share with 38 percent of the total in this category of asset. Again, cars and air-conditioners are proved to be the assets of non-slum areas as 87 percent of the total cars are found at the Lakhudi non-slum.

Rest of the non-slum localities have lower shares. At Lakhudi non-slum, 40 percent of the households have one or more cars. Household coverage by a car is negligible in rest of the localities. Air-conditioners show different picture. At Lakhudi and Machhipir non-slums, 36 and 27 percent of the total air-conditioners are found. Other assets are more at the non-slum of Lakhudi, which accounts for around 48 percent of the total. At Lakhudi slum and Machhipir non-slum too, there are considerable other assets, with 27 and 13 percent of the total respectively. Rest of the localities have a negligible share. These assets are in the form of music system, computers, radio, etc.

11

Health: Utilisation and Preference

Distribution Pattern of Diseases

The distribution of diseases as reported by the respondents in last one year shows that a large number of people are affected by some disease or the other whereas some people are affected by more than one disease within the same period. Disease-wise data indicate that the maximum number, of cases, i.e., 29.1 percent are of cold and fever which many a time are nothing but a symptom of some other disease. The cases of blood pressure, heart trouble and indigestion that are approximately 3.3 percent of the total come next, and the rest of the diseases constitute very small percentage ranging from 0.4 percent to 1.5 percent. The other diseases reported are malaria, jaundice, typhoid, tuberculosis, respiratory problems, joint pain, skin diseases and measles. The primary survey result goes against our recent study (Ray, 1996) where maximum cases of malaria were reported. In some informal talk with private doctors it was reported that malaria cases have declined during 1997-99 period because of several initiatives taken by the Ahmedabad Municipal Corporation (AMC). It is also interesting to note that more people from non-slum areas are suffering from malaria and that is also true for jaundice and typhoid which are purely water-borne.

When compared to the secondary information available from the AMC on diseases, we find that the large numbers of cases related to water-borne diseases are not reflected through the primary survey. The primary survey reveals that cold, fever and to a certain extent blood pressure, heart trouble and indigestion are the most common ailments across all the localities as against the secondary information available showing greater percentage of water-borne diseases. Also, the living environment and disease pattern do not seem to be in tandem, as the physical environment is better in non-slum area as compared to slums. However, it is important to note that AMC is keeping information only for water-borne diseases and there is no other source of information for air-borne and general diseases. Some recent studies by the National Institute of Occupational Health reported a large number of air-borne diseases in some cities of Gujarat. Therefore, a detailed survey needs to be conducted to find out the actual disease pattern in this city.

Persons Affected by Diseases

Of the fifty households surveyed in each of the six localities, it was found that some disease affected 425 people during the period of one year (August 1998 to July 1999). The following trend has been observed: the number of persons affected by diseases varies between a minimum of 65 persons in Lakhudi non-slum area and a maximum of 79 persons in Lakhudi slum area. It is also observed that in the non-slum areas the range varies between 65 and 68 cases, while in the slum areas, between 70 and 79 cases. The second trend that is observed both in the slum and the non-slum areas is that the percentage of male members falling sick is more than females and children. Of the total 425 respondents, 65.2 percent are males, 22.4 percent females and only 12.5 percent children. The percentage of males is greater than the females and children by a wide margin, so much so that in the cases of Lakhudi and Machhipir non-slum areas the male cases constitute 83.1 percent and 86.4 percent respectively. After revisiting these settlements, our observation is that it has happened because of some kind of reporting problem and also due to gender bias or other reason. Both the researcher and field investigators being male might have bearing on female respondents, as the female respondents might not find it comfortable to talk about their own health problem to an unknown person, particularly male. Children are also affected by various diseases on a regular basis which also appears to be underreported for reason not known.

Therefore, across all the locations, male members are reported to be more affected in larger numbers by diseases as compared with the female members and the children. In the non-slum areas, the percentage of male members affected is even greater than both females and children put together and also higher than the male members affected in the slum areas. Again, this is not in tune with the living environment as in the non-slum areas hardly anyone is occupied in doing menial work in unhygienic conditions, while it may be so in case of people living in slum areas.

Table 11.1
Persons Affected by Diseases

Localities	Male	%	Female	%	Children	%	Total
Lakhudi slum	30	38.0	28	35.4	21	26.6	79
Lakhudi non-slum	54	83.1	8	12.3	3	4.6	65
Machhipir slum	43	61.4	15	21.4	12	17.1	70
Machhipir non-slum	57	86.4	9	13.6	0	0	66
Omnagar slum	44	57.1	18	23.4	15	19.5	77
Omnagar non-slum	49	72.1	17	25	2	2.9	68
Total	277	65.2	95	22.4	53	12.5	425

Mode of Treatment

The mode of treatment includes allopathy, homeopathy, ayurvedic, naturopathy and reiki. According to many

respondents allopathic treatment shows quick curative results
compared to homeopathic treatment that is relatively a slow
process. Homeopathic treatment is also believed to be more
suitable for lifelong health disorders like asthma, blood
pressure, diabetes, etc. Of the total 304 responses, allopathic
seems to be the most popular choice of treatment, with 53
percent respondents opting for it. After allopathic, the order of
preference emerges to be homeopathy with 30.6 percent,
ayurvedic with 10.2 percent, naturopathy with 5.3 percent and
in the last reiki with only 1 percent. This trend remains more
or less the same across the six locations, apart from Omnagar
slum and non-slum areas where homeopathy seems to be more
popular than allopathy. In Omnagar slum area, of the 47
respondents, 31.9 percent opt for allopathy and 40.4 percent for

Table 11.2

Mode of Treatment (Multiple Responses)

Treatment		*Lakhudi slum*	*Lakhudi non-slum*	*Machhipir slum*	*Machhipir non-slum*	*Omnagar slum*	*Omnagar non-slum*	*Total*	*Percentage of total*
Allopathy		50	29	30	25	15	12	161	
	%	81.97	60.42	52.63	53.19	31.91	27.27		53.0
Homeopathy		3	11	14	20	19	26	93	
	%	4.92	22.92	24.56	42.55	40.43	59.09		30.6
Ayurvedic		5	4	8	1	7	6	31	
	%	8.2	8.33	14.04	2.13	14.89	13.64		10.2
Naturopathy		3	2	4	1	6	0	16	
	%	4.92	4.17	7.02	2.13	12.77	0		5.3
Reiki		0	2	1	0	0	0	3	
	%	0	4.17	1.75	0	0	0		1.0
Total		61	48	57	47	47	44	304	100

homeopathy. In Omnagar non-slum area, of the total 44 respondents, 27.3 percent prefer allopathy while 59.1 percent homeopathy. Of the total number of respondents, ayurvedic mode of treatment is preferred by only 10.2 percent. Very few people prefer naturopathy and reiki although with the advent of alternative treatment becoming popular, these methods are gaining more followers. Therefore, in general, allopathy emerges as the form of treatment in which most of the respondents show faith. Next emerges homeopathy whereas very few people opt for naturopathy or reiki.

Use of Medical Facilities

Use of medical facilities before 1991 was enquired to find out whether there is any change in utilisation facility in Ahmedabad. Of the total 331 multiple responses, 48 percent were utilising public medical facilities, 38.7 percent private services, 8.2 percent NGOs and trusts and 5.1 percent report no treatment before 1991. Therefore, the overall utilisation of public facilities was greater than that of private facilities before 1991. However, in Lakhudi slum and Omnagar non-slum, private services were utilised more than public services.

Table 11.3
Use of Medical Facilities before 1991 (Multiple Responses)

Localities	Public	%	Private	%	NGO/ Trust	%	No Treat- ment	%	Total
Lakhudi slum	28	42.4	34	51.5	3	4.5	1	1.5	66
Lakhudi non-slum	26	57.8	13	28.9	3	6.7	3	6.7	45
Machhipir slum	30	52.6	14	24.6	8	14.0	5	8.8	57
Machhipir non-slum	25	53.2	20	42.6	1	2.1	1	2.1	47
Omnagar slum	37	51.4	22	30.6	6	8.3	7	9.7	72
Omnagar non-slum	13	29.5	25	56.8	6	13.6	0	0.0	44
Total	159	48	128	38.7	27	8.2	17	5.1	331

As is evident from the responses (Table 11.4), at present, the public and private facilities emerge as the main health care facilities in the city. The dependency on facilities run by NGOs/trusts or others is marginal. However, in many other cities in India, religious organisations are running medical centres and hospitals and some of them are even known at the national level. Of the total 298 responses 43 percent report utilisation of public facilities, 56.4 percent of private health facilities and a marginal percentage of 0.3 percent each report utilisation of facilities run by NGOs/trusts and others.

Table 11.4
Use of Medical Facilities after 1991

	Public	%	Private	%	NGOs/Trusts	%	Others	%	Total
Lakhudi slum	31	64.6	16	33.3	0	0	1	2.1	48
Lakhudi non-slum	3	6.0	46	92.0	1	2	0	0	50
Machhipir slum	37	74.0	13	26.0	0	0	0	0	50
Machhipir non-slum	1	2.0	49	98.0	0	0	0	0	50
Omnagar slum	39	78.0	11	22.0	0	0	0	0	50
Omnagar non-slum	17	34.0	33	66.0	0	0	0	0	50
Total	128	43.0	168	56.4	1	0.3	1	0.3	298

Here, a strong demarcation is observed in the utilisation trend by the slum and the non-slum areas. In the slum areas majority of the respondents report utilisation of public facilities, while in the non-slum areas utilisation of public facilities is very low to the tune of only 6 percent. Since the public services are generally freely available, this is the reason the slum people prefer it to the private services, which are costly. As, the quality of public services remain dubious, the people who can afford prefer to use private services. In case of the Omnagar non-slum, the higher utilisation of public facilities than the other non-slum areas can be explained by the shift from the services of NGOs/trusts and others which had been present before 1991. Otherwise, here too, there has been a greater shift towards private services after 1991. In any case, even before 1991, Omnagar non-slum had shown a higher preference for private services than public services.

Table 11.5
Change in the Use of Medical Facilities

	Public		Private		NGOs/Trusts	
	Before 1991	After 1991	Before 1991	After 1991	Before 1991	After 1991
Lakhudi slum	42.4	64.6	51.5	33.3	4.5	0
Lakhudi non-slum	57.8	6.0	28.9	92.0	6.7	2
Machhipir slum	52.6	74.0	24.6	26.0	14.0	0
Machhipir non-slum	53.2	2.0	42.6	98.0	2.1	0
Omnagar slum	51.4	78.0	30.6	22.0	8.3	0
Omnagar non-slum	29.5	34.0	56.8	66.0	13.6	0
Total	48	43.0	38.7	56.4	8.2	0.3

Another observation through the years is that while the shift in the utilisation of private facilities in great numbers in the non-slum areas, in the slum areas an equally high increase has been observed in the utilisation of public services. It can therefore be concluded that the non-slum people would rather put their health through quality services despite the costs involved while, for the slum people, increasing health costs have forced them to rely on public services and shift away from their earlier preference of private services. Therefore, the picture that emerges is that maximum utilisation is of private facilities in the non-slum areas whereas the slum areas report maximum utilisation of public facilities, though in this case the difference in utilisation is not as marked as in the case of non-slum areas. A shift from public facilities to private facilities, particularly by residents of non-slum areas, is also observed. It is also important to note that low-income households are still using public facilities with all its limitation in Ahmedabad.

So far as the reasons for change in the use of health facilities are concerned, only 78 respondents expressed them and they are mainly from slum areas. Table 11.6 shows that 33.3 percent respondents have shifted to utilisation of private services from public services because they perceived that the services provided would be better, and 32.1 percent because they found the public facilities to be very time-consuming. The other reasons attributed for change in use of medical facilities are inadequate services, lack of medicine and improper behaviour of doctor. Lack of medicines also emerges as an important factor in this regard as this was the reason cited by 18 percent of respondents. Improper behaviour and inadequate services are also the reasons given by a few respondents. Respondents from Lakhudi and Machhipir non-slums have not responded to this question. In some informal discussions some of the respondents from these areas informed that there is hardly any change in last ten years.

If we analyse the data location-wise, we find that in Lakhudi slum area, better service is the clear reason. In Machhipir slum area, the equal number of respondents resorted to change both because of availability of better private services and the public facilities being time-consuming. In Omnagar slum area, 42.62 percent respondents resorted to change because the facility was time-consuming while in the case of Omnagar non-slum area, the clear reason emerges to be better services with 42.9 percent respondents.

Therefore, across all the locations, the main reason for change of use from public to private comes out to be that public facilities are time-consuming and availability of better services with the private facilities. This finding is very important for public heath planning, as service quality along with time taken for providing such services should be improved so that a large number of people can still utilise this facility at a relatively cheaper rate.

Table 11.6
Reasons for Change in the Use of Medical Facilities

	Lakhudi slum	Lakhudi non-slum	Machhipir slum	Machhipir non-slum	Omnagar slum	Omnagar non-slum	Total
Inadequate services	2	0	2	0	2	0	6
%	5.7	0	13.3	0	9.5	0	7.7
Lack of Medicine	6	0	3	0	3	2	14
%	17.1	0	20	0	14.3	28.6	18
Improper behaviour of doctor	4	0	2	0	1	0	7
%	11.4	0	13.3	0	4.8	0	9
Time-Consuming	9	0	4	0	10	2	25
%	25.7	0	26.7	0	47.6	28.6	32.1
Better service	14	0	4	0	5	3	26
%	40	0	26.7	0	23.8	42.9	33.3
Total	35	0	15	0	21	7	78

Medical Expenditure

The medical expenditure in the localities varies between Rs 22,615 per annum in Omnagar slum area and Rs 87,950 in Lakhudi slum area. The average cost per household works out to be in the range of Rs 452.3 per annum in Omnagar slum area to Rs 1,759 per annum in Lakhudi slum area. In Lakhudi slum area, households are spending more on treatment of diseases as compared to non-slum households while it is the opposite in the other two slum areas. At first glance this may seem ambiguous. Non-slums have better living conditions where the incidence of disease should be less thus necessitating less expenditure on medical grounds. However, it can also be such that in the other localities, the slum areas may be facing the problem of high treatment costs resulting in the absence of any treatment. This may partially account for the slums showing less expenditure on medical treatment than the non-slum areas. In general, Lakhudi slum area is reporting things in many different ways and medical expenditure is one such issue. Medical expenditure as reported by the respondents is totally different when total household expenditure is calculated. It is to be noted that details of household expenditure reveals a much lower figure for medical expenditure. The researcher strongly felt that the figure quoted as medical expenditure separately appears to be more realistic than the total household expenditure. Percentage-wise, it comes close to 15-20 percent of the total expenditure for low-income households.

Table 11.7
Medical Expenditure

Localities	Expenditure per Annum	Percent	Average Expenditure per HH per Annum
Lakhudi slum	87950	26.31	1759.00
Lakhudi non-slum	66956	20.03	1339.12
Machhipir slum	30870	9.24	617.40
Machhipir non-slum	83755	25.06	1675.10
Omnagar slum	22615	6.77	452.30
Omnagar non-slum	42125	12.60	842.50
Total	334271	100	1114.20

Place of Last Birth

Place of birth has been used as one indicator to find out health behaviour of people in both urban and rural areas. Traditionally, home was considered as right place for delivery and local *dais* were called for required services. But, gradually, people started using formal health facilities to avoid problems

like deaths during delivery as well as problems after delivery
both for the mother and the new-born. Here, we have collected
information not only to find the place of birth but also the type
of organisation they are using. Of the total 278 cases, the place
of last birth in majority of cases (i.e., 41%) is at private nursing
homes. Then come the government hospitals with 36.7 percent
cases and lastly at home with only 21.9 percent cases. It shows
that about one-fifth of the population is still not using any
formal heath system for delivering child.

Location-wise, a distinction can be seen between the slum
and the non-slum areas. In the slum areas, the place of last birth
in majority of cases is at home. In Lakhudi slum, it is 45.7
percent, in Machhipir slum it is 47.7 percent while in Omnagar
slum it is 32.7 percent. Therefore, in the slum areas, in two out
of three locations, the last place of birth in majority of cases is at
home. However, in Omnagar slum area, the number of cases at
the government hospitals is more than the number of cases at
home and it is probably related to the location of the civil
hospital in this area. Socio-economic conditions, along with
level of literacy, can be seen as reason for such happenings and
health planners should take note of this phenomenon. Those
who are using formal health system mainly visit public
hospitals and maternity homes and it is certainly related to the
heavy difference between the costs of services in public and
private institutions.

In the non-slum areas, there is a major distinction in the
number of cases at the private hospitals and at home. Only in
three cases, particularly in Lakhudi non-slum area, last birth at
home is reported. In the non-slum areas, the number of cases at
the private nursing homes ranges between 26.09 percent in
Omnagar non-slum area and 87 percent at Machhipir non-slum
area. In Omnagar non-slum area, the number of cases at the
government hospitals is the maximum, i.e., 73.9 percent.

Therefore, while in the slum areas, the number of deliveries
is greater at home than in either government or private

hospitals the difference in the number of cases at home and in the hospitals is not as marked as in the case of non-slum areas. In the non-slum areas, clearly, the place of last birth is private nursing home in two of the three locations and in one location, it is the government hospital, but it is certainly not at home. Even after government initiatives to ensure birth in a medical institution, keeping in mind better maternal and child care, the primary survey reveals that it has not been successful in the slum areas. However, according to respondents, in these slums, compared to previous decade, things are improving as more and more people are going to hospitals and clinics for various reasons that include both child-birth and child care.

Table 11.8
Place of Last Birth

Localities	At Home	%	Govt. Hospital	%	Private Nursing Home	%	Unspecified	%	Total
Lakhudi slum	21	45.7	14	30.4	11	23.9	0	0	46
Lakhudi non-slum	3	6.4	8	17	35	74.5	1	2.1	47
Machhipir slum	21	47.7	18	40.9	5	11.4	0	0	44
Machhipir non-slum	0	0	6	13	40	87	0	0	46
Omnagar slum	16	32.7	22	44.9	11	22.5	0	0	49
Omnagar non-slum	0	0	34	73.9	12	26.1	0	0	46
Total	61	21.9	102	36.7	114	41	1	0.4	278

Immunisation

Immunisation is another important indicator of public health in developing countries as maternal and child care is directly related to it. According to Table 11.9 barring both Lakhudi slum and non-slum areas, acceptance of immunisation in all other localities is above 90 percent. No specific demarcation is observed in the trend shown by slum and non-slum areas. This is certainly a very healthy development and will contribute to reduce the IMR, as children are prone to be affected by various diseases before completing one year of age. The pulse polio programme, for polio eradication, promoted by the government, has penetrated every nook and corner of the country. It is for the very first time that an immunisation programme initiated by the government has been successful at the national level. It has achieved not only immunisation but has also been successful in promoting awareness amongst the people.

Table 11.9

Acceptance of Immunisation

Localities	Total Immunised Households
Lakhudi slum	32
Lakhudi non-slum	39
Machhipir slum	48
Machhipir non-slum	45
Omnagar slum	46
Omnagar non-slum	45

Of the total number of 264 households reported immunisation, 188 have utilised public services for this purpose while the remaining 76 have used private facilities. In Lakhudi slum area, all the 25 (100%) households have got immunisation by public facilities, whereas in Machhipir slum area, of the total 48 households, 97.9 percent used public facilities and in Omnagar slum area, of the total 46 households 91.3 percent used public facilities. In Lakhudi non-slum area, of the 50 households, 48 percent have got immunisation done through public facilities and 52 percent through private services. In Machhipir non-slum area, of the 50 cases, 72 percent have got immunisation done at private institutions, whereas in Omnagar non-slum area, 80 percent have got immunisation done at public institutions. It is very interesting to note that non-slum households have used public facilities for immunisation while they use private services for treatment of various diseases.

In general, this shows greater dependency of the slum areas on public facilities as compared to the non-slum areas. Greater dependency on the private facilities by the non-slum areas is also indicated by the place of last birth, which in majority of the cases was private nursing home. Probably, the private immunisation service, which is expensive, is not affordable by the financially weak slum residents. However, the general perception among the slum dwellers is that it is safer to get immunisation done at a private facility.

A clear observation gained so far is the increasing dependency of the slum dwellers on public services although their personal preference would be private facilities which they consider are of better quality and, hence, safe. Yet, when it comes to utilisation, they are depending on the public services – a clear indication of the restrictive costs involved in private services. This is validated by the fact that with growing awareness of the importance of health, people of all classes are willing to spend more in order to remain healthy.

Table 11.10
Immunisation

Localities	Public Facilities		Private Facilities		Total
	Number	*%*	*Number*	*%*	
Lakhudi slum	25	100	0	0	25
Lakhudi non-slum	24	48	26	52	50
Machhipir slum	47	97.9	1	2.1	48
Machhipir non-slum	14	28	36	72	50
Omnagar slum	42	91.3	4	8.7	46
Omnagar non-slum	36	80	9	20	45
Total	188	71.2	76	28.8	264

Number of Days Lost Due to Diseases

When any disease affects a person, it may result in losing mandays, as he will be forced to remain at home. The number of days lost due to diseases appears to be higher in Lakhudi non-slum with 29 percent of the total 17,552 mandays or more than eight mandays per month, followed by Omnagar slum area with 23.8 percent or about seven mandays per month. The number of days lost due to diseases is the lowest in Machhipir non-slum area with 5.1 percent only. In this case, no definite pattern is observed separately for the slum and the non-slum areas. But, the implication of it will vary according to the income category.

Table 11.11
Number of Days Lost Due to Diseases

Localities	No. of Days	Percent
Lakhudi slum	3091	17.6
Lakhudi non-slum	5095	29.0
Machhipir slum	2202	12.5
Machhipir non-slum	896	5.1
Omnagar slum	4176	23.8
Omnagar non-slum	2092	11.9
Total	17552	100.0

Interestingly, Lakhudi non-slum has the lowest incidence of persons affected by illnesses in the observed year in all the localities but is the place where the maximum number of man-days is lost due to illnesses. Again, this is also the place where there is the highest incidence of male members affected by disease within the same period in all localities. But previous observations have shown that Lakhudi non-slum also has the highest presence of public jobs as well as the highest levels of household income (Chapter 10). The implication is, however, similar to all localities. In non-slum area, persons losing days because of illness will have marginal effect or no effect at all on their household income as they belong to upper income group.

In slums, many are daily wage earners, for them the impact will be severe, and hence they are more concerned about it. It shows that every family is losing about five mandays or Rs.500/750 (Rs.100/150 per day) per month per household because of illness. In other words, those with an assured higher income have the luxury of holiday and rest in case of illness.

Deaths in the Localities in the Last One Year

There have been 22 deaths in all the six localities in the last one year. Of these, the maximum deaths (50%) have been from Omnagar non-slum area and no deaths in Lakhudi non-slum area. This clearly shows that Lakhudi non-slum area is a very complex case having very low mortality rate but very high rate of mandays lost due to various diseases. It is happening even though the area is known for its better living environment. It appears that health problems may create some disturbance but probably they have better access to treatment and hence the death rate is quite low. However, based on one-year data, it is extremely difficult to arrive any specific conclusion in this matter.

Table 11.12

Deaths in the Localities in the Last One Year

Localities	No of Cases	Percent
Lakhudi slum	6	27.26
Lakhudi non-slum	0	0
Machhipir slum	3	13.64
Machhipir non-slum	1	4.55
Omnagar slum	1	4.55
Omnagar non-slum	11	50.00
Total	22	100.00

Perception Regarding Government-Owned Health Facilities

Only 145 respondents have expressed their opinion regarding government-owned health facilities in Ahmedabad. About 43.4

percent perceived government health facilities to be good, 24.1 percent to be efficient, and 19.3 percent felt that the medicine given by the doctors were effective. None of the respondents felt that the medical facilities are expensive. It is also important to note that very few respondents felt that the government-owned medical facilities are inefficient, that the behaviour of doctors is bad, that there is problem of timing or that there was no medicine given, etc.

Table 11.13

Perception regarding Government-owned Health Facilities

Perception		Lakhudi slum	Lakhudi non-slum	Machhipir slum	Machhipir non-slum	Omnagar slum	Omnagar non-slum	Slum total	Total
Good		8	1	17	1	27	9	52	63
	%	66.67	33.33	47.22	33.33	37.50	47.37	35	43.45
Efficient		0	1	9	1	19	5	28	35
	%	0	33.33	25.00	33.33	26.39	26.32	19.3	24.14
Inefficient		0	0	2	0	2	1	4	5
	%	0	0	5.56	0.00	2.78	5.26	2.7	3.45
Expensive		0	0	0	0	0	0	0	0
	%	0	0	0	0	0	0	0	0
Good behaviour		1	0	0	0	2	0	3	3
	%	8.33	0.00	0.00	0.00	2.78	0.00	2	2.07
Bad behaviour		0	0	3	0	1	0	4	4
	%	0	0	8.33	0	1.39	0	2.7	2.76
Problem of timing		2	0	0	0	4	0	6	6
	%	16.67	0.00	0.00	0.00	5.56	0.00	4.13	4.14
No medicine was given		0	0	0	0	1	0	1	1
	%	0	0	0	0	1.39	0.00	0.6	0.69
Medicine was effective		1	1	5	1	16	4	22	28
	%	8.33	33.33	13.89	33.33	22.22	21.05	28.53	19.31
Total		12	3	36	3	72	19	120	145

Given the fact that most of the people who utilise the government-owned medical facilities are from the slums, it would be pertinent to observe the reactions of the slum people irrespective of the non-slum people. In this case, a keener picture emerges. The proportion of people considering the services to be good falls down a good 10 to 35 percent. In other cases, only 2.7 percent of the total respondents considered it to be inefficient. However, this is corroborated by the fact that only 19.3 percent consider it to be efficient. The perception that emerges then is that while the people are not unhappy with the services, they are not too happy with it either.

Therefore, the general perception regarding government-run medical facilities comes out to be positive. This is also the scenario, which emerges across all the locations of slum and non-slum areas. The problem may, however, lie with the per capita availability of services to the large number of people.

Perception Regarding Municipal Health Facilities

There are no responses from the non-slum areas regarding perception of municipal health services. Of the total 77 respondents expressed their perception regarding municipal health facilities all are from the slum areas only. While, a total of 44.2 percent of the respondents perceive municipal health services to be good, 26 percent perceive them to be efficient. Very few respondents felt that the municipal health services are inefficient or that there is a problem with the timing. Therefore, the general perception regarding municipal health services as for public health facility is that they are good and efficient. In non-slum areas some people are using municipal health facility mainly for specialised cases and also for indoor services. For the day-to-day problem they prefer to visit a private doctor close to their house and hence refused to give any opinion about municipal services.

Table 11.14
Perception regarding Municipal Health Facilities

Perception		Lakhudi slum	Machhipir slum	Omnagar slum	Total
Good		12	17	5	34
	%	48	42.5	41.7	44.2
Efficient		6	10	4	20
	%	24	25	33.3	26.0
Inefficient		3	1	1	5
	%	12	2.5	8.3	6.5
Good behaviour		1	1	0	2
	%	4	2.5	0	2.6
Problem of timing		1	0	1	2
	%	4	0	8.3	2.6
Medicine was effective		2	11	1	14
	%	8	27.5	8.3	18.2
Total		25	40	12	77

Perception Regarding Private Nursing Homes

Private nursing homes are gradually becoming important health care institutions in Ahmedabad and in many urban centres. The number of such homes is not only increasing but these have also started offering various specialised services, which were available only in the public hospitals. Only 39 of the total respondents expressed their perception regarding private nursing homes. Table 11.15 shows that maximum respondents, i.e., 38.5 percent feel that the private nursing homes are good, and 20.5 percent feel that they are efficient. The difference in the perception as compared to the government-run health facilities and municipal-run facilities is evident through the responses on one criteria, namely, expensive. Of the total, 25.6 percent respondents feel that the private medical facilities in the form of nursing homes are expensive.

Table 11.15
Perception regarding Private Nursing Homes

Perception		Lakbhudi slum	Lakbhudi non-slum	Machbipir slum	Machbipir non-slum	Omnagar slum	Omnagar non-slum	Total
Good		6	1	0	1	6	1	15
	%	40.0	100.0	0	33.3	35.3	33.3	38.5
Efficient		3	0	0	1	4	0	8
	%	20	0.00	0	33.3	23.5	0.0	20.5
Inefficient		1	0	0	0	0	0	1
	%	6.7	0	0	0.00	0.00	0.00	2.6
Expensive		2	0	0	0	6	1	10
	%	13.3	0.0	0	0.0	35.3	33.3	25.6
Problem of timing		1	0	0	0	0	0	1
	%	6.7	0.0	0	0.0	0.0	0.0	2.6
Medicine was effective		2	0	0	1	1	0	4
	%	13.3	0.0	0	33.3	5.9	0.0	10.3
Total		15	1	0	3	17	3	39

Perception Regarding Private Clinics

The private clinics offer general as well specialised heath care services and mainly one doctor is available in one clinic. Such clinics are spread over the city and these doctors receive most of the general health problems. According to Table 11.16, 38.1 percent of the total respondents expressed their opinion as good and useful. They perceived these clinics to be efficient (29.2%). Of the total 11.3 percent felt that the behaviour of doctors is good, 10.2 percent found that medicine given is effective but 10 percent found the facility to be expensive. Very few respondents perceive the private clinics to be inefficient; none of the respondents have found any problem with the time schedule or any other problem.

Table 11.16

Perception regarding Private Clinics (Multiple Responses)

		Lakhudi slum	Lakhudi non-slum	Machhipir slum	Machhipir non-slum	Omnagar slum	Omnagar non-slum	Total
Good		20	47	23	46	33	36	205
	%	44	38	35	37	37	41	38
Efficient		9	42	15	42	23	26	157
	%	20	33.6	22.7	33.6	25.6	29.9	29.2
Inefficient		0	0	1	0	0	0	1
	%	0	0	1.5	0.0	0.0	0.0	0.2
Expensive		12	4	13	0	20	5	54
	%	26.7	3.2	19.7	0.0	22.2	5.7	10.0
Good behaviour		0	17	5	27	3	9	61
	%	0.0	13.6	7.6	21.6	3.3	10.3	11.3
Problem of timing		0	2	1	0	0	0	3
	%	0.0	1.6	1.5	0.0	0.0	0.0	0.6
No medicine was given		0	0	0	0	2	0	2
	%	0	0	0	0	2.2	0.00	0.4
Medicine was given		4	13	8	10	9	11	55
	%	8.9	10.4	12.1	8.0	10.0	12.6	10.2
Total		45	125	66	125	90	87	538

Perception Regarding NGOs/Trusts

There are no responses from the non-slum areas for the perception regarding health services run by NGOs/trusts. Very few responses are received from the slum areas also. Of the total 15 responses, 33.3 percent respondents perceive services run by NGOs/trusts to be good, 26.7 percent to be efficient and acknowledge good behaviour of doctors and 13.3 percent have stated that medicine prescribed is effective.

Table 11.17

Perception regarding NGOs/Trusts

		Lakhudi slum	Machhipir slum	Omnagar slum	Total
Good		3	1	1	5
	%	33.3	33.3	25	33.3
Efficient		2	1	1	4
	%	22.2	33.3	25	26.7
Good behaviour		3	0	1	4
	%	33.3	0	25	26.7
Medicine was effective		1	1	0	2
	%	11.1	33.3	0	13.3
Total		9	3	3	15

To summarise, most people suffer from cold and fever. Other water-borne diseases are reported more from non-slum areas. Across all the locations it is the male members who are affected in large numbers by various diseases as compared to females and children. Allopathic as the treatment system is much more popular. For treatment respondents are using public facilities more in slums whereas non-slum respondents are using private facilities. Some people have changed the institution for health care facility from 1991 and better service and less time are mainly responsible for it. Home is still popular for delivering the child mainly in slum areas. In non-slum areas people prefer private nursing home for delivery. Gradually, people are accepting immunisation as essential for child care. In slum areas respondents are using public system for immunisation. Perception regarding public system shows a positive trend as it comes out to be good and efficient. The private health care system although found to be efficient has been identified as expensive.

12

Education: Utilisation and Preference

To explain the utilisation and preference for education services various parameters, such as number of students at various educational levels, school types, medium of instructions, enrolment scenario and dropout of students, etc., were selected. Data related to perception regarding schools and preference were also collected.

Students at Different Educational Standards

Of the three hundred households surveyed in the six localities, there are 405 students, at various levels of education. The total number of students under all the categories in the six locations ranges between a minimum of 49 students in Machhipir non-slum area and a maximum of 79 in Omnagar slum area. Of the 50 households in each of the six locations, it was only in three locations that we came across college-going students in the course of survey. These three locations are Lakhudi non-slum with seven out of the 77 students in 50 households, Machhipir slum with three out of 68 students and Machhipir non-slum with one student out of 49 students. In Lakhudi slum, of the 67 total students, 92.5 percent are in primary schools and the remaining 7.5 percent in secondary schools.

Figure 12.1
Students in Different Educational Standards

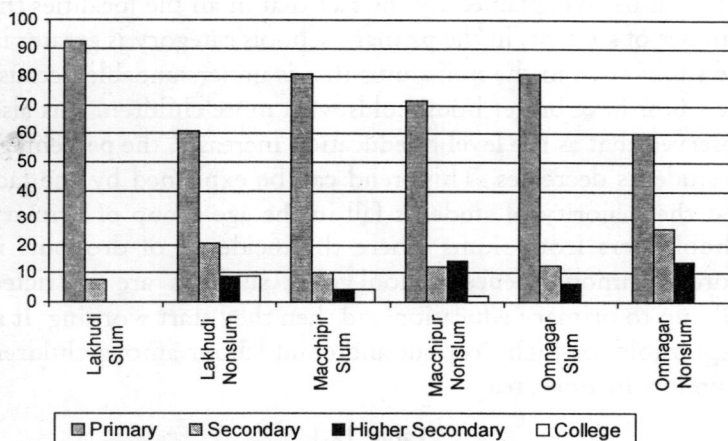

Of the 405 students 74.6 percent are in primary schools. In Lakhudi non-slum, of the 77 students, 61.04 percent and 20.8 percent are in primary and secondary schools respectively while an equal number (9.1%) are in higher secondary schools as well as in colleges. Similarly, in Machhipir slum area, of the 68 students, 80.9 percent and 10.3 percent are in primary and secondary schools respectively, while an equal number (4.4%) are in higher secondary schools as well as in colleges. In Machhipir non-slum area, of the 49 students, 71.4 percent, 12.2 percent and 14.3 percent are studying in primary, secondary and higher secondary schools respectively while 2 percent are studying in colleges. Likewise, in Omnagar slum area, of the 79 students, 81 percent, 12.7 percent and 6.3 percent are studying in primary, secondary and higher secondary schools respectively. And, in the Omnagar non-slum, of the 65 students, 60 percent, 26.2 percent and 13.9 percent are in primary, secondary and higher secondary respectively while none are in college.

The primary survey reveals that the majority of school-going students fall in the category of primary schools. This can be so explained by the fact that in all the localities the number of students in the primary schools category is greater in the slums than in the non-slums that is understandable because the slums have bigger households with more children. It is also observed that as the level of education increases, the percentage of students decreases. This trend can be explained by the fact that the majority of students fall in the age group of primary school goers from slums where the incidence of dropouts is more common. Hence, school-going students are restricted only up to primary education and then they start working. It is responsible for high dropout and child labour among children from low-income area.

Table 12.1
Students in Different Educational Standards

Localities	Primary	%	Secondary	%	Higher Secondary	%	College	%	Total
Lakhudi slum	62	92.54	5	7.46	0	0	0	0	67
Lakhudi non-slum	47	61.04	16	20.78	7	9.09	7	9.09	77
Machhipir slum	55	80.88	7	10.29	3	4.41	3	4.41	68
Machhipir non-slum	35	71.43	6	12.24	7	14.29	1	2.04	49
Omnagar slum	64	81.01	10	12.66	5	6.33	0	0	79
Omnagar non-slum	39	60	17	26.15	9	13.85	0	0	65
Total	302	74.57	61	15.06	31	7.65	11	2.72	405

As the level of education increases, it can be seen that the proportion of students increases in the non-slum areas and decreases in the slum areas. Till higher secondary, most of the localities show a fair share of students except Lakhudi slum. This is doubly unfortunate as Lakhudi slum shows the second highest number of students in the primary schools category in all the localities. On the brighter side, however, Machhipir slum has college-going students figuring a greater percentage than Machhipir non-slum. This is a trend which should be encouraged in the other slums too where there are no college-going students.

School Types

The primary survey of the six locations indicates that the utilisation of type of schools is limited to municipal and private schools only. While the private schools, some of them are privately managed but funded by the state government, are most popular among households living in non-slum areas, utilisation of municipal schools has been reported by majority of the households in slum areas. So, the survey results very clearly indicate that selection of school for children is highly related to economic condition that again determines the settlement type in Ahmedabad. It also shows that municipal primary schools still offer some basic educational service to the poorer segment of city dwellers and special attention should be given for its development.

Settlement-wise information reveals that in Lakhudi slum area, of the total 67 students, 77.7 percent go to the municipal schools, next comes the private schools with 19.4 percent and in the last the government-aided schools with 2.99 percent. Similarly, in Lakhudi non-slum area, of the total 77 students, 96.1 percent go to the private schools, only 2.6 percent go to the municipal schools and 1.3 percent go to the government-aided schools. In Machhipir slum area, of the 68 students in total, 66.18 percent go to municipal schools while the remaining 33.82 percent go to the private schools. Likewise, in Machhipir non-slum area, of the total 49 students 95.92 percent go to the private schools, while the remaining 4.08 percent go to the municipal schools. In Omnagar slum area, of the total 79 students, 65.82 percent go to the municipal schools, and the remaining 34.18 percent go to private schools. And, finally, in

Figure 12.2
Students in Different School Types

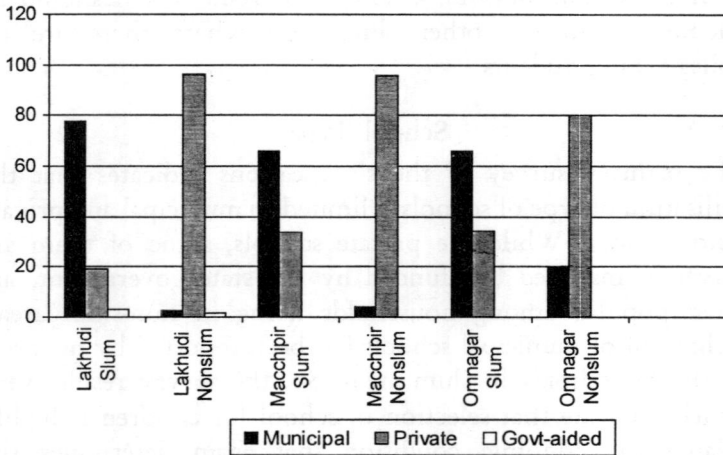

Omnagar non-slum area, of the total 65 students, 20 percent go to the municipal schools, while the remaining 80 percent go to private schools. The table very clearly indicates that all the non-slum areas are not equal in economic terms and hence in some cases students from these areas are also attending municipal schools.

Table 12.2
School Types

Localities	Municipal	%	Govt-aided	%	Private	%	Total
Lakhudi slum	52	77.7	2	2.99	13	19.4	67
Lakhudi non-slum	2	2.6	1	1.3	74	96.1	77
Machhipir slum	45	66.18	0	0	23	33.82	68
Machhipir non-slum	2	4.08	0	0	47	95.92	49
Omnagar slum	52	65.82	0	0	27	34.18	79
Omnagar non-slum	13	20	0	0	52	80	65
Total	168	41.2	3	0.74	237	58.1	405

Medium of Instructions

Of the total 405 students, 90.1 percent across all the locations study in Gujarati-medium schools. In Lakhudi slum, of the 67 pupils, 66 study in Gujarati medium and one in school with English as the medium of instructions. In Lakhudi non-slum also, the largest percentage of students is studying in Gujarati-medium schools. Of the total of 77 students in this area, 53 are in Gujarati medium, 22 in English medium, one in Hindi medium, and again one in schools with other medium of instructions. Therefore, in this locality, 28.57 percent of the students study in English-medium schools. In Machhipir slum area, of the 68 students, 89.71 percent study in Gujarati-medium schools, while 10.29 percent in Hindi-medium schools. In Machhipir non-slum area, of the total 49 students, 93.88 percent study in Gujarati-medium schools while the remaining 6.12 percent in English-medium schools. In Omnagar slum area, of the total 79 students, 76 study in Gujarati-medium schools and the remaining three in Hindi-medium schools. In Omnagar non-slum area, of the 65 students, two are in English-medium schools while the rest in Gujarati-medium schools.

Thus, the spoken language of the state being Gujarati, maximum number of students are studying in schools with Gujarati as the medium of instructions among all the localities. A very slight inclination towards the English-medium schools is observed in the non-slum areas. English-medium schools, which are perceived to provide a better quality of education and are also considered expensive, are not affordable by residents of slum areas with low-income level. A greater percentage of students in English-medium schools is observed in Lakhudi non-slum, which as stated earlier has a higher income level as compared to the rest of the locations. Besides the affordability of the residents, this area is also having some well-known English-medium schools and some them are managed by Christian missionaries that appears to be responsible for sending kids in these schools. Also, English-medium schools are

Figure 12.3

Students in Different Mediums in Instructions

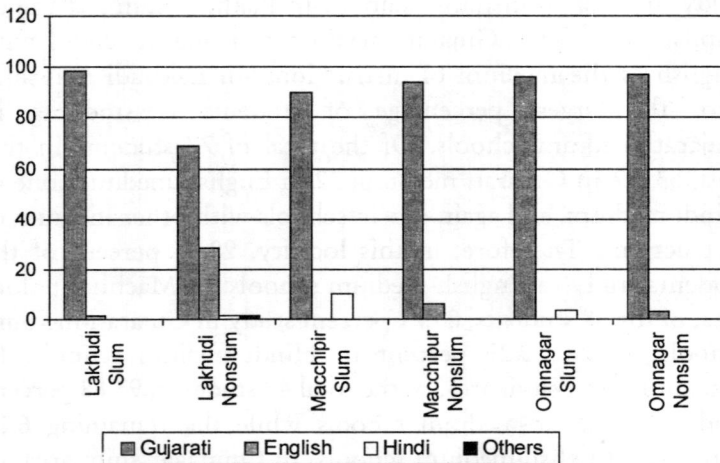

becoming more popular now as competition for job is increasing. Recent developments in IT-related courses have also been identified as a probable reason for diverting towards English-medium education. So, in near future, Gujarati as medium of instructions will be less popular among school-going children.

Table 12.3

Students in Different Mediums of Instructions

Localities	Gujarati	%	English	%	Hindi	%	Others	%	Total
Lakhudi slum	66	98.51	1	1.49	0	0	0	0	67
Lakhudi non-slum	53	68.83	22	28.57	1	1.3	1	1.3	77
Machhipir slum	61	89.71	0	0	7	10.29	0	0	68
Machhipir non-slum	46	93.88	3	6.12	0	0	0	0	49
Omnagar slum	76	96.2	0	0	3	3.8	0	0	79
Omnagar non-slum	63	96.92	2	3.08	0	0	0	0	65
Total	365	90.12	28	6.91	11	2.72	1	0.25	405

Enrolment Scenario

The primary survey reveals that a large percentage of the children in school-going age across all the locations are enrolled. Of the total 259 children, nearly 90.4 percent are enrolled. The highest percent, of enrolment is observed in Lakhudi non-slum area, where this is as high as 97.7 percent of the total 44 households, again indicating a relation between income level and literacy. The lowest percentage of enrolment is observed in Lakhudi slum area, where this is observed to be 78.3 percent of the total of 46 households. Among all the three slum areas, Lakhudi is located in an affluent area but its enrolment rate is lowest. In other slums like in Omnagar only two children were found to be non-enrolled. In general, it shows a good performance in school enrolment although special attention should be given to slum areas where some children are not yet enrolled in any school. It also indicates that economic condition is a very strong factor directly related to the enrolment of children.

Figure 12.4
Enrolment Scenario

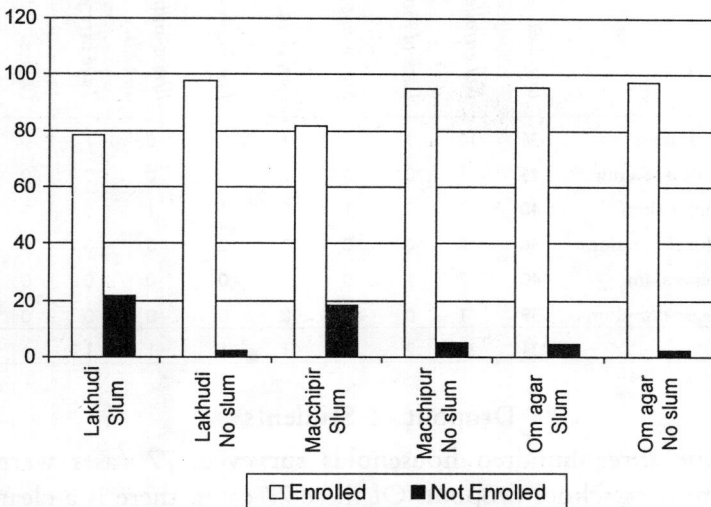

The reasons for not enrolling are reported by a few households and among them include lack of money, education is not important, girl child, little interest in education, illness, taking care of younger children in the household or some other reason. Of all of these reasons no specific reason emerges to be the dominant one. Therefore, the stated reasons are either financial, gender-related, or psychological orientation of the parents that resulted in non-enrolment. At the national level, the present education policy is giving special emphasis on enrolment so that the rate of literacy is increasing. But special initiative should be taken to address the problems like girl child or taking care of younger child and thinking like education is not important in life.

Table 12.4
Enrolment Scenario

Localities	Enrolled	Not enrolled	Reasons for Not Enrolling						
			Lack of money	Edn is not important	Girl child	Less interest	Illness and/or disability	Take care younger	Others
Lakhudi slum	36	10	1	0	1	0	0	1	0
Lakhudi non-slum	43	1	0	0	0	0	0	0	0
Macchipir slum	40	9	0	1	0	1	1	0	1
Macchipir non-slum	36	2	0	0	0	0	0	0	0
Omnagar slum	40	2	1	0	0	0	0	0	0
Omnagar non-slum	39	1	0	0	0	0	0	0	0
Total	234	25	2	1	1	1	1	1	1

Dropout of Students

Of the three hundred households surveyed, 77 cases were recorded of school dropout. Of these 77 cases, there is a clear demarcation of a larger proportion of dropout from the slum areas. If we observe the percentage-wise distribution across localities, 28.6 percent are from Lakhudi and Machhipir slums, and 27.3 percent from Omnagar slum. In the non-slum areas, it is less than 10 percent of the total. The reported dropout from Lakhudi is again a special case as this area is supposed to be better off than other slum areas. It clearly shows that dropout is again related not only to financial condition of the households but also some other reasons as observed for enrolment.

Table 12.5
Dropout and its Reasons

Localities	Dropout	%	For extra earning	Failed in exams	Less interest	Mother's pregnancy
Lakhudi slum	22	28.57	6	2	1	1
Lakhudi non-slum	4	5.19	0	3	1	0
Machhipir slum	22	28.57	10	1	4	1
Machhipir non-slum	2	2.6	0	1	0	0
Omnagar slum	21	27.27	9	0	4	0
Omnagar non-slum	6	7.79	0	0	0	0
Total	77	100	25	7	10	2

Again, the reasons for dropout are mainly financial and no particular reason emerges to be individually responsible. Dropout reasons attributed are: for extra earning, failed in examinations, little interest in studies and mother's pregnancy. The first reason is purely economic where children are required to work for earning as parents cannot earn enough to meet their daily requirements. The failure in examination is also important and recently government is insisting to pass all the students at primary level so that no one is leaving school for this reason. In some states, in final examinations conducted at primary level many students who failed, left school forever. Such examinations have now been withdrawn and it certainly helped in restricting dropouts but the quality of student is suffering. The present condition is very complicated and an easy solution is difficult. In city like Ahmedabad special attention should be given to make education more attractive and parents need some support so that they are not withdrawing their kids from schools. As the problem is found to be more prevalent in low-income settlements NGOs and CBOs working in these areas can help in educating parents against the adverse consequences of dropouts. Many researchers have observed gender bias among student's dropout but in this study we failed to find out any such trend.

Occurrence of School Change

Table 12.6 gives details of school changes during the last five years. In fact, there are very few instances of school changes across all the localities. Of the total 186 responses, 9.7 percent have reported schools change, while the remaining 90.3 percent have not reported any change. The percentage of school change appears to be higher in the case of Machhipir slum and Omnagar non-slum, with 14.3 percent and 21.4 percent respectively. Survey results clearly show that majority of parents do not want any change of school. While talking to some respondents it was noted that it is a very difficult to get admission in higher classes as compared to kindergarten or equivalent level (entry level for most of the schools in Ahmedabad). According to recent press reports, admission in well-known schools, both English and Gujarati medium, is becoming very difficult and some schools even demand donation for admission. So, in case of school change, parents have to pay a lot as donation which is an important reason for continuing in the same school. But, this trend is observed in private schools and admission in municipal schools is relatively easy at any level. Even when there is change of school it is within the same category (public or private).

Table 12.6
Occurrence of School Change

Localities	Yes	%	No	%	Total
Lakhudi slum	2	5.7	33	94.3	35
Lakhudi non-slum	2	7.1	26	92.9	28
Machhipir slum	4	14.3	24	85.7	28
Machhipir non-slum	1	3.3	29	96.7	30
Omnagar slum	3	8.1	34	91.9	37
Omnagar non-slum	6	21.4	22	78.6	28
Total	18	9.7	168	90.3	186

Selection of School

Respondent were asked to specify the criteria for selection of the school for their children. Of the total 376 responses, maximum weightage is given to distance from home with 37 percent, followed by the fee structure with 30.6 percent and quality of teaching with 29 percent. The reason that "other kids study there" has been the deciding factor in only 3.46 percent cases. In general proximity to home appears to be the most important criterion in school selection and it is directly related to the issues like transportation, safety, etc. It is also important to remember that the maximum number of students are in primary schools and parents are not interested to send their kids in long distance places. It also justifies the requirement of neighbourhood level schools as propagated by urban planners. This information is also very useful to look at the location of activities in newly developed area. In the new town planning schemes, provision for primary and secondary schools at neighbourhood should be made compulsory.

But when we analyse the same data based on settlements it clearly shows settlement-wise variations in factors for selection. For the financially weak slum population fees and distance are equally important while the quality of teaching does not matter much to them. Education, even at the primary level, has become quite expensive, as parents have to bear the cost of additional books, notebooks, dress, tiffin and even private tuition free even when their kids are going to municipal schools that have free education. The national and state governments should take note of it and make necessary changes in the allocation of funds for primary education.

In non-slum areas where people are economically well-off have expressed their concern about quality of teaching while deciding the school for their children. Some respondents expressed it very clearly that they want their children to get best education available in this city and they will send them where it is assured. Distance has been expressed as the second important deciding factor in school selection and it is more so in Omnagar as compared to the other two non-slum settlements. Many households in both Machhipir and Omnagar slums have used distance as a factor for school selection.

Table 12.7
Selection of School

Localities	Distance	%	Fees	%	Teaching	%	Others	%	Total
Lakhudi slum	2	5.13	32	82.05	3	7.69	2	5.13	39
Lakhudi non-slum	19	30.16	3	4.76	36	57.14	5	7.94	63
Machhipir slum	32	42.11	33	43.42	8	10.53	3	3.95	76
Machhipir non-slum	20	37.04	4	7.41	28	51.85	2	3.7	54
Omnagar slum	37	48.68	37	48.68	2	2.63	0	0	76
Omnagar non-slum	29	42.65	6	8.82	32	47.06	1	1.47	68
Total	139	36.97	115	30.59	109	28.99	13	3.46	376

School Facilities

School facilities are important factor in determining the standard of education. Of the total 747 responses, toilet and playground come out to be the most common facilities as more than 70 percent of the total schools are having these facilities. Next follows library as about 40 percent of schools are having library in their buildings and almost all of them are working. Computer too seems to be a new facility with 17 percent of the respondents acknowledging computer education in their respective schools. However, very few schools are having transport facility, science laboratory and audio-visual facility. In general, it indicates that many schools are not having enough space for play. The settlement-related information shows very little difference in the availability of facilities between municipal and private schools. Facilities other than those discussed are also present in 16.9 percent of the cases. Some respondents, mainly from the slums, are concerned about the condition of the building in municipal schools, as many buildings are not properly maintained. Private schools are of recent origin and many such schools have moved into buildings constructed recently. Cleanness has also been discussed as many municipal schools are not cleaned properly on a daily basis. These two issues found to be equally responsible for quality of education offered by different types of schools in Ahmedabad.

Therefore, basic facilities that a school should provide apart from education like space for play, infrastructure facility like toilet particularly for girls and library seem to be present in a large number of schools but not in all the schools in Ahmedabad. Computer facilities too seem to have gaining importance in the schools and many schools are planning to have this facility in near future. Private schools are more interested to have computers and also facilities like swimming pool (even a small one) and skating. Transport facility is available in all the schools as many auto-rickshaws are attached with schools and offering this facility as a private service. Only few schools are having their own vehicles. Science laboratory and audio-visual mode of teaching are also identified as facilities and only few schools are having them in their schools. The survey results clearly show difference in the responses from non-slum and slum areas as students attending schools from non-slum areas are having little better infrastructural facilities in comparison to students from slums.

Table 12.8
School Facilities

Facilities		Lakbudi slum	Lakbudi non-slum	Machbipir slum	Machbipir non-slum	Omnagar slum	Omnagar non-slum	Total	% of total
Playground	%	16.2	16.7	17.6	14.8	18.1	16.7	100	
		34	35	37	31	38	35	210	28.1
Library	%	22.1	29.8	10.7	15.3	17.6	4.6	100	
		29	39	14	20	23	6	131	17.5
Toilet	%	15.8	18.1	16.7	14.4	18.1	16.7	100	
		34	39	36	31	39	36	215	28.8
Transport	%	0	80	0	0	0	20	100	
		0	4	0	0	0	1	5	0.7
Computer	%	1.9	61.5	1.9	30.8	0	3.9	100	
		1	32	1	16	0	2	52	7.0
Science lab	%	0	50	0	25	0	25	100	
		0	2	0	1	0	1	4	0.5
Audio-visual aids	%	0	50	0	0	0	50	100	
		0	2	0	0	0	2	4	0.5
Others	%	23.0	2.4	17.5	11.1	22.2	23.8	100	
		29	3	22	14	28	30	126	16.9
Total		127	156	110	113	128	113	747	

Perception Regarding Schools

The quality of educational services has been debated for a long time and many experts are of the opinion that parents' perception regarding quality of education is very important.

During our survey we asked this question to all our respondents but only about 80 percent have expressed their views. It has to be seen in the context that larger utilisation of municipal schools from slum areas and private schools from non-slum areas was reported. The respondents were asked to rate the schools on the scale of good, average and bad. The numbers of respondents, who perceive the municipal schools to be average, are in the range of 63.9 percent in Lakhudi slum,

Table 12.9
Perception regarding Schools

Perception		*Lakhudi slum*	*Lakhudi non-slum*	*Machhipir slum*	*Machhipir non-slum*	*Omnagar slum*	*Omnagar non-slum*	*Total*
Municipal	Good	8	0	4	0	9	1	22
	%	22.22	0	16	0	33.33	16.67	23.16
	Average	23	0	12	1	12	5	53
	%	63.89	0	48	100	44.44	83.33	55.79
	Bad	5	0	9	0	6	0	20
	%	13.89	0	36	0	22.22	0	21.05
	Total	36	0	25	1	27	6	95
Government Aided	Good	0	3	0	0	0	0	3
	%	0	100	0	0	0	0	100
	Total	0	3	0	0	0	0	3
Private	Good	6	34	8	30	16	20	114
	%	46.15	87.18	61.54	96.77	94.12	64.52	79.17
	Average	1	4	5	1	1	11	23
	%	7.69	10.26	38.46	3.23	5.88	35.48	15.97
	Bad	6	1	0	0	0	0	7
	%	46.15	2.56	0	0	0	0	4.86
	Total	13	39	13	31	17	31	144
Grand Total		49	42	38	32	44	37	242

48 percent in Machhipir slum, 100 percent in Machhipir non-slum, 44.4 percent in Omnagar slum and 83.3 percent in Omnagar non-slum areas. Generally, across all the localities, very few respondents feel that the municipal schools are in the category of either good or bad. With the exception of Machhipir slum area, where 36 percent of the respondents feel the municipal schools to be bad and Omnagar slum area where 33.3 percent of the respondents feel the municipal schools to be good, the general perception comes out to be average. Very few responses were received regarding government-aided schools.

With the exception of Lakhudi slum, where six of the respondents feel that private schools are bad, across all the other localities the perception comes out to be good. Respondents from non-slum areas are happy with private schools except one from Lakhudi non-slum area. Therefore, the municipal schools are rated as average while the private schools are good by majority of the respondents.

Perception Regarding School Affairs

School affairs have been explained through parameters like teacher's quality, regularity of classes, behaviour of teachers, individual care, frequency of parents' meeting, extra-curricular activities and physical activities. Of the total 225 respondents, 64.4 percent feel that the teachers are good, 26.7 percent feel that they are average and the remaining 8.9 percent feel that they are bad. This is the opinion across all the localities but for Lakhudi slum where of the 36 respondents 40 percent feel that the teachers are of average, 16 percent feel that they are good and another 16 percent feel that they are bad in teaching. However, people from the nearby non-slum areas expressed happiness over teaching quality in schools where their kids are going. Similar trend is also observed in Machhipir and Omnagar non-slum areas as only one gave negative reply. But respondents from the nearby slum areas do not seem to be very happy, as 20 percent have given very negative opinion regarding teachers. The perception regarding regularity of classes comes out to be a definite 'yes', with 91.6 percent of respondents considering classes to be regular. Some respondents from slum areas have reported that classes are not held regularly in schools. So, with regard to both the teacher's quality and regularity of classes, some differences of opinion among slum and non-slum areas have been observed. This is certainly related to the type of school kids are attending.

The behaviour of teachers is generally perceived to be good, with 64 percent feeling this way. Although, in Lakhudi slum area, the opinion differs, with 19 out of 35 respondents expressed that the teacher's behaviour to be average, nine of them reported it as bad and only seven as good. Individual care is considered to be in the range of good and average, with 40.4 percent and 38.7 percent respectively. In Lakhudi slum and Omnagar non-slum areas, the opinion is definitely average, with 23 out of 36 and 20 out of 37 respectively were of this opinion. In case of Lakhudi non-slum area, the opinion comes out to be definitely good with 40 out of 43 respondents opining this way.

The trend can also be related to the type of school that the students are studying in -- municipal or private. The responses from slum areas can be said to represent municipal schools while those from non-slum areas private schools. It is also important to note that respondents from Lakhudi slum are not really happy with many things in the schools and it is certainly related to municipal schools where most of their kids are studying.

In the slum areas the responses clearly indicate irregular parents' meeting. Of the total 219 responses, 55.7 percent indicate irregular parents' meeting. In case of non-slum areas, 37 out of 43, 29 out of 32 and 14 out of 37 from Lakhudi, Machhipir and Omnagar respectively are of the opinion that parents' meeting are regular. Parents' meeting is an important issue in modern education system as it gives opportunity to

Table 12.10
Perception regarding School Affairs

Perception		Lakhudi slum	Lakhudi non-slum	Machhipir slum	Machhipir non-slum	Omnagar slum	Omnagar non-slum	Total	Percentage of total
Teachers quality	Good	8	41	20	30	24	22	145	64.4
	Average	20	1	10	2	13	14	60	26.7
	Bad	8	1	7	0	3	1	20	8.9
	Total	36	43	37	32	40	37	225	
Regularity of classes	Regular	32	43	27	32	37	35	206	91.6
	Irregular	4	0	10	0	3	2	19	8.4
	Total	36	43	37	32	40	37	225	
Behaviour of teachers	Good	7	38	14	28	21	34	142	64.0
	Average	19	4	13	4	13	2	55	24.8
	Bad	9	1	9	0	6	0	25	11.3
	Total	35	43	36	32	40	36	222	
Individual care	Good	4	40	7	18	15	7	91	40.4
	Average	23	2	17	11	14	20	87	38.7
	Bad	9	1	13	3	11	10	47	20.9
	Total	36	43	37	32	40	37	225	
Parents meeting	Regular	2	37	7	29	8	14	97	44.3
	Irregular	30	6	29	3	31	23	122	55.7
	Total	32	43	36	32	39	37	219	
Extra-curricular activities	Good	10	38	8	14	13	8	91	40.4
	Average	22	4	19	14	17	13	89	39.6
	Bad	4	1	10	4	10	16	45	20.0
	Total	36	43	37	32	40	37	225	
Physical facilities	Good	14	41	16	17	23	7	118	52.4
	Average	16	1	10	12	9	22	70	31.1
	Bad	6	1	11	3	8	8	37	16.4
	Total	36	43	37	32	40	37	225	

both teachers and parents to discuss about child and also helps to resolve if there is any problem. Most of the private schools in Ahmedabad give special importance to such meetings. As students from non-slum areas are going to these types of schools parents' meeting are regular except the Omnagar non-slum area. It shows that same thing is not happening all over the city even for similar socio-economic groups.

Extra-curricular activities like sports, drama and celebration of various festivals are again perceived to be in the range of good to average. Of the total of 225 respondents, 40.4 percent are of the opinion that extra-curricular activities are good, 39.6 percent that they are average and 20 percent that they are bad or inadequate. Physical facilities are generally perceived to be good, with 52.4 percent of 225 responses. The exception again seems to be Omnagar slum area with only seven responses indicating that physical facilities are good.

A picture that emerges from the above observation is that students from the slum area schools and the school affairs are not as good as in the non-slum areas. The responses of the slum areas indicate lesser satisfaction with the school affairs as compared with the non-slum areas across all the categories. This distinction is actually between the types of schools children are attending.

School Preferences

Respondents were asked to specify their preference for schools where they would like to send their children. Of the total 364 respondents, the highest number, i.e., 35.2 percent expressed their preference to proximity to home be the most important criterion in selecting the school. Good teaching environment is preferred by 31.3 percent and then free education by 20.1 percent of the respondents. The criteria of preference of school in various localities show that in the slum areas, the important criteria are proximity to school and free education whereas in non-slum areas good teaching gains the highest priority in all

the three locations. Apart from the quality of education, the
fame of the school has also been an important criterion in
Lakhudi non-slum area. In Machhipir non-slum area proximity
to home turns out to be the next important criterion. In
Omnagar non-slum area proximity to home has equal
importance as quality of teaching. In general, it shows that
people in Ahmedabad are mainly concerned with distance,
quality and cost of education in selecting schools for their
children.

Table 12.11
School Preferences

Criteria of preferences	Lakhudi slum	%	Lakhudi non-slum	%	Machhipir slum	%	Machhipir non-slum	%	Omnagar slum	%	Omnagar non-slum	%	Total	%
Less fees	1	1.6	0	0	2	2.7	0	0	4	5.9	5	9.1	12	3.3
Good teaching	1	1.6	36	59.0	15	20.5	26	56.5	15	22.1	21	38.2	114	31.3
Near home	28	45.9	8	13.1	29	39.7	13	28.3	29	42.6	21	38.2	128	35.2
Free education	26	42.6	0	0	23	31.5	1	2.2	17	25	6	10.9	73	20.1
Part-time at home	3	4.9	0	0	4	5.5	0	0	3	4.4	0	0	10	2.7
Extra-curricular activities	2	3.3	4	6.6	0	0	4	8.7	0	0	2	3.6	12	3.3
Famous school	0	0	13	21.3	0	0	2	4.3	0	0	0	0	15	4.1
Total	61	100	61	100	73	100	46	100	68	100	55	100	364	100

Thus, to summarise it can be stated that a clear demarcation
in trend exists between the slum areas and the non-slum areas.
While majority of the responses from the slum areas show

utilisation of municipal schools, in the non-slum areas show maximum utilisation of private schools. The medium of instructions across all the localities is clearly Gujarati, barring a few responses from the non-slum areas, showing English as the medium of instructions. School dropouts are low, but from the cases observed these are larger in the case of slum areas as compared with the non-slum areas. The criteria for school selection show that in the non-slum areas main weightage is given to the quality of teaching, while in the slum areas, greater importance is given to the fee structure and the proximity of the school from the home. The perception regarding types of schools shows that while the municipal schools are generally rated average, the private schools are considered good, in terms of quality of teaching. This trend is also reflected in locality-wise number of students studying in the municipal and private schools.

13

Summary and Conclusion

The Structural Adjustment Programme (SAP) was introduced in India in 1991. Although it was a result of the balance of payment crisis that India was facing at that time, many believe that such a course of policy change was inevitable and would have happened sooner or later. Despite being a welcome change from the previous protectionist policy, most analysts were cautious about its outcome.

Until at least the 1970s, the Indian economy was seen as a classic case of post-war state-led economic development, within a mixed economy framework (Ghosh, 2001). This approach incorporated the major tendencies of Indian economic planning, including the emphasis on heavy industrial investment until the mid-1960s and the focus on state ownership/control of the 'commanding heights' of the economy (the basic and core infrastructure industries as well as other strategic and economically significant industries), as well as state regulation of many other aspects of economic activity even in the non-core areas. It also meant recognition of the role played in the subsequent decades of Indian development by the state in subsidising private investment activity in both industry and agriculture.

Over four decades, this broad mixed economy approach brought about some significant, if qualified, economic successes, as well as glaring failures. The most striking successes were in terms of the substantial increase in aggregate growth rates over the pre-independence period, as well as the steady diversification of the economy and the building up of a substantial productive base in a range of modern industry. Similarly, the most striking failures were in the persistence of absolute material poverty among a very large section of the population (such that even at present more than 30% of the population is officially described as below the poverty line) and in the inability to achieve basic human development goals such as education and adequate health provision for the entire population.

The basic elements of the changed economic regime since 1991 have included a system of more liberal imports and reduction/elimination of external trade controls generally; a progressive removal of administrative controls over capacity creation, production and prices, including a move to free markets in foodgrains and a cutting down of food subsidies; a strictly limited (and declining) role for public investment even in important infrastructure sectors, the privatisation of publicly-owned assets over a wide field; a focus on reducing implicit subsides by raising user charges over a wide range of public utilities and services; an invitation to MNCs to undertake investment (under substantially liberalised conditions relating to ownership, operation and profit repatriation); and financial liberalisation measures that have substantially reduced priority sector lending and subsidised credit and allowed greater capital market innovation.

Much of the discussion of the SAP package applied in India since 1991 has tended to concentrate on its intellectual origins in the Fund-Bank 'Washington consensus' and its likely consequences in the specific Indian environment (Ghosh, 2001). It is now increasingly evident, however, that this may be an inadequate mode of considering the entire process. Some of the essential ingredients of the package have been retained in Indian practice, for example, in terms of greater emphasis on liberalised markets, a reduced role for direct public investment and a concerted drive to woo foreign investment through numerous concessions. But it is also certainly the case that the Indian combination of economic policies for adjustment has differed in some important ways from the 'textbook' Fund-Bank model, most particularly in the continuing internal imbalances of the government as well as in the possibility of continued external imbalances because of capital inflows, both of which point to the lack of 'adjustment' at least in the standard sense. Focusing on the ideal construct of the standard package is therefore not very illuminating any more. With some of the more recent data that are now available, it is now possible to attempt an assessment of the Indian structural adjustment package since 1991, based not on the supposed model, but on the policies that have actually been pursued.

There are at least two striking features of mainstream analyses of the economic reforms in India since 1991. The first, which is evident not only in official government publications (particularly of the Finance Ministry) but also in the English language financial press, is the generally unsupported statement that the 'reforms' instituted so far by and large have been successful both in achieving the medium-term goals of structural adjustment and in preparing the economy for 'take-off' in the new globalised environment. The second, which is not so much an assessment as a longing and wistful eastward gaze, refers to the bold examples of the successful East and South-East Asian economies, and suggests that emulation of their supposedly 'open' and 'market-oriented' policies would allow India also to benefit from the buoyancy evident in what is economically the most dynamic part of the world today. Not only are the countries in this region constantly cited as examples of the enormous benefits to be derived from 'globalisation', but their rapid growth is seen as a continuous reminder of the failures of our own past development strategy.

The liberalisation process has come in for criticism from two opposite ends. First, there are those who feel that the process has been slow and not sufficiently comprehensive. These critics attribute the current slowdown in the growth rate to this factor. On the other hand, there are critics who view the reform process as misconceived, ignoring the basic realities of our country. There are four aspects of these criticisms, which deserve attention.

The demographic growth in urban India has been projected to be very high because of natural growth of population and inmigration. Population projection across the country by the international agencies like World Bank as well as by several researchers shows that India is poised for rapid urbanisation in next twenty years. It is also argued that structural reforms and the associated development strategy would accelerate rural-urban migration and give boost to the pace of urbanisation. The proponent of this strategy believe that linking of India with global economy will increase the inflow of foreign capital as also facilitate indigenous investment, resulting in rapid development of infrastructure and industries. This is likely to give impetus to the process of urbanisation since much of the industrial growth and consequent increase in employment would be within or around the exiting urban centres.

Liberalisation's impact on urban infrastructure and basic services is not very clear. Recent efforts have been made to change the set-up of local governments by empowering them for the planning and execution of projects. But, as the capacity building process is limited to mega cities only, the gap between the mega cities and small and medium towns is increasing gradually. Increases in the administrative and financial powers do not help the small and medium towns, as these towns are not attractive enough for foreign private investment (as well as from inside the country). On the other hand, after liberalisation, public investments in these towns are decreasing gradually in the expectation of private investment. Due to lack of both private and public investment, small and medium towns may face severe problem of service inadequacies and future development.

There is also an increasing gap between rich and poor even in potential mega cities, where benefits from liberalisation are more. Lack of public investment can cut down the level of basic amenities in the poorer areas in a city and private services may be costlier to afford affecting the utilisation rate as well as increasing cost of living of the poor. Researchers are more critical in monitoring structural adjustment with an apprehension that the investments in social sector will go down as direct returns from this sector is not very high. It will not be favourable for the private investors and, on the contrary, the government will cut investment in the expectation of the private enterprises. There was a deep cut in the level of public investment in the first five years since the reforms, which often make the researchers anxious about the results associated with it. Questions of the sector, which bore the burden of these adjustments and of sustainability of economy often, arise.

From 1999 onwards, the second-generation reforms have been started by the present government headed by the BJP. At present, all the national political parties, except the left front, is broadly supporting the structural adjustment and privatisation of services. International agencies are also influencing the policy framework in favour of new polices at macro as well as micro levels. It appears that the process is going to continue for a longer time and several changes are expected in next few years.

Ahmedabad is the seventh largest city in India. According to Census 2001, the city has a population of 3.5 million. During that time, the population of total urban agglomeration area was around 4.5 million. The decadal growth rate in the Ahmedabad Municipal Corporation (AMC) area during the period from

1981 to 2001 is much lower than in the total urban agglomeration area. There is a spatial variation and differentiation of distribution of population density in the city. Different wards under the AMC exhibit a differential pattern of density. The AMC wards falling under the walled city area show the highest level of density in the city. The average density pattern in the eastern part of the city is higher than that of the western part. The peripheral areas in the city exhibit comparatively lower density levels, but the rate of growth of annual density is very high.

The economy of Ahmedabad is gradually changing from a secondary base to a tertiary base. Now, Ahmedabad has more than five hundred thousand tertiary workers which account for more than 60.72 percent of the total main workers in the city; on the other hand, there are three hundred thousand workers in the secondary sector which is 37.84 percent of the total. It implies the decreasing secondary sector activity or faster rate of growth in tertiary sector activity. There is clear decline in the textile sector, which saw closing down of many of the textile mills during the decades of 1980s and 1990s.

The fall of textile industry also affected other ancillary industries in the city. There is a sectoral shift in industrial growth in Gujarat, after liberalisation and this also exhibits an unequal spatial pattern of distribution. There is rapid growth of chemical and petrochemical industries in South Gujarat districts, such as Bharuch, Surat and Valsad. The South Gujarat districts of Bharuch and Surat, and Jamnagar from Saurashtra, account for 58 percent of the investment envisaged in the state in the year 1995-96. On the other hand, there is a significant decline in the share of industries in and around Ahmedabad. On the other hand, there is rapid growth in the tertiary sector that includes business and commerce, transport and communication, construction activities and other services. In the post-liberalisation era, corporate business and other related activities are booming in the city. Due to rapid growth of the tertiary sector, the growth of employment in Ahmedabad Urban Agglomeration (AUA) area is much higher than in other parts of urban Gujarat. Therefore, the work participation ratio for males in AUA has gone up from 49.6 percent in 1981 to 55.7 percent in 1991 (for urban Gujarat, from 49.8% to 50.8% only). The unemployment rates in AUA have also declined sharply during the early 1990s, although they show still high figures.

Planning, development and maintenance for infrastructure facilities in the city have been exercised by the AMC and the Ahmedabad Urban Development Authority (AUDA). Electrification, sewerage network, drinking water facilities and transport installations are considered as the most important infrastructural requirements by the authorities. All parts of the city are now accessible (spatially) for electricity, which is provided by a private enterprise called Ahmedabad Electricity Company. But still the city does not have complete electrification, as many low-income families cannot afford to have a connection while many enjoy it by unauthorised connections. AMC area has 13,08,453 total connections and the total urban agglomeration area of Ahmedabad has 13,76,870 connections. Ahmedabad has a long history of installing and managing sewerage network. AMC has covered most of its areas by sewerage network. AUDA also has started constructing it in the areas under its jurisdiction. Drinking water in the AMC area has been provided by AMC on hourly basis in a day. Generally flow continues in a day for two hours with varying intensities and at different time. To fulfil the requirements, people of Ahmedabad generally depend upon ground water. Almost all the middle and higher income households have electric motors for ground water draft. Due to the continuous exploitation of ground water and the imbalance between the total draft and refill, the level of ground water is gradually going down and alarming the future situation of water resource management in the city.

Ahmedabad has all sorts of transport facilities, except water transport. The total road length in the city is 1,384 km, out of it 1,103 km is paved and 998 km comes under the jurisdiction of AMC. The hierarchy of roads varies from national highways to the local roads. The National Highway 8 links Ahmedabad to Delhi and Mumbai and an express highway is under construction to link it with Baroda. There are other state highways to connect it with other urban areas in Gujarat and surrounding states. During the early years of the 1990s, a massive road upgradation operation was done in the city by the city authority. Presently upgradation (four-laning) of the state roads is being done by the state government of Gujarat. The city has a congested and overused regional bus terminus in Gita Mandir area in the old part of the city. The only means of public transportation in the city is the city bus service, which has been provided by Ahmedabad Municipal Transport Service (AMTS) -- an AMC operated service. Private auto-rickshaws provide semi-public passenger service in the city.

Rapid industrialisation and urbanisation have also worked as a catalytic factor in mushrooming of low-income localities in Ahmedabad. There are two types of low-income settlements in the city, which differ from one another in terms of their origin and growth. First, out of the two, is the 'slums', which can be found in any other city with a similar nature of occupants and with identical physical conditions. The second type of these settlements in Ahmedabad is known as 'chawls'. Initially, chawls were built to house the industrial workers, mainly associated with the textile industry in the early decades of the last century. Now, they are occupied by the workers of the closed mills in the city and due to their old age, lower income occupants and the initial design, they are in dilapidated condition. Their physical status and their occupants' economic status today are more alike slums. According to the census of 1991, within the limit of AMC, there are 91,188 families with 474 thousand persons lived in slums. Population in chawls in the city transcended the upper limit of that in the slums and around 133 thousand families with 696 thousand persons lived in them. Therefore, a total of 225 thousand families with more than 1,170 thousand population are distributed over 2,432 low-income localities which accounts for nearly 41 percent of the total population in the city.

Ahmedabad is the largest city in the state and provides a good network of medical services in the form of hospitals, dispensaries and maternity homes. AMC is providing basic amenities according to the provisions of Bombay Municipal Corporation Act, 1949. Along with the obligatory functions like water supply and solid waste management, it provides a large number of voluntary services like hospital services, medical education, etc. The Corporation manages three general hospitals, one ophthalmic hospital, one TB hospital, five referral hospitals and 22 allopathic dispensaries. It also provides 18 maternity homes, three ayurvedic dispensaries, two unani dispensaries and four dental clinics. It has also taken many measures to provide special health care services for low-income areas in the city. AMC has decided to improve the primary health care and family welfare services with the financial assistance of the World Bank.

According to the AMC budget, the average health expenditure is increasing every year but the percentage of the total expenditure for health has remained constant for the last few years. Special allocation for slums has been made since 1997-98 onwards which is the new feature of health expenditure in Ahmedabad. Allocations for dispensaries and referral services have reduced over a period of time and it is very clear that AMC is not interested in continuing these services for a long time. Road cleaning appears to be the most important activity of the health department as two-thirds of the expenditure goes for this activity. The solid waste management is part of this activity and hence very essential to keep the city clean.

The AMC is also maintaining records of some diseases treated by the municipal health services. The available information shows that more people are dying owing to diseases like gastroenteritis ranging between 58 in 1991 and 9 in 1997. But, a large number of people are suffering from this disease. The month-wise information shows that a large number of cases are reported during the months of June, July and August. The viral hepatitis cases range between a maximum of 2,591 in 1993 and a minimum of 512 in 1998. These were reported more during the months of November and December in 1993. The maximum number of deaths also occurred in 1993 (80 deaths) and minimum of five deaths in 1999. Typhoid cases were reported more in 1991 while these were minimum in 1995 and very few deaths are reported during the period from 1991 to 1999. Cholera cases were reported more in 1996 while these very few in previous year. During 1991 to 1999, only one death due to cholera has been reported in Ahmedabad in the year 1994.

The AMC is providing the primary education through different types of schools within its jurisdiction. The Primary School Board is responsible for the management of these schools. Its activities are divided into five zones. Zone 1 consists of Kankaria area, zone 2 consists of Jamalpur area, zone 3 consists of Ellisbridge area, zone 4 consists of schools of other mediums like Urdu and Hindi and the last zone 5 consists of the east zone which was transferred from the Zilla Panchayat to the Corporation when it was merged within the municipal limit.

Municipal primary schools run on 80 percent grants and the Corporation provides 20 percent of the expenditure. The Corporation also provides uniforms to some children, free textbooks to all and scholarships to those belonging to SCs/STs/OBCs. In each of the 43 wards of the city, there is at least one primary school. Each year, the best teacher award, also known as the Mayor's Award, is given to a teacher from the primary school who is recognised for his/her efforts towards education, has started some innovative activity for students or the results of the students make evident the quality of education provided by that teacher.

In addition, the primary education department has ten part-time doctors, who visit schools, examine the student's eyes, nose, ears, skin, teeth etc., and if a student is affected by some ailment, they fill a yellow card for the student. They administer medicines and an affected student is supervised regularly. A supervisor is the person who is directly responsible for schools falling under his bid. One bid consists of around 20-30 schools. The supervisors make daily visits to the schools falling under their bid, supervise proper functioning, and report to the assistant administrative officers.

The municipal expenditure on education has been in the range of 16.8 percent to 24.4 percent of the total expenditure, between 1986-87 and 1998-99, with the lowest being in 1998-99. In absolute terms, the expenditure on education ranges between a minimum of Rs 151 million in 1986-87 to a maximum of Rs 577 million in 1995-96. In fact, the expenditure on education has been slowly decreasing ever since 1991-92 with the exception of the year 1995-95. The number of primary educational institutions, including the municipal and private primary, has increased over the years. The private primary schools that were lesser in number than the municipal primary schools from 1986 to 1990, exceeded in number since 1990-91 and ever since their number has remained higher. Barring the year 1986-87, when the student-teacher ratio was 36.6 students per teacher, it is observed to be in the range of 39.7 in 1989-90 and 43.4 in 1998-99. As of 1996-96, there are about 2,39,273 students. Over the years, the number of girls studying in both municipal and private schools has increased in number. In fact, the number of girls has marginally exceeded the number of boys in the private primary schools from the year 1991-92 onwards. It is also observed that there is a shift in the total number of students studying at municipal primary schools to private primary schools in Ahmedabad. The secondary schools declined in early 1990s reported to be increasing from 1996 onwards. The numbers of students and teachers are also increasing.

Household survey of the six settlements revels that Hindus are the dominant religious group in these localities and it is true for entire city. Hindu society is divided into caste that is both a ritual as well as economic grouping. People living in slums are mainly from the low-caste categories while in non-slum areas majority are from higher castes. Quality of housing is good in non-slum areas and it is quite unsatisfactory in slum settlements. In terms of ownership people are living in their own houses and it is true for both slum and non-slum settlements. The average unit size is big in non-slum areas but there are variations among three locations. Other infrastructural facilities like toilet, bathroom, sewage connection and electricity are available almost in the entire non-slum houses. On the other hand, in slums, very few are having these facilities. In slums people are still using firewood and kerosene for cooking which pollute the indoor air quality. The literacy level is quite satisfactory in non-slum locations only. A large number of people are unemployed and they are more in non-slum settlements. In slums more people are self-employed and also working as daily wage labourers. The monthly average income differs among settlements and it is much lower in slums in comparison to average of all the respondents. The average household expenditure is much lower than the household income. Asset holding is more in non-slum areas that clearly shows the economic differences between these two types of settlements.

According to primary survey results, most people suffer from cold and fever. Other water-borne diseases are reported more from non-slum areas. Across all the locations, it is the male members who are affected in large numbers by various diseases as compared to females and children. Allopathy as the treatment system, is much more popular. For treatment respondents are more using public facilities in slums whereas non-slum respondents are using private health care facilities. Some people have changed the institution for health care facility from 1991 and better service and less time are mainly responsible for it. Home is still a popular place for delivering the child mainly in slum areas. However, in non-slum areas, people prefer private nursing home for delivery. Gradually, people are accepting immunisation as essential for child care. In slum areas, respondents are using public system for immunisation. Perception regarding public system shows a positive trend as it comes out to be good and efficient. The private health care system, although found to be efficient, has been identified as expensive.

A clear demarcation in trend exists between slum and non-slum areas. While majority of the responses from the slum areas show utilisation of municipal schools, in the non-slum areas show maximum utilisation of private schools. The medium of instructions across all the localities is clearly Gujarati, barring a few responses from the non-slum areas, showing English as the medium of instructions. School dropouts are low, but from the cases observed school dropouts are larger in slum areas as compared with the non-slum areas. The criteria for school selection show that in the non-slum areas main weightage is given to the quality of teaching, whereas in the slum areas, greater importance seems to be given to the fee structure and the proximity of the school from the home. The perception of type of schools shows that while the municipal schools are generally rated average, the private schools are considered good, in terms of quality of teaching. This trend is also reflected in locality-wise number of students studying in the municipal and private schools.

Since the year 1991-92 when there were about 210 institutions, secondary education institutions declined in the year 1992-93 to 166 institutions. After which, the number increased again to around 175 and remained the same for a couple of years. In the year 1996-97, the number increased to 219 and further to 228 in 1998-99. The number of students studying at the secondary schools has also decreased considerably since the year 1991-92.

From the survey of the six localities, one point which emerges conclusively is that, as far as the low income households are concerned, it is the cost factor that differentiates private facilities from public facilities. Their perception regarding the municipal health and education facilities is that they are either good or average or mediocre but never of poor quality. The assumption is that the availability of public health facilities is much lesser than required and, as a result, they do not get the desired individual attention that is the cornerstone of most private facilities. And, with decreasing expenditure on public facilities, this gap between need and availability will further widen. In the case of education, parents were more critical of the municipal schools judging the private schools to be more modern and of better quality. The parents in the slums are found more concerned with distance and free education while choosing the schools for their offspring, the educational standards of private schools are not up to their expectations and they would prefer to send their children if they had the financial ability.

Differences in growth rates among states have become more pronounced after liberalisation. Judged by the standard criteria of growth rates of national income and per capita income, external balance and inflation rate, the Indian economy has done well since liberalisation. Between 1981-82 and 1990-91, the growth rate of the economy was 5.6 percent per annum. The sum of spending on health, education, housing and social services has remained constant at 2.9 percent of GDP during the period between 1992 and 1995 while sectors witnessing bulk of spending cuts are defence and economic services. There is a strong case for public involvement in health and education matters from the viewpoint of equity and rights. However, there was a remarkable neglect of elementary education in India, and this has now forced her to recognise the importance of basic education for the economic development of the country. Literacy levels have risen in India. Basic health facilities have not reached everyone. The need for expanded state intervention in areas of education, health and sanitation cannot be underestimated.

The government should realise this and attempt to increase public investment in the social sector because the sustainability of economic development is dependent on the successful nature of human development. Lack of public investment can cut down the level of basic amenities in the poorer areas in a city and private services may be costlier to afford affecting the utilisation rate as well as increasing cost of living of the poor.

States like Gujarat, located on the western coast, have become popular for industrial and urban development. The successive state governments in Gujarat have taken the initiative for economic reforms by constituting the State Finance Commission and prepared the agenda for reforms. All leading political parties in the state have accepted the agenda for reforms prepared by the State Finance Commission. Infrastructure development was identified as a necessary step for the overall development of the state. It indicates that reforms at the state level are going to be little more difficult and social services are going to be more affected as these services are in the state list.

Bibliography

Ahluwalia, I.J. (1991), *Productivity and Growth in Indian Manufacturing*, Oxford University Press, New Delhi.

Ahmedabad Municipal Corporation (1997), Statistical Outline of Ahmedabad City 1996-1997, Ahmedabad.

Ahmedabad Municipal Corporation (1994), Augmentation of Primary Health Care and Family Welfare Services in the City of Ahmedabad, Ahmedabad.

AUDA (1997), Revised Draft Development Plan of AUDA-2011AD, Part 1, Vol.2, Surveys, Studies and Analysis, AUDA, Ahmedabad.

Awasthi, D. (2000), Recent Changes in Gujarat Industry: Issues and Evidence, *Economic and Political Weekly (EPW)*, August 26, pp. 3181-3192.

Banerjee, D. (1974), Social and Cultural Foundation of Health Services Systems, *EPW*, Special Issue, pp. 1333-1346.

Banerjee, D. (1983), National Health Policy and its Implementation, *EPW*, pp. 105-108.

Basu, A.M. (1992), *Culture: The Status of Women and Demographic Behaviour*, Clarendon Press, Oxford.

Basu, K. (1993), Structural Reforms in India – 1991-93: Experience and Agenda, *EPW*, November 27, 1993.

Berman, P. and M.E. Khan (eds.) (1993), *Paying for India's Health Care*, Sage Publications (India), New Delhi.

Bhat, R. (1996), Regulation of the Private Health Care Sector in India, *Health Planning and Management*.

Bhat, Ramesh (1993), The Private/Public Mix in Health Care in India, *Health Policy and Planning*, Vol. 8, No. 1, pp. 43-56.

Bhat, R. (1999), Characteristics of Private Medical Practice in India: A Provider Perspective, *Health Policy and Planning*, Vol. 14, No. 1, pp. 26-37.

Bhat, R. (1999), Public-Private Partnership in the Health Sector: Issues and Prospects, Working paper 99-05-06, IIM, Ahmedabad.

Bhalla, G.S. (2000), Political Economy of Indian Development in the 20th Century: India's Road to Freedom and Growth, Presidential address delivered on December 30th 2000 at the 83rd Annual Conference of the Indian Economic Association held at Jammu under the auspices of the University of Jammu, Jammu and Kashmir.

Caldwell, J. (1986), Routes to Low Mortality in Poor Countries, *Population and Development Review*, Vol. 12, No. 2.

Care in India, 1986-87, Gujarat Institute of Development Research, Ahmedabad.

CEPT (1995), *Comparative Environmental Risk Assessment of Ahmedabad*, Ahmedabad

CEPT, (1997), *Urban Profile of Gujarat*, Ahmedabad.

Chandrasekhar, S., et al., (1989), *Towards 2000 AD: Indian Health Economy and Policy*, Chugh Publisher, Allahabad.

Datt, Gaurav (1999), Has Poverty Declined Since Economic Reforms? Statistical Data Analysis, *EPW*, Special Articles. December 11-17.

Desai, A.R. (1986), *Social Background of Indian Nationalism*, Popular Prakashan, Bombay.

Desai, B.N. and Namboodri, N.V. (1979), Determinants of Total Factor Productivity in Indian Agriculture, *EPW*, Vol. 32, No. 52.

Deshpande, S. and Deshpande, L. (1998), Impact of Liberalisation on Labour Market in India: What do Facts from NSSO's 50th Round Show, *EPW*, Vol. 33, No. 22, pp. L31-L39.

Dev, Mahendra, S. (2000), Economic Liberalisation and Employment in South Asia – I & II, *EPW*, Vol. 34, No. 1 & 2.

District Primary Education Department, Annual Report (1998-99), Ahmedabad.

Dreze, Jean and Amartya Sen (eds.) (1996), 'Radical needs and Moderate Reforms' in *Indian Development: Selected Regional Perspectives*, UNU/WIDER, Oxford University Press, New Delhi.

----, 2002, *India: Development and Participation*, Oxford University Press, New Delhi.

Duggal, R. and Amin, S. (1989), Cost of Health Care: A Household Survey in Indian district, Foundation for Research in Community Health, Mumbai.

Duggal, R. et al (1995), Health Expenditure Across States - Part I and II, *EPW*, Vol. 30, No. 15 & 16, pp. 834-838, 901-908.

Duggal, R. (1997), Health Care Budgets in a Changing Political Economy, *EPW*, May 17-24, 1197-1200.

---- (2000), The Private Health Sector in India: Nature, Trends, and a Critique, Voluntary Health Association of India. New Delhi.

Economic Survey, (1998-99), Ministry of Finance, New Delhi.

Forbes, N. (1999), *Technology and Indian Industry: What is Liberalisation Changing?* Technovation, 19, pp. 403-412.

GEC (Gujarat Ecology Commission) (1997), Ecological Degradation Around Gulf of Khambat, Gujarat: A Status Report, Vadodara.

GIDB (1999), Gujarat Infrastructure Agenda: Vision 2010, Vol. II, Sector Reports, Gandhinagar.

Giridhar, et al (1987), Study of Health Care Financing in India, Indian Institute of Management, Ahmedabad.

Gopalkrishnan, R. and Sharma, A. (1999), Education Guarantee Scheme: What Does It Claim? *EPW*, Vol. 34, No. 12, pp. 726-728.

---- (1998), Education Guarantee Scheme in Madhya Pradesh: Innovative Step to Universalise Education, *EPW*, Vol. 33, September, pp. 2546-2551.

Government of Gujarat (1984), District Gazetteer, Ahmedabad District, Directorate of Government Printing and Publication, Gujarat State, Gandhinagar, India.

Government of India (1946), Health Survey and Development Committee (Bhore Committee) Manager Publication, Calcutta.

Government of India (1966), Report of the Study Group on Medical Care Services (Jain Committee) Ministry of Health, New Delhi.

Government of India (1975), Report of the Group on Medical Education and Support Manpower (Srivastava Committee) Ministry of Health, New Delhi.

Government of India, Census of India (1991), District Census Handbook, Village and Town Directory, Ahmedabad District, New Delhi.

Gulati, A. and Sharma, A. (1997), Freeing Trade in Agriculture: Implication of Resource Use Efficiency and Cropping Pattern Change, *EPW*, Vol. 32, No. 52.

Haq, M. and Haq, K. (1998), *Human Development in South Asia 1998*, Oxford University Press, Karachi.

Hema, R. and Muraleedharan, V.R. (1993), Health and Human Resources Development, *EPW*, October 23, 1993.

Heredia, R.C. (1995), Education and Mission: School as Agent of Evangelisation, *EPW*, Vol. 30, No. 37, pp. 2332-2340.

Hesselberg, Jan (ed.) (2002), An Urbanizing World, in Jan Hesselberg (ed.), *Issues in Urbanisation: The Case of Ahmedabad*, Gujarat State, Rawat Publications, Jaipur.

Hesselberg, J. (1995), Urban Poverty and Shelter: An Introduction, *Norwegian Journal of Geography*, Vol. 49. pp. 151-160.

Heston, A. (1982), "National Income" ed. Dharma Kumar, *The Cambridge Economic History of India*: Vol.II, Orient Longman & Cambridge University Press.

Hirway, I. and Mahadevia, D. (1999), *Gujarat Human Development Report, 1999*, Mahatma Gandhi Labour Institute, Ahmedabad.

Hirway, I. (2000), Dynamics of Development in Gujarat: Some Issues, *EPW*, August 26, pp. 3106-3120.

Industrial Credit and Investment Corporation of India (1994), Productivity in Indian Manufacturing: Private Corporate Sector, 1972-73 to 1991-92, ICICI, Bombay.

International Commission on Education for the Twenty-first Century (1996), Learning: The Treasure Within, Report to Unesco of the International Commission on Education for the Twenty-first Century (Jacques Delors et al), Unesco (Delors Commission), Paris.

Iyenger, Sudarshan (2000), Level and Pattern of Economic Growth in Gujarat, Occasional Paper Series, No. 1 DTLM Trust, GIDR, Ahmedabad.

Jamison, D. and Lau L. (1982), *Farmer Education and Farm Efficiency*, Baltimore, Johns Hopkins University Press.

Joshi, V. and Little, I. (1998) *India's Economic Reforms 1991-2001*. Oxford University Press, New Delhi.

Joshi, Vidyut (1998), 'Genesis of Tribal Problem' in Vidyut Joshi (ed.), *Tribal Situation in India*, Rawat, Jaipur.

—— (2000), Cultural Context of Development, *EPW*, August 26, pp. G61-G65.

Kashyap, A. (1998), 'Parameters of Tribal Development' in Vidyut Joshi (ed.), *Tribal Situation in India*, Rawat Publications, Jaipur.

Khan, M.A.Ali (1995), Financing, Cost and Efficiency of Public Hospitals in Gujarat, Report of FDPM, IIM, Ahmedabad.

Khan, M.E. and Prasad C.V.S. (1988), Utilisation of Health and Family Planning Services in Bihar, Gujarat and Kerala, Indian Council for Medical Research, New Delhi.

Kolhatkar, M.R. (1988), Education Expenditure in India in Relation to National Income (1980-88): Trends and Implications, *Journal of Education and Social Change*, 2 (2): 104-127.

Kundu, A. (1983), Theories of City Size Distribution and the Indian Urban Structure: A Reappraisal, *EPW*, July.

Kundu, A. (1994), *Urban Development and Urban Research in India*, Khama Publication, New Delhi.

Kundu, A. (1999), Urban Poverty in India: Issues and Perspectives in Development. Paper presented at the Seminar on Social Dimensions of Urban Poverty in India, National Institute of Urban Affairs, New Delhi, 3-5 March.

Kundu, A. (1999), Urbanisation, Employment Generation and Poverty under the Shadow of Globalisation: The Case of Gujarat, India. Paper presented at the Seminar on Dynamics of Development in Gujarat, Centre for Development Alternatives, Ahmedabad, 23-24 April.

Kundu, A. (2000), Globalising Gujarat: Urbanisation, Employment and Poverty, *EPW*, August 26, pp. 3172-3181.

Kundu, A. and Mahadevia, D. (2002), *Poverty and Vulnerability in a Globalising Metropolis Ahmedabad*, Manak Publishers, New Delhi

Lal, R.B. (1998), 'Tribal Situation in Gujarati' in Vidyut Joshi (ed.), *Tribal Situation in India*, Rawat Publications, Jaipur.

Madaswamy, Moni (2002), Impact of Economic Reforms on Indian Agricultural Sector: Application of Geomatics Technology to Reduce Marginalisation and Vulnerability of Small Farmers in India, GIS Development.

Mahadevia, D. (1999), Health for All in Gujarat: Is it Achievable? Paper presented at the Seminar on Dynamics of Development in Gujarat, Centre for Development Alternatives, Ahmedabad, 23-24 April.

Mahadevia, D. (1998), Development Dichotomy in Gujarat, RFSTE, New Delhi.

Mahadevia, D. (2000), Health for All in Gujarat: Is it Achievable? *EPW*, August 26, pp. 3193-3204.

Mahal, A., Srivastava, V. and Sanan, D. (2001), Decentralisation and Public Service Delivery in Health and Education Services: Evidence from Rural India, Forthcoming in Dethier, Jean (ed.), Governance and Development in China, India and Russia, Kluwer Academic Publishers.

Mahal, A. and Gumber, A. (2000), Who Benefits from Public Health Spending in India? National Council of Applied Economic Research, New Delhi, October 2000.

Malik, J.K. (1997), Growth of Agriculture in Independent India: 50 Years and After, Occasional Paper, Vol. 18, Nos. 2 & 3, Reserve Bank of India, Mumbai.

Mathew, E.T. (1999), Growth of Literacy in Kerala: State Intervention, Missionary Initiative and Social Movements, *EPW*, Vol. 34, No. 39, pp. 2811-2820.

Mathur, N. and Kashyap, S.P. (2000), Agriculture in Gujarat: Problems and Prospects, *EPW*, August 26-September 2, 2000.

MHRD (1998), Analysis of Budgeted Expenditure on Education 1994-95 to 1996-97, Ministry of Human Resource Development, Government of India, New Delhi.

Ministry of Health and Family Welfare (2000), Bulletin on Rural Health Statistics in India, New Delhi, Rural Health Division, Ministry of Health and Family Welfare.

Mukhopadhyay, M. (ed.) (1997), Report of the Independent Commission on Health in India, Voluntary Health Association of India Press, New Delhi.

Nagraj, R. (1997), What has Happened Since 1991? Assessment of India's Economic Reforms, *EPW*, November 8, 1997.

Naik J.P. (1975), *Equality, Quality and Quantity: The Elusive Triangle in Indian Education*, Allied Publisher, Mumbai.

National Institute of Public Finance and Policy (1993), Structural Adjustment Programme: Its Impact on the Health Sector (Draft Report), New Delhi.

National Sample Survey Organisation (NSSO) (1998), Morbidity and Treatment of Ailments: NSS Fifty-Second Round (July 1995-June 1996).

Nayar, K. Rajasekharan (1998), Old Priorities and New Agenda of Public Health in India: Is there a Mismatch, Centre of Social Medicine and Community Health, JNU, New Delhi.

NCAER (1994), Non-Enrolment, Dropout and Private Expenditure on Elementary Education: A Comparison Across States Population Groups, September, New Delhi.

Neogi, C. and Ghosh, B. (1998), Impact of Liberalisation on Performance of Indian Industries: A Firm Level Study, *EPW*, Vol. 33, No. 9, pp M-16 to M-24, New Delhi.

Mathur, N. and Kashyap, S.P. (2000), Agriculture in Gujarat: Problems and Prospects, *EPW*, August 26, pp. 3137-3146.

Panchamukhi, P.R. (1990), Private Expenditure on Education in India: An Empirical Study, Indian Institute of Education, Pune.

Pangotra, Prem (1998), City Monitor, 1996-97 Ahmedabad-Bangalore-Hyderabad-Pune, Ahmedabad Management Association, Ahmedabad.

Patnaik, Prabhat (1999), 'The Political Economy of Structural Adjustment: A Note', in Rao Mohan (ed.), *Disinvesting in Health: The World Bank's Prescriptions for Health*, Sage, New Delhi.

Planning Commission, 1998. Ninth Five Year Plan 1997-2002, Volume II, New Delhi, Government of India.

Pudasini, S. (1982), Education and Agricultural Efficiency in Nepal, World Bank Discussion Paper 82-83, Washington, D.C.

Purohit, B.C. and Sidiqui, T.A. (1994), Utilisation of Health Services in India, *EPW*, Vol. 29, No. 18, pp. 1071-1080.

Qadeer, Imrana (1999), 'The World Development Report 1993: The Brave New World of Primary Health Care', in Rao Mohan (ed.), *Disinvesting in Health: The World Bank's Prescriptions for Health*, Sage, New Delhi.

Ramachandran, V. (1999), Adult Education: A Tale of Empowerment Denied, in *EPW*, Vol. 34 No. 15, pp. 877-880.

Ramachandran, R. (1989), *Urbanization and Urban Systems in India*, Oxford University Press, New Delhi.

Randawa, N.S. and Sundaram, K.V. (1990), Small Farmers Development in Asia and the Pacific: Some Lessons for Strategy Formulations and Planning, FAO Economic and Social Development Paper No. 87, FAO/UN, Rome, 1990.

Rangarajan, C. (2001), Economic Reforms: An Assessment, *The Indian Economic Journal*, Special Number in Monetary Economics, July-September 2001-2002, Volume 49, No.1.

Rao, C.H.H. (1998), Agricultural Growth, Sustainability and Poverty Alleviation: Recent Trends and Major Issues of Reforms, *EPW*, Vol. 33, No. 29-30, pp. 1943-1948.

Rao, C.H.H. and Radhakrishna, R. (1997), National Food Security: A Policy Perspective for India, Paper Presented in Conference of Agriculture Economics, August 10-16, California.

Rao, M. (1998), Food Prices and Rural Poverty: Liberalisation Without Pain, *EPW*, Vol. 33, No. 14, pp. 799-800.

Rao, V.M. (1998), Economic Reforms and the Poor: Emerging scenario, in *EPW*, Vol. 33, No. 29-30, pp. 1449-1454.

Ravllion, M. (1998), Reforms, Food Prices and Poverty in India, *EPW*, January 10, 1998.

Raval, Vijay (2000), Ahmedabad Green Partnership: An Urban Community Forestry Model, unpublished dissertation, School of Planning, CEPT, Ahmedabad.

Ray, C.N. (1996), *Comparative Health Risk Assessment of Ahmedabad*, CEPT, Ahmedabad.

Reddy, K.N. and Selvaraju, V. (1994), *Health Care Expenditure by Government in India*, 1974-75 to 1990-91, Seven Hills Publication, New Delhi.

Reddy, K.N. (1992), Health Expenditure in India, Working Paper No. 14, National Institute of Public Finance and Policy, New Delhi.

Rohde, J. and Viswanathan, H. (1995), *The Rural Private Practitioner*, Oxford University Press, Delhi.

Rosegrant, M.W. and R. Evenson (1993), Agricultural Productivity Growth in Pakistan and India: A Comparative Analysis, Mimeograph. Pakistan Institute of Development Economics.

Saldanha, Denzil (1999), Residual Illiteracy and Uneven Development-I: Patterned Concentration of Literacy, *EPW*, July 3-9, 1999.

Satia, et al (1999), Progress and Challenges of Health Sector: A Balance Sheet. Paper presented at a Seminar on India, Balance Sheet of a

Nation, Indian Institute of Management, Ahmedabad, 13-15 September.

Shah, V.P. and Sheth N.R. (1998), 'Swadhaya: Social Change through Spirituality' in Dantwala et al (eds.), *Social Change Through Voluntary Action*, Sage, New Delhi.

Shariff, A. and Ghosh P.K. (2000), Indian Education Scene and the Public Gap, *EPW*, Vol. 34, No. 16, pp. 1396-1406.

Srivasatava, V. (1996), *Liberalisation, Productivity and Competition: A Panel Study of Indian Manufacturing*, Oxford University Press.

Subbarao, K. and Raney, L. (1995), Social Gains from Female Education: A Cross-National Study, *Economic Development and Cultural Change* 44, pp. 105-20.

Sundar, Ramamani (1995), Household Survey of Health Care Utilisation and Expenditure, Working Paper No 53, National Council of Applied Economic Research.

Sundram, K.V. (2000), The Small Farmer Development Strategies for the Next Millennium, presented at National Institute of Rural Development, Hyderabad, 2000.

Swamy, Subramanian (2002), Assessing India's Economic Reforms, *India's National Magazine*, Volume 19, Issue 2, January 19 - February 01, 2002.

Tejada-de-Rivero (1987), Primary Health Care World Strategy, Keynote address delivered at the Third International Congress on Primary Health Care: World Strategy, (February 23 - March 6), organised by the World Federation of Public Health Association and Public Health Association, Calcutta.

Tilak, J.B.J. (1999), National Human Development Initiative Education in the Union Budget, *EPW*, March 6-13,1999.

—— (1994), *Education for Development in Asia*, Sage Publication, New Delhi.

—— (1996) How Free is Free Primary Education in India? *EPW*, Vol. 31, No. 6, pp. 355-366.

Tripathy, D. (1998), *Alliance for Change: A Slum Upgrading Experiment in Ahmedabad*, Tata-McGraw Hill Publication, New Delhi.

Trivedi, Harshad (1998), 'Tribal Land in Gujarat' in Vidyut Joshi (ed.), *Tribal Situation in India*, Rawat Publications, Jaipur.

Umashankar, P.K. and Mishra, G.K. (eds.) (1993), *Urban Health System*, Reliance Publishing House and IIPA, New Delhi.

UNCHS (1996), *An Urbanizing World, Global Report on Human Settlements 1996*, Oxford University Press, Oxford.

UNCHS (2001), *Cities in a Globalizing World*, Global Report on Human Settlements 2001, Earthscan, London, citation p. xxxii.

UNDP (1998), *Human Development Report 1998*, Oxford University Press, New York

UNFPA (2001), *The State of World Population 2001*, United Nations Population Fund, New York.

United Nations (2000), *World Urban Prospects: The 1999 Revisions*, UN Population Division.

Vaidya, Chetan and Johnson, Brad (2001), Ahmedabad Municipal Bond: Lessons and Pointers, *EPW*, Vol. 36, No. 30, pp. 2884-2891.

Visaria, P. and Gumber, A. (1994), Utilization of and Expenditure on Health Care in India; 1986-87, Gujarat Institute of Development Research, Ahmedabad.

World Bank (1993), *World Development Report 1993*, Oxford University Press, New York.

World Bank (1995), India: Policy and Finance Strategies for Strengthening Primary Health Care Services. Washington, World Bank, Report No. 13042-IN.

World Bank (1997), *Primary Education in India*, Washington, D.C.

World Bank 1997, India: New Directions in Health Sector Development at the State Level: An Operational Perspective, Washington: World Bank, Report No. 15753-IN.

World Bank (1999), *Human Development Report 1999, Knowledge for Development*, Oxford University Press, New York.

World Bank (2000), *Cities in Transition*, Washington D.C.

World Bank (2001), *World Development Indicators*, Washington D.C.

Yesudian, C.A.K. (1990), Utilisation Pattern of Health Services and its Implication for Urban Health Policy, Harvard School of Public Health (draft).

— (1994), The Nature of Private Sector Health Services in Bombay, in Health Policy and Planning, *EPW*, Vol. 32, No. 52.

Index